BTEC
Level 3

edexcel
advancing learning, changing lives

CREATIVE MEDIA PRODUCTION LEVEL 3

BTEC National

Paul Baylis | David Brockbank | Andy Freedman | Ken Hall
Philip Holmes | Dan Morgan | Natalie Procter | Pete Wardle

Published by Pearson Education Limited, a company incorporated in England and Wales, having its registered office at Edinburgh Gate, Harlow, Essex, CM20 2JE. Registered company number: 872828

www.pearsonschoolsandfecolleges.co.uk

Edexcel is a registered trademark of Edexcel Limited.

Text © Pearson Education Limited 2010

First published 2010

13 12 11

10 9 8 7 6 5 4 3 2

British Library Cataloguing in Publication Data

A catalogue record for this book is available from the British Library.

ISBN 978 1 846906 72 5

Edited by Sally Clifford and Helen Kemp
Designed by Wooden Ark
Typeset by Phoenix Photosetting, Chatham, Kent
Original illustrations © Pearson Education Limited 2010
Cover design by Visual Philosophy, created by eMC Design
Picture research by Emma Whyte
Cover photo/illustration © Image Source Ltd
Back Cover photos © Shoosmith Collection/Alamy; Zsolt Nyulaszi/Shutterstock; Jules Selmes/Pearson Education Ltd
Printed in Malaysia (CTP-VP)

Websites

The websites used in this book were correct and up to date at the time of publication. It is essential for tutors to preview each website before using it in class so as to ensure that the URL is still accurate, relevant and appropriate. We suggest that tutors bookmark useful websites and consider enabling students to access them through the school/college intranet.

Disclaimer

This material has been published on behalf of Edexcel and offers high-quality support for the delivery of Edexcel qualifications.

This does not mean that the material is essential to achieve any Edexcel qualification, nor does it mean that it is the only suitable material available to support any Edexcel qualification. Edexcel material will not be used verbatim in setting any Edexcel examination or assessment. Any resource lists produced by Edexcel shall include this and other appropriate resources.

Copies of official specifications for all Edexcel qualifications may be found on the Edexcel website: www.edexcel.com

Contents

Photo credits

The publisher and authors would like to thank the following individuals and organisations for permission to reproduce photographs:

(Key: b-bottom; c-centre; l-left; r-right; t-top)

Acknowledgements

The publisher and authors would like to thank the following individuals and organisations for permission to reproduce their materials:

- **p. 10** PEGI/www.isfe.eu
- **p. 11** PEGI
- **p. 43** Rentrak EDI, UK Film Council
- **p. 45** www.ofcom.org.uk
- **p. 46** From BBC News at bbc.co.uk/news
- **p. 52** The Ramblers, www.getwalking.org.uk
- **p. 53** UK Film Council. Graph drawn by Hardwick Studios/www.hardwickstudios.com
- **p. 114** Department for Business Innovation and Skills/Digital Britain Final Report/Crown Copyright click-use licence number C2008002221
- **p. 116** Realtime Worlds Ltd
- **p. 119** From BBC News at bbc.co.uk/news
- **p. 138** From BBC News at bbc.co.uk/news
- **p. 142 Film:** Skillset/www.skillset.org: Skillset Employment Census 2009 and secondary analysis of unit lists for feature film productions (80 minutes or longer and minimum budget of £500K) involving UK based crew that were shot during 2006; Skillset/UK Film Council Feature Film Production Workforce Survey 2008 and the Skillset Creative Media Workforce Survey 2008
- **p. 142 Television:** Skillset/www.skillset.org: Skillset Employment Census 2009
- **p.170** Copyright 2010 members of the Audacity development team Creative Commons Attribution License, version 2.0
- **p. 197** Skillset/www.skillset.org
- **p. 200** Skillset/www.skillset.org
- **p. 204** Northcliffe Media
- **p. 213** Skillset/www.skillset.org
- **p. 234** PEGI

The publisher and authors would like to thank the individuals and organisations in the case studies in this book for their kind permission to feature material about them.

The publisher would like to thank the authors for their kind permission to use/adapt their artworks in this book.

Every effort has been made to trace the copyright holders of material reproduced in this book and we apologise in advance for any unintentional omissions. We would be pleased to insert the appropriate acknowledgement in any subsequent edition of this publication.

About the authors

Paul Baylis

Paul Baylis is Director of Curriculum at North Nottinghamshire College. He has over 20 years' history in the educational sector, specialising in Creative Studies. Paul has combined his extensive experience of the media industry with his work with Awarding Organisations to become an established author and trainer.

David Brockbank

David Brockbank is the course director for the BTEC Level 3 National Diploma in Creative Media Production (Games development) at the Northern Regional College in Northern Ireland. He has been involved in writing related units for this qualification. Alongside his 30 years' teaching experience, David has worked in the industry with Games Publisher Eidos Wimbledon, working on PC and Xbox Live Casual and Mobile Games such as Tomb Raider Legend.

Andy Freedman

Andy Freedman has been a media lecturer and trainer for 25 years with a background in producing and screenwriting. Head of Media at Cirencester College, part of the Skillset Media Academy network, Andy is also an experienced author and has been involved in developing qualifications. As a director of the Gloucestershire Media Group he is directly involved in training for media industry professionals.

Ken Hall, MA, BSc, Dip PCE, Cert Ed

Formerly Head of faculty at a leading FE college, Ken Hall is a retired senior academic with significant classroom experience. He has combined his background in the media industry with a publishing career, and brings his in-depth knowledge of the BTEC qualification to these resources.

Philip Holmes

Philip Holmes is an established author and trainer in the media sector, and has been involved in developing the BTEC Creative Media Production qualifications. Philip runs his own media production company, PMH Productions.

Dan Morgan

Dan Morgan is curriculum co-ordinator for Performance, Music and Media at West Herts College. He has been teaching in the post-compulsory sector around the country for 20 years, in all areas of sound recording and reinforcement. He has also worked in education as a Moderator, Internal Verifier and Technology Co-ordinator for national music organisations. Dan has also amassed extensive experience in areas of the sound recording and reinforcement industry and currently is director of a music technology company specialising in music practising aids.

Natalie Procter

Natalie Procter is Head of Media at Bishop Ullathorne RC High School and Humanities College as well as being the Course Organiser for BTEC Level 2 First Creative Media Production at City College Coventry. She studied Communication, Culture and Media at Coventry University, and has worked in the print industry, having specialised in journalism and TV. She has been involved in developing the BTEC Creative Media Production qualifications.

Pete Wardle

Pete Wardle leads the Media Team at Trafford College near Manchester. He has over 20 years' experience both within the creative media production sector, as a designer and creative director working on print, web and video projects, and within education. His primary interest is interactive media and he has exhibited interactive installations in the UK and at the Tech Museum in San Jose. He is currently undertaking a PhD part time at the University of Salford, researching aspects of identity within virtual worlds and has recently presented at the University of Nevada.

About your BTEC Level 3 National Creative Media Production course

Choosing to study for a BTEC Level 3 National Creative Media Production qualification is a great decision to make for lots of reasons. It can lead you into a whole range of professions and sectors and allows you to explore your creativity in many different ways.

Your BTEC Level 3 National in Creative Media Production is a **vocational** or **work-related** qualification. This doesn't mean that it will give you all the skills you need to do a job, but it does mean that you'll have the opportunity to gain specific knowledge, understanding and skills that are relevant to your chosen subject or area of work.

What will you be doing?

The qualification is structured into **mandatory units** (ones that you must do) and **optional units** (ones that you can choose to do). How many units you do and which ones you cover depend on the type of qualification you are working towards.

Qualifications	Credits from mandatory units	Credits from optional units	Total credits
Edexcel BTEC Level 3 Certificate	10	20	30
Edexcel BTEC Level 3 Subsidiary Diploma	20	40	60
Edexcel BTEC Level 3 Diploma	50 (unendorsed)	70 (unendorsed)	120
	60 (endorsed)	60 (endorsed)	
Edexcel BTEC Level 3 Extended Diploma	60 (unendorsed)	120 (unendorsed)	180
	70 (endorsed)	110 (endorsed)	

At Diploma and Extended Diploma levels, you may have chosen a general creative media production route or you may be following a pathway/endorsed route, and the units you study will reflect this. Whatever your choice, you will need to complete a mix of mandatory units and optional units.

General creative media production route (unendorsed), or		
Pathways (endorsed routes):	Television and film	Print-based media
	Radio	Interactive media
	Sound recording	Games development

How to use this book

This book is designed to help you through your BTEC Level 3 National Creative Media Production course.

All of the Creative Media Production mandatory units are covered in this book. Your programme of study may cover these in different ways, and the projects that you work on may cover learning outcomes and content from a range of units. However, this book will help you to develop the knowledge, skills and understanding that you need.

- Section 1 covers units 1 to 7 that everyone must complete if they are taking the BTEC Level 3 Extended Diploma and following the 'unendorsed' route.

- Section 2 covers the pathways (endorsed routes) including the specialist mandatory units for Television and film, Radio, Sound recording, Print-based media, Interactive media and Games development. This section also includes a reference section with assessment and grading criteria.

This book contains many features that will help you use your skills and knowledge in work-related situations and assist you in getting the most from your course.

Introduction

These introductions give you a snapshot of what to expect from each unit – and what you should be aiming for by the time you finish it!

Assessment and grading criteria

This table explains what you must do to achieve each of the assessment criteria for each unit. For each assessment criterion, shown by the grade button **P1**, there is an assessment activity.

Assessment

Your tutor will set **assignments** throughout your course for you to complete. These may take the form of projects where you research, plan, prepare, produce and evaluate reports, presentations, copy and media productions. The important thing is that you evidence your skills and knowledge.

Stuck for ideas? Daunted by your first assignment? These learners have all been through it before…

How you will be assessed

Assessment for this unit can take many forms, from assignments requiring written reports and documentation to observed oral presentations. It is very likely that the work required for this unit will be undertaken in other units such as the optional practical production units chosen by your centre. Your tutor will track your progress in an integrated assignment, rather than by separate assessment.

Your assessment could take any of the following forms:

- undertaking written assignment work including production paperwork
- pitching your ideas to the tutor/client
- presenting the results of your investigations in written and oral formats
- undertaking annotated research work.

Zander, creative media production student

When I first started the course I didn't realise how much planning and research was involved in production work. I may have been a little naïve but I really thought that if I had a good idea then I could just go ahead and make a product using the technical skills I had been taught.

When I thought about it, it made sense that there should be a level of planning and preparation. In the real world I would be working for someone who would have clear ideas about what they wanted and why.

Proposals and treatments are a good way of planning a production and presenting your ideas to a client. It gives them a clear and detailed understanding of what the production is about and what your intentions are.

Now I start by outlining everything in a proposal such as my idea, the narrative or story and the target audience. Then I pass that over to the client for approval.

The proposal is a bit like putting in a bid: you offer the client an idea and then they decide whether they want to see more. If they like your ideas you then go into more detail and produce a treatment which forms the basis of the production.

Finally you really need to sell your ideas and try to convince the client to let you make their product for them. It's all a process and it needs to be well planned and researched if you are going to get the job!

Over to you!

- Why is it important to produce production paperwork?
- What is a proposal?
- What is a treatment and how is it different from a proposal?
- Why do you have to present a pitch to the client?
- What will happen if the client likes your treatment and pitch and approves your ideas?

Activities

There are different types of activities for you to do: **Assessment activities** are suggestions for tasks that you might do as part of your assignment and will help you develop your knowledge, skills and understanding. **Grading tips** clearly explain what you need to do in order to achieve a pass, merit or distinction grade.

Assessment activity 2.1

When addressing this learning outcome you will be required to undertake research for a production activity and extract relevant information from a range of written sources. The work for this unit will be assessed in an integrated way, meaning that it will be done as part of your work in other units.

You have been provided with a client brief to generate ideas for a new teen magazine that will be distributed nationwide.

Look into the current market and use your annotation and note taking skills to extract information from a range of relevant sources, such as the Internet, books and current publications, that will help you to generate effective ideas. You could also conduct your own primary research, such as interviews and questionnaires, and present your findings for the client. Outline some initial ideas for the new magazine, drawing on your research.

- Use appropriate techniques to extract relevant information from written sources. **P1**
- Use appropriate techniques to extract information from written sources with some precision. **M1**
- Use appropriate techniques to extract comprehensive information from written sources. **D1**

Grading tips

For a merit grade, you will need to use your skills to extract information that is relevant to your production and that will clearly move forward your ideas and project planning.

For a distinction grade, you will need to use your skills to extract detailed and targeted information that is highly relevant to all the important aspects of your production ideas and planning processes.

There are also suggestions for **activities** that will give you a broader grasp of the industry, stretch your imagination and deepen your skills.

Activity: Profile your class!

The members of your class are likely to include a range of people of different genders, cultures and tastes. Although it is likely that you will all share a broadly common age range it is also likely that you will have very different likes and dislikes.

Over the years, teen culture has been defined in many ways, according to age, musical tastes and dress preferences, and sometimes even race or gender, for example, Teddy Boys, Rockers, Mods and punks.

More common youth culture groups today might include Emo, Indie, Ravers, Gangsta and so on. Again, many of these classifications can be related to musical tastes but can also be related to the type of clothes people wear, their hairstyles and even a tendency towards body piercing.

- As a group, have a go at profiling several volunteers from your class by looking at their mannerisms, the way they dress and how they 'style' themselves. In the first instance you will be relying on a form of stereotyping and making assumptions about these people and their consumption habits.

- Once you have outlined your profiles, ask the volunteers some questions to see if you can get a more detailed picture of them and their interests and tastes.

- Try to link your questions to some of the profiling factors outlined above and see if you can find things that link as well as separate people.

- What have you found to be the most unifying factor between the people you profiled (for example, age, race, gender)?

- When did your profiles start to narrow down and become more defined?

- What did you find difficult about this activity?

Personal, learning and thinking skills

Throughout your BTEC Level 3 National Creative Media Production course, there are lots of opportunities to develop your personal, learning and thinking skills. Look out for these as you progress.

PLTS

Undertaking your pre-production work in your chosen area of creative media production will help you to develop your skills as a **creative thinker**.

Functional skills

It's important that you have good English, mathematics and ICT skills – you never know when you'll need them, and employers will be looking for evidence that you've got these skills too.

Functional skills

Developing the presentation of your research will help you to improve your **ICT** skills in entering, developing and formatting information.

Key terms

Technical words and phrases are easy to spot. You can also use the glossary at the back of the book.

Key term

Recce – a planned and structured visit to a potential production location during pre-production to ascertain its suitability for use.

WorkSpace

Case Studies provide snapshots of real workplace issues, and show how the skills and knowledge you develop during your course can help you in your career.

There are also mini-case studies throughout the book to help you focus on your own projects.

WorkSpace Kieran Clark
Researcher

When the company I work for decides to make a new product, it is important to conduct research into audience tastes and consumption in order to understand how well that product will be received.

If we were making a new reality TV show, for example, we would need to know how popular these types of shows are with current audiences to see whether they are still interested or are suffering from reality fatigue! Television programmes cost a lot of money to make – there is the studio, cast, crew and equipment to be paid for – so producers need to be sure that they are not spending money out that they will never get back.

One of the places I would go to in order to find out audience viewing figures is BARB. We receive regular updates on audience viewing trends and use them to work out what types of programmes are most popular. We can also see if there is a gap in the market for a specific genre of programme that is not currently being produced.

Various kinds of send-ups, particularly of the documentary format, have been popular in recent years but it gets to a point where even the spoof itself becomes so familiar that it just enters the mainstream and doesn't feel so edgy and exciting any more. So then the hunt is on for new ideas that the audience will find fresh and exciting again. Producers are constantly looking for new ways to surprise the audience, whether by finding a new way to play with familiar conventions, or something that breaks with the norms completely.

Think about it!

- At what stage of production does audience research begin?
- Where does Kieran say he gathers information from?
- How does this information help with decisions?
- How can an understanding of the existing conventions of a medium contribute to the development of new ideas?

109

Just checking

When you see this sort of activity, take stock! These quick activities and questions are there to check your knowledge. You can use them to see how much progress you've made or as a revision tool.

Edexcel's assignment tips

At the end of each unit, you'll find hints and tips to help you get the best mark you can, such as the best websites to go to, checklists to help you remember processes and really useful facts and figures.

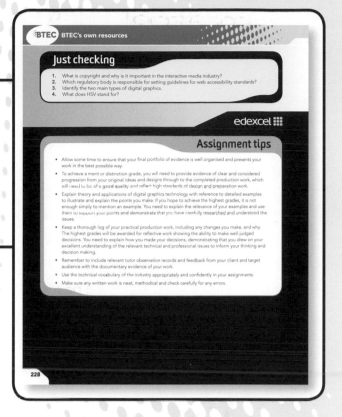

Have you read your **BTEC Level 3 National Creative Media Production Study Skills Guide**? It's full of advice on study skills, putting your assignments together and making the most of being a BTEC Creative Media Production student.

Ask your tutor about extra materials to help you through your course. You'll find interesting videos, activities, presentations and information about the Creative Media Production sector.

Your book is just part of the exciting resources from Edexcel to help you succeed in your BTEC course.

For more details visit:
- www.edexcel.com/BTEC
- www.pearsonfe.co.uk/BTEC 2010

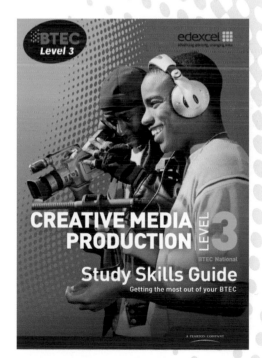

1 Pre-production techniques for the creative media industries

Creative media production is a complex process that requires lots of different elements to come together for it to be a success. Careful planning and preparation at the pre-production stage is important so that you have everything in place to monitor and control the production process itself.

The aim of this unit is to introduce you to the pre-production processes that underpin any successful media product so that you will then be able to develop and apply these to your own production work.

You will learn about the key activities, documentation and sources of information that you will need to understand and be able to use in order to work in pre-production within your chosen media sector. You will then have the opportunity to practise and apply your knowledge and skills to the production work that you are undertaking in some of your other practical units. All of them will benefit from a carefully structured and planned approach to the work. A comprehensive and well-managed pre-production stage should provide a firm foundation for the production itself and ensure that you are able to deal effectively with any issues or problems that crop up along the way.

Learning outcomes

After completing this unit you should:

1. understand requirements for a specific media production
2. be able to prepare pre-production documentation for a specific media production
3. be able to apply pre-production planning for a specific media production.

Assessment and grading criteria

This table shows you what you must do in order to achieve a **pass**, **merit** or **distinction** grade, and where you can find activities in this book to help you.

To achieve a **pass** grade the evidence must show that you are able to:	To achieve a **merit** grade the evidence must show that, in addition to the pass criteria, you are able to:	To achieve a **distinction** grade the evidence must show that, in addition to the pass and merit criteria, you are able to:
P1 outline requirements and sources of requirements for a specific media production **See Assessment activity 1.1, page 12**	**M1** explain in some detail and competently present requirements and sources of requirements for a specific media production **See Assessment activity 1.1, page 12**	**D1** comprehensively explain and present to a quality that reflects near-professional standards fully detailed requirements and sources of requirements for a specific media production **See Assessment activity 1.1, page 12**
P2 generate outline pre-production documentation for a specific media production with some assistance **See Assessment activity, 1.2 page 16**	**M2** generate competent, carefully presented and detailed pre-production documentation for a specific media production with only occasional assistance **See Assessment activity 1.2, page 16**	**D2** generate thorough and comprehensively detailed pre-production documentation for a specific media production, working independently to professional expectations **See Assessment activity 1.2, page 16**
P3 apply pre-production planning to a specific media production working with some assistance **See Assessment activity 1.3, page 18**	**M3** apply pre-production planning to a specific media production competently with only occasional assistance **See Assessment activity 1.3, page 18**	**D3** apply pre-production planning to a specific media production to a quality that reflects near-professional standards, working independently to professional expectations **See Assessment activity 1.3, page 18**

How you will be assessed

This unit will be assessed by a number of internal assignments designed to allow you to show your understanding of the unit outcomes. These relate to what you should be able to do after completing this unit. Most of the assignments that you will complete for this unit will relate to the practical production work that you are doing in some of your other units. This means that the pre-production work that you undertake will relate directly to the media products that you are developing and producing within the other practical units of this course.

Your assessments could be in the form of:

- presentations
- case studies
- practical tasks
- written assignments
- pre-production documentation.

Karen, creative media production student

My college's marketing department gave us a presentation on the services that they provide and they highlighted the need for a new area of the website that specifically targeted 16–19-year-olds. A group from our class decided we would form a production team and use this idea as one of our main production projects.

Because the website had lots of different elements to it, the pre-production stage was particularly important to us as it allowed us to think about all of the things that we needed to get into place before production could begin.

This was quite a high-profile project that would be seen by hundreds of potential learners at the college. The pressure was on to get it right and so we were really pleased that we had the time to go through a pre-production stage.

Some people in the team were impatient and just wanted to start producing the video clips, photographs, written content and graphics for the website but we soon realised that this simply would not work and we were all really glad that we had the time to plan and prepare things properly. It really did make a difference and the production stage ran so much more smoothly than some of our earlier projects had done.

Over to you!

- Why do you think a pre-production stage is so important?
- What processes and activities do you need to undertake in the pre-production stage?
- What skills do you think you will need to develop and then apply throughout this important stage?

1. Understand requirements for a specific media production

Pre-production skills

The process of pre-production is a vital one that you and your team will need to undertake in all of your practical units before the actual production stage begins.

To start you thinking about this process, list all the practical units that you will be undertaking on this course. For each unit identify the potential production projects that you might be involved in.

Discuss with your class all of the activities that you will need to do during the pre-production process before you actually get your hands on the production equipment.

Write the list on the board and discuss with the rest of the class what order you think they should go in and which ones are the most important. Are all of them generic (do they apply to any sort of creative media production) or are some specific to particular types of production?

Discuss what skills you already have that will help you with this stage and also what skills you will need to develop.

1.1 Type of production

In the Set up activity you should have identified the range of different types of production that you will be involved with throughout the course. It does not really matter which pathway you have chosen, or what products you have chosen to work on, as pre-production is a vital stage of any creative production process.

The processes and activities that you learn about in the early parts of this unit should be applied to one or more of the productions that you are working on in your optional practical units. All of them will benefit

Case study: Single-camera drama

When a filming budget is tight, one way to reduce costs is to shoot using a single camera. This reduces the equipment costs and crew costs.

Single-camera production methods are often used in dramas, documentaries and comedies. Two examples of comedy shows that used single-camera techniques for filming are *My Name is Earl* and *The Office*.

Careful pre-production planning needs to be in place for low-budget productions to save time and money during the shoot. Locations need to be carefully chosen to minimise set-up and travel times. Using natural lighting where possible can also reduce crew and equipment costs and again save set-up time.

1. In what ways can careful pre-production planning help if you have a small budget?
2. What are the advantages of undertaking a single-camera production?
3. What problems might be encountered when planning a single-camera production?

from a carefully structured and planned approach to the work, and a comprehensive and well-managed pre-production stage should provide a firm foundation for the production itself.

1.2 Finance

An important part of the pre-production process is to assess the financial viability of the proposed production. There are two aspects to this: first, the potential sources of finance (such as advertising, sponsorship, subscription fees, cover price, sales, rental charges) and second, the expenditure (covering such elements as equipment, materials, transport costs, crew, personnel, facility hire, clearances and legal costs).

It is likely that the productions that you will undertake for your practical units will be subsidised by your college, as you will be using their equipment and materials and you will not have to pay for the personnel on your team. This means that your financial needs will be minimal and you will not necessarily need to secure funding for your projects.

However, you need to demonstrate that you are able to work in a realistic vocational context and you should explore the potential funding for your project as well as the potential costs, as both of these factors are critical to all creative media productions if they are to be viable.

Activity: Sources of finance

Research the potential sources of finance that would be available for your type of media product.

1. How much income do you think you could generate from these sources?
2. How would you go about securing this income?

Write up your findings in the form of a short report.

1.3 Time

The timescale is an important factor for any media production and deadlines can often be very tight. A journalist working on a daily newspaper will have a very tight deadline to research and write a story for the next edition of the paper; the production team who plan and produce the evening television news programmes must have all of the news items completed and ready for broadcast by the specified schedule time.

The timescale and deadlines for your practical projects are likely to be less pressured, but you will still need to think carefully about the availability of your crew and equipment, the timings of the different stages of the production process and the final deadline for the project when you are undertaking your pre-production planning.

Case study: TV drama

TV drama can be expensive to make and the timing of the different aspects needs to be carefully controlled.

The American TV series *Lost* was a high-profile production that had over 250 people working on it, with each episode having a tight three-week production schedule.

This schedule included:

- five days of pre-production planning and preparatory work on scripts, sets and locations followed by three days getting all of the technical aspects in place
- nine days of shooting, with most of this taking place on location in Hawaii
- four days of post-production work, including editing and adding the soundtrack and any special effects.

1. How does the breakdown of time for this programme reflect the timings for your own productions?
2. Why does a series like *Lost* need so many people working on it?
3. Does the fact it was filmed mainly on location add any extra complications to the pre-production process?

1.4 Personnel

Sourcing the right personnel for a media production is another important aspect of the pre-production process and you will need to ensure that your production team is the right size for the job and that each member has the right balance of knowledge, skills and experience to undertake the specific role that is needed.

An important first step is to assess the initial skill level that each member of your team has. You will then be able to plan what skills you need to develop further and how you will be able to do this. This process can also help identify any skills gaps you have and those areas in which you might require extra help and support from other people.

Activity: Skills audit

Carry out a skills audit of your production team.

To do this you need to:

- list all the equipment each member of the team already has experience of using
- identify the level of media production skills and techniques they already have for each item of equipment
- identify any gaps and any areas that you need to develop further.

Draw up an action plan to further develop the team's existing skills and to fill any gaps that you have identified.

Try to use **SMART** targets in your action plan. This means the targets need to be **S**pecific, **M**easurable, **A**chievable and **R**ealistic, and carried out within an appropriate **T**imescale.

You might wish to use a **SWOT** analysis when doing your initial skills audit. Here you identify your **S**trengths and **W**eaknesses, the **O**pportunities that are available to you (resources, workshops, support) and any **T**hreats (barriers) that might get in the way.

1.5 Facilities

Any creative media production will involve the use of production equipment and facilities to capture, record, edit and manipulate the raw material into the finished product. Moving image, audio and photographic products will need equipment and perhaps studios to record and capture the sounds and images that you

Why is pre-production work vital for complex TV productions?

require. Computer hardware and software is now at the heart of the production and post-production processes that are used to create all digital media products.

Professional production companies will either use their own equipment and facilities or hire what they need for a specific production from facility houses. They might even outsource some of the work, such as post-production special effects, to a specialist company.

Activity: Facilities

1. What will you need for your own project?
2. What is available within your school or college?

Do some research to find out what your local facility houses offer and what the costs are.

Are you aware of what equipment and resources you will have available to you when developing your ideas?

1.6 Materials

All media products require raw material for the actual content and you can plan to gather and generate this raw material in various ways.

Some will be original material that you are planning to produce yourself. Undertaking a series of test shoots or recordings can help you further develop your ideas during the pre-production stage, help you to decide what original material you will be able to include in your final product and what is the best way to get the effect that you want.

For example, for a multimedia production project you might need some country sounds, so you would need to look for a suitable location to undertake the recording. After doing a test recording in a local park you might discover that the traffic noise is too loud and, through additional research, discover that you can use some copyright-free sound effects instead.

You may also want to use some existing archive material, such as photographs or film footage, material from a sound or photographic library or sourced from the Internet, or some existing music or graphics. In all of these cases you will need to be aware of **copyright**. Copyright owners can choose to grant permission or license others to use their work, usually for a fee, while retaining ownership over the rights themselves. Like other forms of intellectual property, copyright can be bought and sold.

When you are developing your ideas, think about the permissions that you will need to get before the production process can begin. This might include clearing rights, agreeing royalties or paying fees for copyright material that you are planning to include.

You will need to write to the copyright holder and ask for permission to use the material. You will often have to make a payment for the right to use the material.

You can find more information on copyright and other forms of intellectual property, such as logos and trademarks, on the Intellectual Property Office website (www.ipo.gov.uk).

Key term

Copyright – an automatic right that protects a piece of written or recorded work from being copied or used by anyone else without the copyright owner's permission.

Activity: Test shoots and recordings

If your practical production involves photography, moving image or audio recording, write down a list of the test shoots or recordings that might help you to develop and test your ideas.

Plan what you will need to do to undertake the test shoots or recordings and discuss your ideas with your tutor.

Did you know?

Performing rights royalties are paid to a writer, composer or publisher whenever their music is played or performed in a public space such as on television, radio, on the Internet, in a shop or restaurant, or at an event such as a concert or a football match.

Mechanical rights royalties are paid to a writer, composer or publisher when music is reproduced and used in a physical product or artefact such as a television programme or a video game.

1.7 Contributors

As well as needing a production team, you may also need other people to contribute to your project. You might be able to acquire the services of actors, presenters or voice-over artists (referred to as **talent**) to make your product look and sound more professional and might also include contributions from experts in the area that you are dealing with in your media production or the general public.

Remember that you will need to get permission from people who are featured or quoted in your media production and you should get them to sign a release and consent agreement form so that you have documentary evidence of their permission to be featured. You should also include a biography of the contributors in the supporting documentation that you produce.

Key term

Talent – the professional people who feature in a production such as actors, presenters, dancers and voice-over artists.

Release Form

Model's Name: .... Model's Age: ....

Photographer/Recorder's Name: ....

Contact Number: ....

Project Title: ....

I hereby agree to the use of my Photograph and/or the recording of my voice in the above-mentioned project (the name of which may change), the nature and content of which have been fully explained to me.

I agree that [INSERT NAME] does not have to use the Photograph but, if they do so, they may cut and edit it as they wish and use it in any manner including in any publicity or advertising for the project.

I understand and agree that, unless I give my express permission to the contrary, the Photograph is not specifically intended to represent me and will be used to represent a fictional person.

I hereby grant a licence for use in this project in print and electronic format to [INSERT NAME].

The term "Photograph" as used herein includes still photographs, voice recordings and video recordings.

Signed by the Model: .... Date: ....

Signed on behalf of [INSERT NAME]: ....

Print name: .... Date: ....

Figure 1.1: An example of a release form. How might you need to adapt the wording of a release and consent agreement form to cover different situations and uses?

1.8 Locations

It is important to check out appropriate locations during the pre-production phase. This can save lots of time and money during the production stage.

Having crew, talent and equipment out on location can be very expensive and so you need to maximise the amount of material that you can produce in the shortest time possible. You also need to ensure that the locations are suitable for your purpose, that you can obtain permission, if necessary, to work at the location, and that you are aware of any risks and health and safety issues that may be present. You will also need to secure permission from any people who might feature in your product (for example, people working at a location that you intend to use).

A location reconnaissance (or **recce**) is a visit to a potential production location that is carried out during pre-production to ascertain its suitability. The information that you bring back from the recce will inform the production schedule as you will be able to find out about distance, access, power supply, potential problems over weather, health and safety issues and any costs associated with using that particular location.

Details from the recce should be recorded on a location visit sheet and attached to your production schedule so that all members of the production team are aware of the information that has been gathered.

Key term

Recce – a planned and structured visit to a potential production location during pre-production to ascertain its suitability for use.

1.9 Codes of practice and regulation

One of the reasons that media companies undertake pre-production work is to make sure that what they are planning to produce adheres to the relevant codes of practice, laws and regulations that govern and control their industry.

We have already looked at some of the legal issues that you must consider during pre-production, including obtaining permission to use any copyright material, the health and safety considerations that you

should be aware of before production can begin, and gaining permission from people who may appear in your work.

Public liability

Public liability is another legal requirement for companies and organisations who are involved in creative media production, particularly when they are recording on location where members of the public may be at risk from the production activities. Because you are a learner, your school or college should already have public liability insurance for your production work, but you should check this out just to be sure. Commercial companies will also have a range of other forms of insurance to cover their employees, their equipment and even the products that they are working on.

Activity: Filming in London

London is the third busiest city in the world for filming and there is a film or TV crew on the streets almost every day of the year.

The Film London website is an important source of information for companies in the pre-production stage who are looking to film in the capital and contains lots of invaluable information and links to support the planning process.

Visit the Film London website (www.filmlondon.org.uk) and find out more information about the clearances, permissions and legal requirements that are needed before a crew can start filming.

Regulatory bodies, trade unions and trade associations

During pre-production you also need to be aware of the relevant codes of practice and industrial guidelines and regulations that relate to your specific area of production. You will need to undertake some careful research to find out what the constraints are for the media sector that you are working within.

Table 1.1 shows some of the main regulatory bodies that limit and control what a media sector can and cannot produce. Table 1.2 lists some of the trade unions and associations that represent people working in media industries.

Table 1.1: Main regulatory bodies in the media sector.

Media sector	Regulatory body	Website
Television and radio	Ofcom	www.ofcom.org.uk
Film	British Board of Film Classification (bbfc)	www.bbfc.co.uk
Computer games	Pan European Game Information (PEGI)	www.pegi.info
	Entertainment Software Rating Board (ESRB)	www.esrb.org
Newspapers and magazines	Press Complaints Commission (PCC)	www.pcc.org.uk
Advertising	Advertising Standards Authority (ASA)	www.asa.org.uk
Internet	W3C (World Wide Web Consortium)	www.w3.org

Table 1.2: Trade unions and associations in the media sector.

Trade union / association	Website
Pact (Producers' Alliance for Cinema and Television)	www.pact.co.uk
NUJ (National Union of Journalists)	www.nuj.org.uk
BECTU (Broadcasting Entertainment, Cinematograph and Theatre Union)	www.bectu.org.uk
TIGA (The Independent Games Developers' Association)	www.tiga.org
ELSPA (The Entertainment and Leisure Software Publishers Association)	www.elspa.com
BIMA (The British Interactive Media Association)	www.bima.co.uk

Visit the websites of the organisations associated with your area of interest to find out what they do.

Did you know?

Computer games are becoming an increasingly popular form of digital entertainment all over Europe, though they are more popular in some countries than others. In 2010 the Interactive Software Federation of Europe (ISFE) reported that 32 per cent of the UK population aged 16–49 described themselves as 'active gamers', playing games on a console, a handheld device, a mobile phone or a PC. In comparison, in Spain and Italy the equivalent figure was respectively 24 per cent and 17 per cent. (Source: *Video Gamers in Europe 2010*, ISFE).

Computer games are becoming ever more sophisticated. Do some research to find out what the next generation of computer gaming is likely to bring.

Case study: Pan European Game Information

In June 2009 the Department of Culture, Media and Sport made the decision that the Pan European Game Information (PEGI) would be the sole classification system for computer games and interactive software in the UK. In the past the British Board of Film Classification (bbfc) classified some computer games as well as films and DVDs.

The PEGI system is now used in more than 30 European countries and is based on a self-regulatory code of conduct to which every games publisher is contractually committed.

The PEGI classification consists of five age categories and eight content descriptors that give advice on the suitability of a game for a certain age range based on the game's content.

Icons are used to indicate each of the content descriptors in Table 1.3.

1. Why is it better to have a pan-European classification rather than each country having its own system?

2. Find out from the PEGI website what the age classifications are, and what they mean. Do you think that the age classification system works?

3. Can you think of examples of computer games that fit each of the content descriptors?

Table 1.3: PEGI classification system.

Icon	Content descriptor	Explanation
	Violence	May contain scenes of violence and people getting injured or dying, often by use of weapons.
	Profanity (bad language)	May contain swearing and sexual innuendo.
	Fear	May contain scenes that are considered too disturbing or frightening for younger or more emotionally vulnerable players.
	Sex	May contain nudity and references to sexual activity.
	Drugs	May contain references to illegal drugs.
	Discrimination	May contain scenes of cruelty or harassment based on race, ethnicity, gender or sexual preferences.
	Gambling	May contain games that are played for money (real or simulated).
	Online	Contains an online game mode.

(Source: Adapted from information on PEGI website: www.pegi.info/en/index/id/23)

Assessment activity 1.1

P1 M1 D1 **BTEC**

Choose one of the production projects that you are undertaking in one of your practical option units. Take the role of production co-ordinator for this project and plan and produce a report that describes the requirements and the sources of requirements for the specific media production you are undertaking. You should make sure that your report covers all of the following aspects:

- type of production you are undertaking
- finance
- timescale
- personnel
- facilities
- materials
- contributors
- locations
- codes of practice and regulations.

Your report should be well written, using appropriate terminology, and be carefully checked through for accurate spelling, punctuation and grammar.

Grading tips

For a merit grade, your report needs to demonstrate good understanding of the relevant issues. These should include the relevant codes of practice, laws and regulations that apply to the production work that you are planning, together with a detailed explanation of where the information can be sourced from. Your report should be clearly and carefully produced and explain in some detail the relevant pre-production requirements for your proposed production and why they are important.

For a distinction grade, your report needs to reflect near-professional standards and be fully considered and detailed. It should demonstrate an excellent understanding of the requirements for the proposed production and explain fully why each aspect is required. This includes a full and detailed consideration of the relevant codes of practice, laws and regulations that apply to the production work that you are planning, together with a fully detailed explanation as to where the information can be sourced from.

PLTS

Investigating the relevant pre-production requirements for your proposed production will help develop your skills as an **independent enquirer**.

Functional skills

Producing your written report on the relevant pre-production requirements for your proposed production will help you to develop your **English** skills in writing.

2.   Be able to prepare pre-production documentation for a specific media production

Having established which key aspects of pre-production are important to your particular production, you can now begin to plan it in more detail and begin to prepare the appropriate documentation.

2.1 Procedure

The specific pre-production processes and procedures that you follow will be dictated by the particular production that you are planning. However, whatever your production is you should ensure that you cover all of the following key areas.

- Identify finance, personnel and resources that are required and are available to you and your production team.
- Prepare a budget.
- Book personnel and resources.
- Prepare a detailed production schedule.
- Identify relevant health and safety issues, risk to the project and any legal issues.

A **production schedule** is a planning document that brings together all of the information needed for a particular production. It is referred to and monitored throughout the production stages and shows the production team where they are against the planned schedule and what resources and personnel they need to have in place for the next part of the process. It is an important document for you to include in your final portfolio and you will need to ensure that it is detailed and comprehensive if you are aiming for a high grade.

A production schedule should contain the following key elements:

- details of the original proposal
- key dates as agreed with the client for the different stages of pre-production, production and post-production, together with a final completion date
- details of production equipment required and where it is being sourced from
- location details and any transport required
- full details of the crew, talent and other personnel with contact details
- any props and other resources required.

The production schedule is often supplemented with a sheet that details the specific plan and resources for a single day of production – this is called a **call sheet**. A call sheet is often given to the crew, talent and personnel required for each day of production so that everybody is clear who is needed where and what they need to do.

Key terms

Production schedule – a planning document that brings together all of the information needed for a particular production. It gives an overview of the whole production.

Call sheet – details the specific plan and resources needed for a single day of production.

Activity: Production schedule

Start to put together the production schedule for one of the practical projects that you are working on in your other units. Make sure that you include all of the elements identified above and that it is clear and detailed.

2.2 Documentation

The pre-production documentation that you develop will vary depending on which production medium you are working in and will form an important part of your completed portfolio.

For example, if you are planning a moving image production you will develop and refine your ideas through a storyboard and script. For a printed product such as a magazine or newspaper you will produce ideas sheets, rough drafts, concept drawings, sample designs and thumbnails of the pages you are planning to produce. For an interactive media product you might use all of the above together with a mood board to give you an idea about the overall look and feel of the product. A web-based interactive product might also need a structure diagram (a way of planning out the structure of the different web pages that need to be produced) to show the links between the different web pages and the order in which they are accessed by the user.

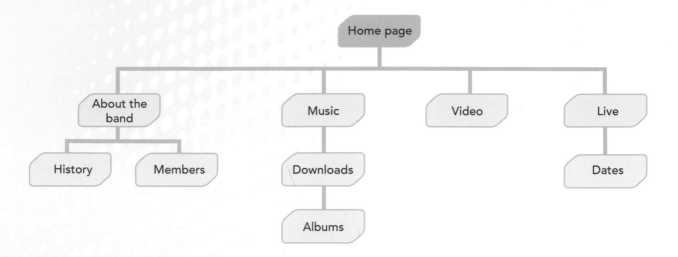

Figure 1.2: This is a structure diagram that a learner produced for a website for a band. What additional pages could be added to the structure to further improve the website?

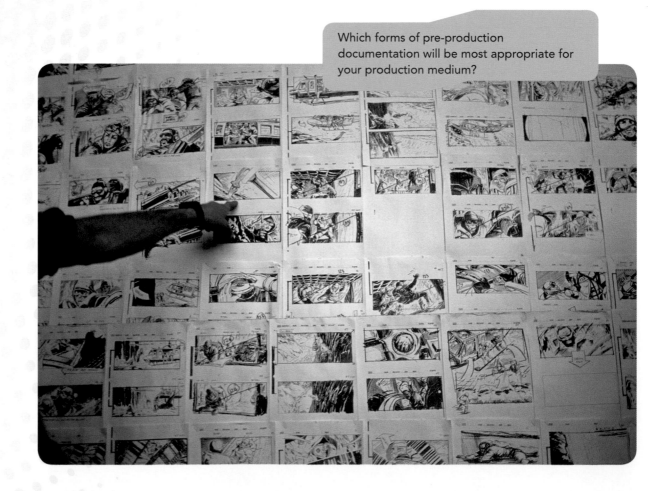

As your plans come together, and before you actually start the production process itself, you will need to put together a detailed production schedule showing what you are going to do and when and how you are going to do it. This schedule is the plan that you will take with you through to the production stage. It will help you to keep track of where you are in the process and what you need to do next.

You will also need to undertake risk assessments and consider the relevant health and safety issues. You should also have a contingency plan just in case things go wrong.

The contingency plan should cover all aspects of the production including personnel, equipment and locations. You need to have alternative arrangements ready in case things do not quite go to the original plan so that your project stays on track and will still be completed within the specified time frame.

Table 1.4 shows you examples of the types of pre-production documentation you might use for each production type, together with an explanation.

Table 1.4: Pre-production documentation.

Production type	Pre-production documentation	What is it?
All types of production	Production schedule	A detailed plan that brings together all the information needed for your particular production to take place.
	Call sheet	A document that details the specific plan and resources needed for a single day of production.
	Risk assessments	Details of things that could go wrong and relevant health and safety issues (see Unit 4, Creative media production management project for more information).
	Contingency plan	This links to your risk assessment and shows what your alternative plan is if some of the things that could go wrong actually do.
	Permissions	Forms that give you permission to film in the places that you want to and to include the people that you want in your final product.
Moving image	Storyboard	A visualisation of each shot of your finished programme that includes timings and details of the soundtrack.
	Script	What the people in the programme are going to say, together with how they are going to say it and any music or sound effects.
	Shooting script	A more detailed script that includes camera angles, locations, types of shot, dialogue and soundtrack.
Radio and sound recording	Script	What the people in the programme are going to say, together with how they are going to say it and any music or sound effects.
Print and interactive media	Concept drawings	Drawings of what a picture or page might look like.
	Thumbnails	Rough sketches of a proposed page layout.
	Mood boards	Collection of different examples of colour, text and styles to show how the finished product will look and feel.
Web-based interactive media and games	Structure diagrams	Similar to a storyboard for a web-based interactive product; shows the hierarchy of the pages and the links between them.

Assessment activity 1.2

P2 M2 D2 BTEC

The assessment activity for this element of the unit will be the pre-production work that you undertake for your specified media production.

The evidence for the achievement of the learning outcome will be the pre-production documentation and paperwork that you complete, together with a production log that contains records of pre-production meetings, discussions and research, supported by tutor observations and witness statements where appropriate.

Grading tips

To achieve a merit grade, your pre-production work must be carefully presented, well developed and well organised, and demonstrate some depth and detail in the pre-production documentation produced, with only occasional assistance.

To achieve a distinction grade, you must generate thorough and comprehensively detailed pre-production documentation, working independently to professional expectations. This means that you must demonstrate good self-management skills, showing that you can work on your own initiative and work positively and cooperatively with others to meet deadlines.

PLTS

Undertaking your pre-production work in your chosen area of creative media production will help you to develop your skills as a **creative thinker**.

Functional skills

Producing your pre-production documentation will help you to develop your **English** skills in writing.

3.   Be able to apply pre-production planning for a specific media production

Everything should now be in place so you can apply and use the pre-production planning as you work through the production and post-production stages of one of your option units.

The creative process is a complex one and the logistics can be difficult to control at times, but this is one reason why the pre-production planning is so important.

3.1 Elements of production

The pre-production work that you completed earlier in this unit should provide a secure framework for the production to be undertaken, but the production process will still need careful management if it is to produce a successful final product.

You will need to keep a careful eye on the finance as the production unfolds and ensure that the different elements such as crew, talent, personnel, equipment and resources all come together in the right way, at the right time and in the right place.

3.2 Project management

Clear communication and good organisational skills are perhaps the two most important aspects to successful production management. You should ensure that you fully record and document all of the meetings and briefings that you have with your team and keep all the relevant paperwork and documentation up to date. Make sure that all decisions are noted and any action points for individuals are clearly written up so that everyone knows exactly what is expected of them.

Did you know?

James Cameron, the director of *Titanic* (2007), forfeited his $8 million director's salary and his percentage of the gross profits when the studio that had set the budget and provided the finance became concerned at how much over budget the film was running. The film was initially budgeted at $135 million but after going two months over schedule required an additional $65 million to be completed.

Activity: Most expensive film?

James Cameron's film *Avatar* (2009) is reported to be the most expensive film ever made with estimates of the budget ranging from $230 million to $500 million.

1. How would you keep track of your project budget?
2. What plans do you need to make for contingency?

FROM THE DIRECTOR OF "TITANIC"

AVATAR

What difficulties do you think there are in managing costs for a big budget film?

Assessment activity 1.3

P3 M3 D3 BTEC

For the assessment activity for this element of the unit you will apply your pre-production planning to the production of your specified media product that was the focus of the first two assessment activities.

The evidence for the achievement of the learning outcome will be a production log which documents and records the ways in which you used and applied the pre-production planning throughout the production process. You should also include a personal evaluation in your final portfolio together with any relevant tutor observations and witness statements where appropriate.

Grading tips

To achieve a merit grade, you must apply your pre-production planning to your particular media production competently and with only occasional assistance. This means that you need to demonstrate good organisational skills in the work that you are undertaking.

To achieve a distinction grade, you must apply your pre-production planning to your particular media production to a quality that reflects near-professional standards, working independently to professional expectations. This means that you must demonstrate good self-management skills, showing that you can work on your own initiative and work positively and cooperatively with others to meet deadlines.

PLTS

Applying your pre-production planning to your media production work will help you to develop your skills as a **creative thinker**, a **team worker** and a **self-manager**.

Functional skills

Producing your production log and records will help you to develop your **English** skills in writing.

Isaac Williams

Production assistant in television broadcasting

My role as a production assistant (PA) for a broadcasting company is very varied and I am involved with all stages of the pre-production and production processes.

I have to work closely with other members of the team and get involved with lots of different aspects of production. Being a PA means that I have to have a good overview of the whole production and have good technical, creative and administrative skills and knowledge. I also have to be a good communicator as I have to deal with lots of different sorts of people and make sure that information doesn't get lost or confused.

This means I have to be very organised and listen carefully to what the production team want me to do and what information they need next. I also have to keep the pre-production documentation well organised as a member of the team will often ask me for the production schedule, to see what is happening next, or the latest version of a storyboard or script so that some changes can be made.

I also have to get the call sheets out to the relevant people in time for them to get themselves organised and make sure that they are at a location on time.

I have learned that having a positive attitude and a 'can do' approach is very important to working in the industry and that you have to be able to work well on your own as well as being an effective team member.

Think about it!

- What skills do you have already that would help you to play a positive role in a pre-production team? Discuss with the rest of your class and then produce a written summary of your key points.
- What further skills might you need to develop to be successful in pre-production? Write a list and discuss with the rest of the class.
- Why is pre-production such an important stage of the creative media production process?

Just checking

1. Why is the pre-production stage so important?
2. Identify the main aspects that need to be considered when undertaking pre-production.
3. Why is copyright an important issue to consider?
4. What is a recce and why can it be an important part of the pre-production process?
5. Identify the main regulatory bodies for your chosen media sector and explain what their remit is.
6. Identify the eight content descriptors used in the PEGI classification system.
7. What is a production schedule and what should it contain?
8. What pre-production documentation should you use for your chosen area?
9. What evidence should you generate to show that you have successfully applied your pre-production planning to your media production work?

edexcel

Assignment tips

- Link the work you are doing for this unit with one of the practical productions that you are undertaking in one of your optional units.

- Make sure your team meetings are minuted so people know what was decided and what is expected of them, and to ensure you have good evidence of pre-production work and team work for your final portfolio.

- Spend time planning your production and use the correct pre-production documentation to help you develop your ideas.

- Make sure your production schedule and other written documents are detailed and comprehensive and cover all of the required elements.

- Allow some time at the end of the unit to ensure that your final portfolio of evidence is well organised and presents your work in the best possible way.

Credit value: 5

2 Communication skills for creative media production

Effective communication skills are required in all businesses and industries around the world but are especially important when working in the creative and media sector where whatever your job, you'll need to communicate with lots of different people for different purposes. You are required to communicate with your colleagues and co-workers, you need to communicate your ideas and concepts to clients and you need to be able to communicate effectively with your audience, who will receive and consume your products.

This unit has been designed to target these essential skills and to help you to develop them in a vocational context. Here you will be required to undertake sound written and oral communication and to use your skills and knowledge to undertake effective research into your production work, extracting targeted and relevant information through use of annotation.

All your production work will require the use of relevant documentation. Outline briefs and treatments will be an intrinsic part of that work. You should produce these documents in response to a client brief and they should be detailed, well written and free from errors; they are representative of professional practice within the industry and will be a marker of your own professional conduct and ability to respond to client needs.

You will also be required to undertake presentations or 'pitches' to clients according to a set brief and you will need to be able to outline for them your ideas for your production using relevant technology and vocational and specialist language and terminology.

Learning outcomes

After completing this unit you should:

1. be able to extract information from written sources
2. be able to create a report in a media production context
3. be able to pitch a media production proposal using appropriate technology.

Assessment and grading criteria

This table shows you what you must do in order to achieve a **pass**, **merit** or **distinction** grade, and where you can find activities in this book to help you.

To achieve a **pass** grade the evidence must show that you are able to:	To achieve a **merit** grade the evidence must show that, in addition to the pass criteria, you are able to:	To achieve a **distinction** grade the evidence must show that, in addition to the pass and merit criteria, you are able to:
P1 use appropriate techniques to extract relevant information from written sources **See Assessment activity 2.1, page 26**	**M1** use appropriate techniques to extract information from written sources with some precision **See Assessment activity 2.1, page 26**	**D1** use appropriate techniques to extract comprehensive information from written sources **See Assessment activity 2.1, page 26**
P2 present a media production report which conveys relevant information **See Assessment activity 2.2, pages 30–31**	**M2** present a structured and detailed media production report which conveys information and explains conclusions with clarity **See Assessment activity 2.2, pages 30–31**	**D2** present a well-structured and substantial media production report which conveys information with precise exemplification and justifies conclusions with supporting arguments **See Assessment activity 2.2, pages 30–31**
P3 review reports to make changes with occasional beneficial effects **See Assessment activity 2.2, pages 30–31**	**M3** review reports to make changes with frequent beneficial effects **See Assessment activity 2.2, pages 30–31**	**D3** review reports to make changes with consistently beneficial effects **See Assessment activity 2.2, pages 30–31**
P4 deploy and manage appropriate technology to pitch a media production proposal **See Assessment activity 2.3, page 36**	**M4** deploy and manage technology to pitch a media production proposal effectively and with some imagination **See Assessment activity 2.3, page 36**	**D4** deploy and manage technology to pitch a media production proposal with creativity and flair and to near-professional standards **See Assessment activity 2.3, page 36**
P5 employ appropriate forms of address in a media production pitch to communicate ideas **See Assessment activity 2.3, page 36**	**M5** employ forms of address in a media production pitch to communicate ideas effectively **See Assessment activity 2.3, page 36**	**D5** employ forms of address in a media production pitch with flair to communicate ideas with impact **See Assessment activity 2.3, page 36**

How you will be assessed

Assessment for this unit can take many forms, from assignments requiring written reports and documentation to observed oral presentations. It is very likely that the work required for this unit will be undertaken in other units such as the optional practical production units chosen by your centre. Your tutor will track your progress in an integrated assignment, rather than by separate assessment.

Your assessment could take any of the following forms:

- undertaking written assignment work including production paperwork
- pitching your ideas to the tutor/client
- presenting the results of your investigations in written and oral formats
- undertaking annotated research work.

Zander, creative media production student

When I first started the course I didn't realise how much planning and research was involved in production work. I may have been a little naïve but I really thought that if I had a good idea then I could just go ahead and make a product using the technical skills I had been taught.

When I thought about it, it made sense that there should be a level of planning and preparation. In the real world I would be working for someone who would have clear ideas about what they wanted and why.

Proposals and treatments are a good way of planning a production and presenting your ideas to a client. It gives them a clear and detailed understanding of what the production is about and what your intentions are.

Now I start by outlining everything in a proposal such as my idea, the narrative or story and the target audience. Then I pass that over to the client for approval.

The proposal is a bit like putting in a bid: you offer the client an idea and then they decide whether they want to see more. If they like your ideas you then go into more detail and produce a treatment which forms the basis of the production.

Finally you really need to sell your ideas and try to convince the client to let you make their product for them. It's all a process and it needs to be well planned and researched if you are going to get the job!

Over to you!

- Why is it important to produce production paperwork?
- What is a proposal?
- What is a treatment and how is it different from a proposal?
- Why do you have to present a pitch to the client?
- What will happen if the client likes your treatment and pitch and approves your ideas?

1. Be able to extract information from written sources

Choosing the right materials

Deciding where to source information can be as complicated as actually extracting the information itself. Before you decide where to look for information you need to think about what you want to find out and how it will help you with your production.

First read through your assignment brief carefully and look for key words to help you to identify your research parameters. Establish what you are looking for and think about the kind of sources that might provide the information you need.

- What type of product are you being asked to produce?
- What is the specified target audience?
- Have you been given a specific genre to work in?
- Are you required to look at budgeting?
- Can you foresee any constraints being placed on your product?

Remember that the Internet is not the only source of information. Books, magazines, newspapers and so on can also provide useful information. You may also need to carry out your own research using questionnaires and interviews, and collate the data so that you can then extract relevant information.

For this learning outcome you will be required to undertake research for your production work, which is likely to be linked to Unit 3, Research techniques for the creative media industries. You will need to be able to extract targeted and relevant information from a variety of different sources that will be beneficial to your production work throughout.

You should use sound and established methods to extract the required information, such as targeted searches and annotation, which will allow you to generate materials that are clear and concise and contain only relevant information.

1.1 What information am I looking for?

You will need to sift through your research to locate information that will help you to generate ideas and produce the required production documentation for submission to the client. The following types of information will prove helpful.

Similar products – looking at products similar to the one you have been asked to produce will allow you to get ideas about content, style and format. If you are looking at print production, for example, you could get a similar magazine and begin highlighting content such as cover styles, contents pages – what is in them? – use of photography, writing style and use of fonts.

Costing/budgeting – all productions from the largest to the smallest cost money! A **budget** is what your production is going to cost. This needs to be broken down and detailed for the client so they know how much they will be spending and what they are getting for their money. You will be asked to work on a client brief and you will be expected to treat it like a 'real' project. You want to get this job and produce this product for the client so you need to be competitive,

Key term

Budget – what your production is going to cost.

yet realistic. If you are planning a media production, although you will be using college/school facilities you will need to research the costs of production equipment and resources in real terms. How much does it cost to hire camera equipment, editing or filming studios, lighting and sound equipment and actors? What about printing costs? Are you using copyright material and if so how much will it cost?

Legal and ethical constraints – all media production work will be subject to legal and ethical constraints. Being **ethical** means ensuring that you are working within accepted social 'norms' – that you are being principled in your actions and making sure that rules and values are upheld. **Constraints** are the limits put on your production – what you can and cannot do – and they must be taken into consideration at all times. You are producing something that will be supplied to the public and it has to be suitable for their consumption. You have to think in terms of your target audience and ensure that your content is age appropriate. You cannot be sexist or racist and you must consider issues such as scheduling and product placement.

Distribution/commissioning – this relates to who is paying you to make a product and where that product will ultimately be released to the public. If, for example, you are being commissioned by the BBC, you will need to look at where and when they schedule similar products and gain an understanding of the commissioning process. If you are working independently and are producing a product for your own purposes you must consider who will buy it and how they can access it. For example, a DVD would need to be distributed to relevant shops and outlets either locally or nationwide; similarly a magazine or newspaper would need to be available in newsagents, supermarkets and so on.

How will this information help me?

The information you gather will help to inform your entire production. It will help you to generate ideas and to plan and lay out your proposals and treatments.

1.2 Where do I source relevant information?

Information (mainly sources for **secondary research** – research using information that has already been gathered by other people or organisations) can be found in many different places. Remember that you will always have to sift through the information to find what is relevant to you and your production.

Books – school, college and local libraries should have a range of books relevant to your studies. Sections can be photocopied and taken away for annotation.

Internet – there are many websites available but take care to use trustworthy sites if you need accurate factual information. Avoid getting overwhelmed by the volume of material by keeping firmly in mind the questions you want to answer and sifting carefully through the information for relevant details. Remember to give references for your sources and any quotations, and add them to your bibliography.

Newspapers/magazines/journals – trade journals for your chosen industry and newspaper and magazine articles can often have useful articles.

Television – you can use the wide range of entertainment media to research similar products, but also refer to factual productions such as documentaries and news programmes for information.

Primary research – **primary research** is original research to obtain new information. You can gather the thoughts and opinions of others using questionnaires and interviews, then collate and present relevant findings as appropriate in reports and so on.

1.3 How do I extract relevant information?

The method that you use to extract information from texts and other sources will depend on the activity you are undertaking. It is important to have a clear idea of what you are looking for in the first place. Try writing down some questions you want the answers to or making an outline plan of the information you need to help you to focus on identifying relevant details in your sources.

Key terms

Ethical – ensuring that you are working within the accepted social 'norms' and that rules and values are upheld.

Constraints – the limits put on your production.

Primary research – original research to obtain new information using techniques like interviews, questionnaires and focus groups.

Secondary research – research using existing information that has already been gathered by other people or organisations.

For the most part you will be reading through documents and it is important that you ensure you do so in a space where you can concentrate, that you allow yourself time to read through the material and that you have a focus for your work.

Different reading methods will help you to locate the required information.

- **Skim-reading** – quickly skimming over a text to get the gist of it, so that you can decide whether to read it in more detail. Does it look as though it might have some of the answers you are looking for?

- **Scanning** – searching through the text looking for specific key words or phrases. When you have spotted the relevant terms you can then read that section in more detail.

- **Using an index** – in print products, the index allows you to find where a topic is mentioned so you can go straight to the page you need.

- **Using word and phrase search** – these are electronic search methods. You can 'google' words and phrases to find relevant websites, or use 'search' or 'find' commands to find specific terms used in electronic texts (for example, online journals).

Once you have located useful information, you need to extract the relevant details. You could do the following.

- Highlight text or underline passages in books (if they are your own!), on photocopies, on printouts and so on. This will help you to focus on relevant information which can then be written up into notes.

- Copy and paste extracts from web pages and electronic texts. Remember that this is only a means of extracting information and should never be used within your own work, as that would be plagiarism.

- Write notes. These should summarise relevant details from the information that you have found, in your own words.

Try using these methods in the activity on the next page and see if you can extract useful information.

Assessment activity 2.1   P1 M1 D1 · BTEC

When addressing this learning outcome you will be required to undertake research for a production activity and extract relevant information from a range of written sources. The work for this unit will be assessed in an integrated way, meaning that it will be done as part of your work in other units.

You have been provided with a client brief to generate ideas for a new teen magazine that will be distributed nationwide.

Look into the current market and use your annotation and note-taking skills to extract information from a range of relevant sources, such as the Internet, books and current publications, that will help you to generate effective ideas. You could also conduct your own primary research, such as interviews and questionnaires, and present your findings for the client. Outline some initial ideas for the new magazine, drawing on your research.

- Use appropriate techniques to extract *relevant information* from written sources. **P1**

- Use appropriate techniques to extract *information* from written sources *with some precision.* **M1**

- Use appropriate techniques to extract *comprehensive information* from written sources. **D1**

Grading tips

For a merit grade, you will need to use your skills to extract information that is relevant to your production and that will clearly move forward your ideas and project planning.

For a distinction grade, you will need to use your skills to extract detailed and targeted information that is highly relevant to all the important aspects of your production ideas and planning processes.

PLTS

Planning and carrying out research which involves gathering information from written sources will help develop your skills as an **independent enquirer**.

Functional skills

Gathering and annotating research from a variety of sources will help you to develop your **English** skills.

Activity: Extracting information from a document

The following information outlines how front covers of fashion magazines, teen magazines, music magazines and so on are laid out. Read through the information and make a note of what you feel would be relevant to you if you were designing a fashion magazine cover for a client. Focus on aspects such as cover design layout, use of colour, use of fonts and use of pictures, as well as use of text and captions.

Table 2.1: Items included on a magazine cover.

Masthead or logo	This must be distinctive, eye catching and relevant to the magazine genre.
Publication date	This must show when the magazine is published, for example, weekly, fortnightly, monthly or quarterly.
Main image	This usually relates to the main 'feature' within the publication and again should catch the eye of the reader or target audience.
Cover lines	These are the sections of text that are spread over the front page and again relate to the features and content of the magazine.
Main cover line	This should go alongside the main image and relate to the main 'feature article'.
Bar code	All magazines have a bar code that is scanned at point of purchase; thought needs to go into its placement so that it does not interfere with the main features of the front cover.
Selling line	This is what will sell the magazine to the consumer. It needs to be punchy and give the reader a reason to pick up the product and buy it. Consider it in the same terms as, say, a headline in a newspaper as a summary of the content.

1. Which method (for example, skim-reading, underlining) did you find most useful for identifying key information?
2. How relevant is the information you have extracted?
3. Could you edit down that information further still?

Which magazines do you think make the best use of layout?

2. Be able to create a report in a media production context

In your media production work you will be asked to produce many different types of document. Some will be for research and planning purposes, some will be based on pre-production and production work and may only be relevant to a specific medium, or you may have to complete post-production paperwork. You may also be required to write essays or reports outlining the result of your investigations into a particular medium or genre.

Whatever the purpose, you need to ensure that your work is relevant and fits the purpose for which it was intended. You also need to check your work on a regular basis and make any changes necessary to improve the content and quality. This section gives guidance on how to do this and provides examples of documents you may see.

2.1 Create report

When creating content for a report or document you need to consider the overall structure, how you want the work to be presented and what you are trying to convey to the reader. Begin by making rough drafts of the content and sketch out where you could add graphics, charts and graphs to illustrate any research or other information you have gathered.

Be sure to use an appropriate tone for the document and take care not to use slang or text talk, unless it is for an illustrative example. This informal type of language has no place in formal reports or professional documentation and will have a damaging effect on the overall content and presentation of your work.

When writing reports, provide a summary of your main points in the conclusion and provide a contents list, an index and a bibliography so that the reader can find specific information and knows where you found your information.

Using charts and graphs to represent the results of primary and secondary research helps the reader to understand what you are saying quickly and easily. Bar charts can provide a good comparative illustration (for example, showing how many men and how many women watch television at different times of day), whereas pie charts are good for showing proportions, for example, how much of the viewing audience is

Activity: Creating charts and graphs

Here are the results of a questionnaire on what people think about graffiti, carried out by a learner who was doing research for a new magazine about graffiti.

Gender					
Female	**13**	Male	**12**		
Age					
10–13	**3**	14–16	**6**	17–19	**10**
20–25	**4**	20+	**2**		
Do you like graffiti?					
Yes	**7**	No	**11**	Some of them	**7**
Do you think that graffiti is vandalism?					
Yes	**5**	No	**5**	Depends	**15**
What do you think about designated places for graffiti ('legal walls')?					
Good	**22**	Bad	**3**	Don't care	**0**
Would you consider graffiti as a form of art?					
Yes	**12**	No	**3**	Sometimes	**10**
Do you know any graffiti artists?					
Yes	**7**	No	**18**		
Do you like to draw?					
Yes	**11**	No	**5**	Sometimes	**9**
Have you ever tried to make graffiti (including on paper)?					
Yes	**9**	No	**16**		
If yes, at what stage do you think you are?					
Amateur **5**		Advanced **4**		Professional	**0**
Would you like to learn how to create graffiti?					
Yes	**11**	No	**14**		

Figure 2.1: There is a lot of information here that is relevant to the proposed product. How would you present it?

1. Extract and present relevant information for a range of purposes, such as which gender or age group the magazine should be aimed at, what level of experience of graffiti the readership might have. Create and appraise both bar and pie charts for each aspect you want to represent. Which works best for this purpose?

2. Can you think of suitable titles and labels to explain the relevance of each section of your chart?

3. Does the questionnaire give you all the information you want? If not, what do you still need to know? How would you change the questionnaire if you did it again?

watching a particular programme. Charts are especially relevant in media studies as you will often need to interpret and display your research into the views of a mass audience in a way that can be readily understood.

2.2 Contexts

You will be asked to produce reports and documentation for a range of reasons so you need to ensure that your work is always relevant and suitable for the context.

Your report may be for a client who is commissioning you to undertake work for them. Or you may have been asked to produce work for your employer as a member of a production team. In both cases you need to present your work professionally using accurate specialist terms, an appropriate formal 'register' (tone) and concise, clear language, free from errors.

You may also need to present the results of research into areas such as market assessment, market analysis or product analysis using charts or graphs. Again you need to be clear and concise and ensure that your work is relevant, useful and accurate.

You will often be asked to carry out some form of self-evaluation at the end of your production projects. You will need to be able to write a reflective assessment that shows you have thought carefully about your performance and can stand back from your work and conduct a critical analysis which will help you learn from your experience next time.

Figure 2.2 is an example of the type of document that you may produce during the course of your studies: a proposal. A proposal would be followed by a treatment that provides more detail and information and takes into consideration the response and feedback from the client or your tutor.

How would you change it? How well does the proposal relate to the results of the questionnaire research (Figure 2.1 on the previous page)?

PROPOSAL

Outline of Production

I am going to make a print production. It is going to be a graffiti magazine with contents page and article pages. My magazine is going to be a graffiti fan magazine. I am going to include in there some tutorials, tips etc. My idea is to create magazine which is for both professionals and amateurs who would like to start to create urban art.

Purpose of Production

The purpose of my production is to show that graffiti is not always vandalism. It can be a kind of art when made in designated areas and it is not offending anyone. Another purpose is to encourage people to do something creative with their time.

As I said I want it to be a magazine for everyone from beginners to advanced artists so another aim is to develop skills of those less familiar with the techniques.   And as it is a magazine the obvious purpose of it is to earn money. Shops (selling like sprays etc) can earn money on that project as well through advertising in my magazine.

Target Audience

My target audience are mainly young people aged between 10-25 with some exceptions in both boundaries. But I am going to focus on this age group. I believe that more boys are interested in graffiti making than girls so I have to make the magazine attractive especially for boys because boys will not like it pink where girls interested in urban art won't mind a magazine created with boys in mind.

So basically my typical consumer is boys/men in age of 10-25 interested in graffiti art, amateur or professional, probably in subculture connected to urban art.

Other details

Cast
I am going to need only a few people to be models for tutorials of graffiti making and maybe in photo shoots in front of already existing graffiti. I am going to work with D**** because he is really interested in graffiti art style and he can make some simple but very attractive ones so it would be good for first issue as a starting point.

Meaning
My aim is to interest people in the form of art represented by graffiti and to show it in other way than horrible vandalism.

Locations
Most of my shots are going to be in closed spaces probably in D****'s room or my own. I will have to find some nice graffiti in town for the pictures for the cover and for an illustration of articles and others needs.

Figure 2.2: How effective do you think this document is?

Remember

When you are carrying out a self-evaluation, ask yourself questions about the strengths and weaknesses of the production and try to think of evidence or examples of them.

- How effective were your working practices?
- How effective was your product?
- How well was it received by the target audience?
- Ask for the views and opinions of others to get a more objective opinion.
- Be sure to avoid the trap of simply outlining what happened and whether you think it was good or bad. If some things went well, try to identify why. What can you learn from things that didn't go well?

2.3 Revision

Checking and making revisions to your work is of the utmost importance. You should do this regularly, but most certainly before final submission.

You can do this manually, or by using a mixture of your own manual checks and electronic checks performed by the computer. The computer can review spelling, punctuation and grammar and offers a thesaurus. These are all useful, and the computer will often provide alternatives that will make your work more readable, but you must check these suggestions very carefully. The computer cannot put your work into context and so a correctly spelled word used in the wrong place may not be identified, for example, 'of' instead of 'off' and 'them' instead of 'then'. Always check the checker!

As a final check you should proofread your work to ensure the correct use of spelling, punctuation, grammar, clarity of expression and structure of content. Try to do this on paper, using a highlighter or red pen to mark any errors so that you can go back and make corrections to your document.

Activity: Proofreading

Here is an extract from a treatment produced by a learner. A treatment is a production document that will be handed to a client for approval and so must be professionally produced and free from errors.

1. Can you spot the spelling errors?

2. Can you spot the grammatical errors?

3. How could readability of the first paragraph be improved?

4. Are the language and register correct or can they be improved?

Distribution

I intend my music video to be distributted via several music channels. The video ideally, would be aired on Kerrang, NME, and MTV2 due to the genre of the music, research showing me that the viewers of these channels fit the criteria of target audience for the band. However as the band are not signed to a label it is unlikely for them to be considered for air time on all of these channels. Bearing this in mind I do believe that the video would receive sufficient audiences from the NME channel as they are known to show new and un-signed talent, this is also the case on MTV2 on occasions. As well as this the video will be distributed via DVD accompanying the single.

One restriction that the video may have for being aired on these channels, is that it does contain one swearword and therefore would need to be either aired after the watershed or edited so that the swearword is muted or overdubbed. However the release of the DVD with the Single will not be an issue as the single itself will already have been regulated.

The competition that I face is predominantly from other bands or artists of the same calibre as Jealous Fingers. There is a heavy competition for air time in the music industry therefore the quality of the video will have to be to off a certain standard. As well as this, however, the band has been gaining local press, such as radio air time and coverage in the local paper. As well as this they have done fairly well in several nationwide competitions therefore they do seem to have some sort of an edge over there rivals.

Figure 2.3: Treatments should be produced for all production work.

Assessment activity 2.2

P2 P3 M2 M3 D2 D3 **BTEC**

For this learning outcome you need to produce written documents that are appropriate and relevant to your chosen area of study, such as proposals and treatments. You must be able to check them for accuracy and detail and make changes to improve the content and quality.

In Assessment activity 2.1 you came up with some ideas for a new teen magazine. Write a first draft of a proposal, including an outline of your product and its purpose, the target audience and other relevant details such as production costs and distribution requirements. Get feedback from your tutor or client and then rework your proposal, responding to comments and adding more detail to produce a final treatment for presentation to the client.

- Present a media production report which conveys *relevant information* and review reports to make changes with *occasional beneficial effects.* **P2 P3**
- Present a structured and detailed media production report which *conveys information and explains conclusions with clarity* and review reports to make changes with *frequent beneficial effects.* **M2 M3**
- Present a well-structured and substantial media production report which *conveys information with precise exemplification and justifies conclusions with supporting arguments* and review reports to make changes with *consistently beneficial effects.* **D2 D3**

Grading tips

For a merit grade, you will need to be able to construct reports that are of a good quality and that are helpful to the production process. You should be able to review your work and find ways to improve it.

For a distinction grade, you will need to be able to construct reports that are of an excellent quality and that are helpful to the production process. You should be able to review your work and find ways to improve the information and quality that are almost always beneficial to the overall content.

PLTS

Organising time and resources to create effective reports or proposals will help develop your skills as a **self-manager**.

Communicating ideas for different audiences using oral presentations and written formats will help you to become a **reflective learner**.

Functional skills

Producing work in a relevant written format such as essays, reports, computer-based presentations and production documentation will help you to develop your **English** skills.

3. Be able to pitch a media production proposal using appropriate technology

Once you have formed and structured your ideas and produced the necessary paperwork you will need to present your ideas to the client and hope that they will provide you with the required funding to make your product. You will need to present your ideas in a formal yet engaging manner and you will have to provide a detailed description to your client of all areas of the production process. This section looks at the areas you will need to consider when constructing and presenting your ideas.

3.1 Proposal

Your pitch will need to include some essential information. You could begin by mind-mapping the main points you need to cover.

- **Outline your idea** – what do you plan to do or produce? What medium are you working in and what is your intention or message?

- **Costs** – how much is your client going to have to pay to get this product produced and on the market? Include detailed costings of all production requirements and a **contingency** plan in case things go wrong. Things can always go wrong even with the best planned projects and so it is always advisable to cover all eventualities. What return or benefit can your client realistically expect? How will they make money from this?

- **Production requirements** – outline what you will need in terms of locations, talent, crew and equipment. What is the timescale for the production?

Key term

Contingency – the back-up plan or reserve pot of money.

- **Target audience** – your **target audience** are the people you want to consume your product, usually defined in terms of age groups, social classes, race, gender, etc. You will have researched this in detail and you will probably have been provided with a profile of the audience the client wants to reach in the first place. However, they need to know that you understand this audience's needs and can target them effectively with your product.

- **USP** – your **USP** is your unique selling point. What makes you and your ideas different? Why will your production stand out from the crowd and be the right one to choose? Sell your ideas!

Key terms

Target audience – the people you want to consume your product.

USP – unique selling point. Often used in advertising, it relates to the originality of your idea or concept that will make it different to anything else already on the market.

Then review your notes. Is anything essential missing? Is there anything irrelevant you could leave out?

Once you know what information you want to include, you need to think about how you are going to get it across. You will need to speak to your audience and you may need to prepare some useful and interesting visuals. Remember that the aim is to capture the audience's interest by providing relevant information in the most interesting way possible.

It can be nerve-racking to speak to an audience, but if you prepare well and find a method that works for you it will help you feel relaxed and confident.

You could begin by writing a full script, and planning your use of technology and any visuals you need to produce. Organise your presentation into a clear introduction, a middle, where you present your main information, and an end, where you conclude your points and invite questions from the audience. Be sure to allow time to prepare any technology or visuals that you need.

Finally, condense the script into an easy-to-follow format, such as cue cards with brief bullet points, including reminders of when to show any visuals. This will prompt you about what you need to cover, and in what order, but will allow you to speak spontaneously and naturally to the audience.

3.2 Technology

Presentation technology can range from a simple printed handout to a complex PowerPoint® presentation with imported clips and animations. There are many places you can look for animations, add ins, clip art, photographs, etc. Some will come with the software you are using. Others can be sourced from the Internet, or you may want to create your own.

However, it is important to remember that any presentation technology you use is supposed to help the audience understand your points. If it is too flashy or complicated it might be distracting; if it is too dull it will not appeal to your audience. Keep your audience in mind at all times and think about the ideas and concepts you are trying to put across. What information is in the presentation and how can it be best presented and illustrated?

Activity: Computer slide shows

Create some slides for a computer-based presentation, making sure that you think about the style, layout, content and graphics for each slide. Evaluate your presentation by considering the following questions.

1. Does the use of colour enhance the presentation?

2. What would you say are the good points about each slide?

3. What would you change in order to improve each one?

Backgrounds

The background that you use for your work is the 'base' on which you are displaying your ideas and will say a lot about you and your concepts.

- Many learners make the mistake of working on very dark backgrounds that can seem alienating to an audience. Lighter, more neutral colours are warm and welcoming, and often much easier on the eye.
- How does the font colour fit the background? How readable is it? What may seem funky and interesting to you could be too dazzling, difficult or painful for others to read. Look for universal colours such as white and black which people are used to seeing.
- How well will your colour combinations print out? This will affect the quality of any handouts and the printed copy you hand in for assessment.

3.3 Rehearsing the presentation

Use your cue cards and your technology to rehearse as often as possible beforehand so that you are clear on what you want to say, can speak fluently to your audience, and are confident about using any technology or other visuals. Try practising your presentation with a friend and ask them for feedback.

It is important for you to engage the audience, to ensure that you maintain their attention and interest throughout and that you get them as excited about your ideas as you are. Engaging your audience is probably the biggest issue facing any presenter. The following guidelines will help you to do this effectively.

Maintaining eye contact

Making eye contact with people makes you come across as confident, knowledgeable and truthful (you may have noticed that when someone is lying they will look away!). The client wants to know that you know what you are talking about and what you are doing, and this will give them confidence in you.

Try to focus on your audience and maintain eye contact with them at all times. Of course, you will sometimes need to look at the screen behind you or refer to your cue cards, but look your audience in the eye when you are addressing them and be sure to include each member of the audience with this eye contact.

Using your voice

Your voice is the most powerful tool you have in a presentation and your pitch and tone can really make a difference. For example, if your voice wobbles or sounds stressed, the audience will pick up on it and the client may lose interest or confidence in you and your ideas. If you speak too quickly, they may miss important details in what you say. If you speak too slowly, they may become bored. Experiment to find a speaking style you are comfortable with, which works for you and will keep the audience's interest.

- Try using your voice to emphasise important words and sentences.
- Try using a more light-hearted and conversational tone to put your audience at ease.
- Try using a touch of wit to engage the audience on a personal level, but do not act up or joke around too much; you want to put them at ease and get them interested, not think you are a joke!
- Take charge but do not be too overpowering.

Using positive body language

Make sure you use open and positive body language. This means you should open your hands outwards and look relaxed and at ease, and maybe move about a bit instead of being static and rigid.

Gestures that can be construed as negative by the audience will alienate them from you and your ideas. Remember always to face your audience, do not turn your back on them, and make sure you arrange yourself and the rest of the room so that it should never be necessary to do so. Do not stand with your arms crossed and be careful not to frown or shrug when asked questions.

The two photographs at the top of the next page show two very different examples of body language.

Tips for engaging an audience

- Project your voice – but do not shout!
- Speak slowly and clearly – do not gabble.
- Speak directly to the audience, spontaneously and naturally.
- Maintain eye contact with the audience at all times, without staring.
- Keep an open and natural expression on your face.
- Use an appropriate style, tone and register; for example, be calm, professional and in control for the most part, but try to inject a little humour to engage with the audience and put them at ease.
- Use handouts and on-screen information to keep the audience engaged.

3.4 Preparing the room

If possible, rehearse your presentation in the room you will finally be using so that you can familiarise yourself with the space, think about how best to set up the room and practise using the technology available.

- Set out the seats to allow plenty of leg room and ensure everyone has a good view.

- Decide where to stand so you will not block the view of the screen or any visuals.

- Arrange yourself and the rest of the room so that it is never necessary to turn your back on your audience.

- Allow yourself plenty of room at the front so that you are not tripping over fixtures or people, and are not 'in their face' too much.

3.5 Giving the presentation

Allow time before your presentation to set up the room as you wish and check that the technology is working properly. Have your first screen ready for display so that you are not fumbling with controls at the start of your presentation. Have a glass of water to hand in case you get a dry throat as you are speaking.

Opening

Open your presentation by greeting your audience with a friendly 'Good morning' or 'Good afternoon' and remember to introduce yourself and the topic of your presentation.

Conclusion

Make sure that the audience knows that you are drawing things to a close so that they can follow what is happening. Say something like 'So in conclusion' before you make your final point.

End by thanking the client for their time, and inviting any questions. Listen carefully to their ideas, thoughts, opinions and questions and be ready to respond to their suggestions or clarify any points they may not have understood.

Case study: Elaine, pitching ideas

When giving presentations I have found that the best thing to do is to plan very carefully what I am going to say. I begin by writing a few notes on prompt cards that relate to key points in my presentation and that helps keep me on track. I also create and print out handouts with pictures and information on so that the audience have something that they can refer to during the presentation. It is always a good idea to give them a chance to look through this before you start speaking, otherwise they may be distracted and not listen to what you are saying; a good way of doing this is to bring their attention to it and describe what it contains and how it is relevant.

I often use a PowerPoint® format for my presentation as I can add in written information as well as charts, graphs and animations. This makes the presentation more interactive and entertaining, and allows me to really put my point across to the audience.

As nerve-racking as presentations can be it is always worth it in the end. I enjoy the feedback from the client/audience as it helps inform my production and it is always nice to hear if someone liked my ideas. I think doing presentations has helped build my confidence in all areas; I have found it helpful in team work as I am now more able to put my ideas forward, I feel that I can express them clearly and that people will understand my point of view better.

1. Have you ever done presentations before?

2. How strong do you think that your communication skills are?

3. What skills do you think you need to improve and how could you go about it?

4. How do you think good communication skills will help you in the creative and media sector?

Assessment activity 2.3

P4 P5 M4 M5 D4 D5 BTEC

For this learning outcome you are assessed on your ability to take part in presentations, using appropriate formats and interaction with your audience. As with the previous learning outcome, you will be assessed using an integrated assignment as part of another unit, probably a production unit where you may be required (in a mock scenario) to undertake work for a client, such as the one below.

Now that you have completed your proposals and treatments you will need to 'pitch' your ideas to the client and gain their approval in order to move forward to the production phase. Create a presentation using PowerPoint® or other software and write up a script or cue cards to help you present your ideas.

- Deploy and manage appropriate technology to pitch a media production proposal and *employ appropriate forms of address* in a media production pitch to *communicate ideas.* **P4 P5**

- Deploy and manage technology to pitch a media production proposal *effectively and with some imagination* and employ forms of address in a

media production pitch to *communicate ideas effectively.* **M4 M5**

- Deploy and manage technology to pitch a media production proposal *with creativity and flair and to near-professional standards* and employ forms of address in a media production pitch *with flair to communicate ideas with impact.* **D4 D5**

Grading tips

For a merit grade, you need to provide a presentation that includes written information for your audience to follow as well as slides and animations to help illustrate your point. You need to communicate effectively with your audience throughout, showing some imagination in your use of the technology.

For a distinction grade, you need to provide a presentation that includes slides and animations, possibly even links, that effectively illustrate your point and which are imaginative and visually appealing as well as containing relevant information. You must show confidence and flair when interacting with your audience throughout.

PLTS

Supporting conclusions when presenting information orally, using reasoned arguments and evidence, will help you to become an **independent enquirer**.

Generating imaginative ideas for presentations will help you to become a **creative thinker**.

Communicating information and ideas in relevant ways for different audiences, using oral presentations and written formats will help you to become a **reflective learner**.

Functional skills

Using ICT to plan and prepare oral and written presentations in a variety of formats will help you to develop your **ICT** skills.

Checking and evaluating information used in charts and graphs will help you to develop your **Mathematics** skills.

Nina Jones
Advertising intern

I have always been interested in advertising and after completing my degree I was taken on as an intern at a large advertising company in London. As I hold a junior position I am still learning the ropes, so to speak, but I am still required to prepare proposals for clients and to take part in team pitches.

It is important to ensure we have our facts right and that we provide the clients with all of the relevant details for the proposed production. We have to make sure we are familiar with the client, their product or service and their overall requirements; what they want to achieve from the project.

We must always keep in mind the target audience for the product and our proposals must be relevant and engaging to them as well as in keeping with the way the client wants to be perceived by the consumer.

Obviously part of my work involves taking through and presenting these ideas to clients from all areas of industry and I always have to keep in mind that I am representing my company when I speak to them. After all, we want the client to like our ideas and commission us for their campaign, that's how the company makes money!

Professional conduct is vital. There is no room for a fit of the giggles in the middle of a pitch and I certainly can't forget what I am talking about. I must know my proposals inside out; I need to be able to respond to clients' questions and be prepared for anything they may ask.

Preparation and confidence are key factors when working in this industry and without it you could end up with a lot of disappointed clients. It is also important to remember to be relaxed, though, to be able to react and interact with the client and to respond to them on a human as well as professional level. Good communication and interpersonal skills are essential.

Think about it!

- Why is it important for Nina to ensure that she has her facts right?
- What are some of the tasks Nina has to undertake as an advertising intern?
- Can you find three key attributes that Nina mentions as important in order to work effectively with a client?

Just checking

1. When would you use annotation and how is it beneficial?
2. Why is it important to review your work?
3. Name two methods you can use to review written work.
4. What are the key points to look for when you are checking your work?
5. What formats and documents might you need to use during production planning?
6. Name some of the presentation technologies you could use for presenting your ideas.
7. What are animations and how could they enhance your presentation?
8. Why is it important to practise your presentation before presenting to the client?
9. What positive body language can you use to engage your audience?
10. Why is it important to maintain eye contact with your audience?
11. What should you do at the end of a presentation?
12. How will you know if you have successfully presented your ideas to your audience?

edexcel

Assignment tips

- When carrying out research, always keep in mind the information you are looking for and focus on key words that can help you locate it.

- For proofreading, invest in a highlighter pen! Whenever you have finished writing a piece of work, print it out and check it carefully. Highlight the areas where you have made mistakes and then make the necessary corrections to your document.

- When planning your presentation, try to condense your script into key words or bullet points written on cue cards. They are small and easy to handle as you refer to them during the presentation, and they will free you up to speak naturally to your audience.

- When constructing a presentation, search for interesting materials such as pictures, clips and links. The Internet is a great resource, so use it.

- Rehearsing your presentation is essential. You will be assessed on your performance as well as the content of your presentation, so you need to appear calm, clear, concise and confident.

3 Research techniques for the creative media industries

As you will know from your own practical work, creative media production can be a complex process with many different stages of development. The starting point of any successful production process is research and media producers put a lot of time and effort into planning and researching their creative media products to make sure that they are successfully targeted at the right audience, in the right market and can be produced within budget and by the required deadline.

The films and television programmes that we watch, the radio programmes and podcasts that we listen to, the newspapers and magazines that we read and the websites and computer games that we interact with have all been thoroughly researched and planned to try to ensure that the production process runs smoothly and the final product is successful.

This unit provides you with the opportunity to learn about the nature and purposes of the research undertaken within the creative media industries. You will be able to develop your research skills and apply a range of different research methods and techniques in the pre-production work that you are undertaking in your other practical units. You will then have the opportunity to summarise your findings and present the results of your research.

Learning outcomes

After completing this unit you should:

1. understand the nature and purposes of research in the creative media industries
2. be able to apply a range of research methods and techniques
3. be able to present results of research.

Assessment and grading criteria

This table shows you what you must do in order to achieve a **pass**, **merit** or **distinction** grade, and where you can find activities in this book to help you.

To achieve a **pass** grade the evidence must show that you are able to:	To achieve a **merit** grade the evidence must show that, in addition to the pass criteria, you are able to:	To achieve a **distinction** grade the evidence must show that, in addition to the pass and merit criteria, you are able to:
P1 describe the nature and purposes of research in the creative media industries with some appropriate use of subject terminology **See Assessment activity 3.1, pages 46–47**	**M1** explain the nature and purposes of research in the creative media industries with detailed illustrative examples and with generally correct use of subject terminology **See Assessment activity 3.1, pages 46–47**	**D1** comprehensively explain the nature and purposes of research in the creative media industries with elucidated examples and consistently using subject terminology correctly **See Assessment activity 3.1, pages 46–47**
P2 apply research methods and techniques with some assistance **See Assessment activity 3.2, page 54**	**M2** apply research methods and techniques competently with only occasional assistance **See Assessment activity 3.2, page 54**	**D2** apply research methods and techniques to near-professional standards working independently to professional expectations **See Assessment activity 3.2, page 54**
P3 present results of research **See Assessment activity 3.3, page 56**	**M3** present results of research competently **See Assessment activity 3.3, page 56**	**D3** present results of research to near-professional standards **See Assessment activity 3.3, page 56**

How you will be assessed

This unit will be assessed by a number of internal assignments designed to allow you to show your understanding of the unit outcomes – what you should be able to do after completing this unit. Most of the assignments that you will complete for this unit will relate to work that you are doing in some of your other units. This means that the research you undertake will relate directly to the media products that you are studying and the media products you are producing.

Your assessments could be in the form of:

- presentations
- case studies
- practical tasks
- written assignments.

Sarah, creative media production student

This unit helped me to understand that all types of creative media production take careful planning and research to be successful. You need to know your target audience, your market and the purpose of your product before you can start planning the production process itself.

I enjoyed learning about the different types, methods and sources of research used in the industry. I could see a direct relevance for my own production work and was able to apply these methods and techniques in my other practical units. This helped my products to be more successful and made the production process run smoothly.

Because I am a practical, outgoing person I particularly enjoyed conducting my own questionnaires, interviews and surveys for my video production project and I also ran my own focus group. This took a lot of organising but I gained valuable information about what my audience really wanted to see. I also liked using the Internet and my college's learning resource centre to find out more information about the creative media sector.

I was a little nervous about the final presentation of my research results to the rest of my class, but it went really well and I was really happy with the positive feedback I got.

Over to you!

- Which section of the unit are you most looking forward to?
- What areas of this unit might you find challenging?
- Which practical units do you think this unit links to?

1. Understand the nature and purposes of research in the creative media industries

Types and methods of research

Playing computer games has become one of the most popular pastimes and a multi-million pound games industry has grown to develop and produce ever-more sophisticated games to feed this expanding market.

If you were going to develop a new computer game, what would you want to find out before you invested lots of time and money in your product? What methods and techniques would you use to get this information?

In small groups, write down what you want to find out about the audience, the market and the production process, and the methods you could use to get this information.

Discuss your findings with the rest of the class.

1.1 Types of research

To undertake successful research for your own creative media productions you need a good understanding of the main types of research used within the industry and the methods and sources employed.

In the Set up activity you may have said you wanted to find factual information such as the sales figures and audience profile for a particular game, or what gamers think about the games that they play – what they like and what they find boring.

To find out the answers to these questions you need to use two different types of research: **quantitative research** and **qualitative research**.

Key terms

Quantitative research – research based on measurable facts and information that can be counted, producing numerical and statistical data.

Qualitative research – research based on opinions, attitudes and preferences rather than hard facts and figures.

Quantitative research produces data and information that is measurable and quantifiable and includes programme ratings, box-office takings, readership circulation figures and website hits, as well as the counting and measuring of items or space in a content analysis of a media product. The data generated from quantitative research can usually be represented numerically and is often presented in the form of tables, charts and diagrams (see, for example, Table 3.1).

Activity: Box-office figures

Visit the UK Film Council website (www.ukfilmcouncil.org.uk) and find out the latest box-office figures. How many UK films are in the top 15?

Qualitative research, on the other hand, produces information on people's opinions, views and preferences about something (see, for instance, Table 3.2). Qualitative data is important to the media industry as it is used to find out what individuals and groups think and feel about a particular media product such as a new computer game, television programme or film. It is also used by advertisers to obtain people's responses to an advertising campaign.

Table 3.1: Top five UK box-office figures for the weekend of 27–29 November 2009.

Rank	Title	Country of origin	Weekend gross	Distributor	% change on last week	Weeks on release	Number of cinemas	Site average	Total gross to date
1	The Twilight Saga: New Moon	USA	£4,303,257	E1 Films	−63	2	504	£8,538	£20,320,686
2	Paranormal Activity	USA	£3,593,762	Icon		1	394	£9,121	£3,593,762
3	A Christmas Carol	USA	£1,935,283	Disney	−13	4	455	£4,253	£11,333,978
4	2012	USA/ Can	£1,834,817	Sony Pictures	−48	3	465	£3,946	£16,217,379
5	Law Abiding Citizen	USA	£1,488,143	Paramount		1	353	£4,216	£1,488,143

(Source: Rentrak EDI, UK Film Council)

Table 3.2: Some of the results from qualitative research into a proposed new social networking site.

Individual	Response
Tanya	Site was easy to navigate through and I really liked the way it was designed. Good content. Colours and graphics were bright and made me feel very positive. Very tempted to become a member.
Ishmael	Hated it. Too busy. Colours and graphics were too bright. Difficult to navigate around and kept getting lost. Link to home page was too small. Not enough interactive features. Don't think I'll be using it again.
Raj	Loved the design but found it a bit tricky to use. Prefer Bebo as a networking site to this one but it does have some good elements to it. Lots of information and features though some of the buttons didn't seem to work. Colours reminded me of the countryside. Overall I like it and will visit again.

Depending on the questions asked, it is not always possible to analyse the resulting information statistically, particularly if the responses are personal and subjective.

1.2 Methods and sources of research

A range of different research methods, sources and techniques can be used to obtain both quantitative and qualitative information. A basic distinction to make is between **primary research** and **secondary research** methods.

Key terms

Primary research – original research to obtain new information using such techniques as interviews, questionnaires and focus groups.

Secondary research – research using existing information that has already been gathered by other people or organisations.

Primary research is original research carried out for a specific purpose. It involves the use of a range of different sources and techniques to obtain new data. Asking people questions during an interview, conducting a survey, using a questionnaire, participating in an Internet forum and running a focus group are all examples of techniques used in primary research.

Case study: Protecting your rights and earnings

It is now very easy to download and share music via the Internet. Although this is welcome for many reasons, it can present problems for songwriters, musicians and agents who want to keep track of potential earnings and ensure that copyright in their work is not breached.

The Performing Rights Society (PRS) helps to protect performers' rights, and is involved in campaigns over royalty payments for music and video content. It runs a website (www. fairplayforcreators.com), where songwriters, artists and people working in the music industry post their views on issues related to rights, earnings and copyright. This primary research is an important source of information for the PRS and also helps to get the message across to the wider public on rewarding artists properly for their work.

In September 2009, a licensing deal was struck between the PRS and YouTube over royalty payments for online content.

1. Why do you think music artists and other people working in the media are concerned about the digital reproduction of their work?

2. Why is a website such as this a help to organisations like the PRS?

3. What might happen if sites like YouTube are forced to pay too much money to show digital media content on their website?

Activity: Further research

The debate about royalty payments for digital media content is an ongoing issue. Research the latest position regarding royalty payments for producers of media content that is accessed through the Internet.

Secondary research involves the use of data and information that has already been published or is already available within an organisation. Looking in books, journals, archives, photo libraries, and searching on the Internet for information that already exists are all examples of secondary research.

Many media organisations will use data and information that has been gathered and analysed by another company or a data-gathering agency to add to and support, sometimes even to replace, their own primary research.

Activity: Media research organisations

Undertake some Internet-based research of your own by visiting the websites of the following data-gathering agencies and finding out what information they have available about different media products.

- National Readership Survey (NRS)
- Broadcasters' Audience Research Board (BARB)
- Audit Bureau of Circulations (ABC)
- Radio Joint Audience Research Limited (RAJAR)
- Office of Communications (Ofcom)

Write a short report on each agency and include some data on specific media products from each site to illustrate your report.

Some of the data is only available to subscribers. Why do you think this might be?

Figure 3.1 is an example of quantitative data from Ofcom showing the revenue generated by different types of programme on commercial television. What does the data tell you?

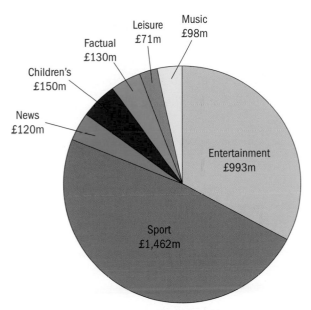

Figure 3.1: Which genre produces most television revenue? (Source: Ofcom report on The Communications Market (Television) 2008.)

1.3 Purposes of research

Research undertaken within the media industries has three main purposes: **audience research**, **market research** and **production research**. It is important that you understand what these forms of research involve as you will need to apply all three to the practical production work that you will be undertaking in your other units.

Key terms

Audience research – the collection and analysis of information about the target audience for a particular media product or sector of the media industry.

Market research – the collection and analysis of information about the market within which a particular product will compete with other products for an audience and for revenue.

Production research – the collection and analysis of information for the content and production of a media product.

Audience research

Effective and successful media products target the right audience and communicate to them in an effective way. As the media industry becomes more fragmented, competition for a share of the audience becomes even more intense. Knowing who your target audience is, and what makes them tick, is therefore increasingly important.

Audience research is about investigating:

- statistical data about the size and profile of the audience for a particular media product
- the extent to which potential audience members are aware of a particular media product or service
- what members of the target audience think about particular products and services and their patterns of behaviour and potential use of the products.

Choose a national newspaper and see what you can find out about its readership and what they think about the paper.

Market research

The media marketplace is highly competitive. Media producers often undertake detailed market research into their target market or commission other companies to undertake research on their behalf. They are interested in what the market looks like, who the other competitors in that market are and what their products are like. They are particularly interested in the economic factors within the market and what potential revenue is available.

Production research

If the audience research goes well and the market analysis is favourable a media company might decide to launch a new product into that market. Production research is needed to:

- provide content and gather material to allow the company to develop the new product
- research the commercial viability of actually making the product
- investigate the technology and personnel available
- check out suitable recording and production locations
- thoroughly research and plan production and post-production stages to ensure that it all runs as smoothly as possible.

You will have an opportunity to undertake your own audience, market and production research in the next section of this unit and link it to the practical production work that you are planning and developing in some of your optional units.

Case study: BBC Worldwide

BBC Worldwide is the main commercial arm of the British Broadcasting Corporation (BBC) and has a wide range of commercial activities, mostly connected with the BBC's broadcast output, in order to maximise the value of the BBC's assets for the benefit of the UK licence payer.

BBC Worldwide undertakes a great deal of research to ensure it provides the right products for the right audience and market. For example, it identified a market demand for magazines that supported popular programmes such as *Top Gear* and *Gardener's World*. But there have also been some failures, such as magazines linked to the children's television programmes *Tweenies* and *Balamory*, which were both pulled due to falling sales.

In 2008/9 BBC Worldwide generated profits of £103 million for the BBC to reinvest in its public service broadcasting. However, the BBC has sometimes been criticised for the amount of money it makes from BBC Worldwide. Commercial rivals are not happy at the advantage the company has from its links to the BBC and its ability to exploit the programme catalogue and resources.

1. **Visit the BBC Worldwide website (www.bbcworldwide.com) and find out more about the products and commercial activities that they are involved in.**

2. **Why is research such an important activity for them?**

3. **Can you understand why some commercial rivals are unhappy with BBC Worldwide's operations?**

Assessment activity 3.1

P1 **M1** **D1** BTEC

You have applied for a job as a researcher with a local media company. As part of the selection process they have asked you to produce a report for them on the nature and purposes of research in the creative media industries.

- In your own words *describe* the main types, methods and sources of research that can be used in a research project and the main purposes of research in the creative media industries. **P1**

- *Explain* the main types, methods and sources of research that can be used in a research project and the main purposes of research undertaken within the creative media industries. Include some examples to support your explanations. **M1**

- *Comprehensively explain* the main types, methods and sources of research that can be used in a research project, and the main purposes of research undertaken within the creative media industries. Include precise and detailed examples to support what you are saying. **D1**

Grading tips

For a merit grade, you need to explain rather than simply describe the main types, methods, sources and purposes of research. This means saying not just what is involved but also why and how. Include relevant examples, perhaps from your own research as well as examples from the creative media industries, to support what you are saying. Make sure you use correct subject terminology in your report.

For a distinction grade, your explanation needs to be fuller and more comprehensive than at merit level and you need to compare and assess the different types, methods, sources and purposes of research. You also need to justify the points being made through the use of clear examples. You need to use correct subject terminology throughout the report and show evidence of a confident approach to the task.

PLTS

Investigating the main types, methods and sources of research will help you to develop your skills as an **independent enquirer**.

Functional skills

Describing the main types, methods and sources of research will help you to develop your **English** skills in writing.

2. Be able to apply a range of research methods and techniques

Planning a successful research project is about choosing the right research methods and techniques so that you get the correct information and then applying these in an effective way.

Get organised

A word of warning before you start! You may gather a large amount of information in your research and you will need to organise, collate and store your material carefully as you go along.

Collating your material means sifting through it to identify what is useful and what can be disregarded, then organising it into categories that will allow you to access it easily, evaluate it and summarise your findings.

It is best to store all your relevant research material in a folder. This needs a clear index system so that you can easily find a piece of information. Use highlighting and annotation to keep track of what you have used and how.

Keep a written log that explains to the tutor and moderator what is in your research folder, how it was

obtained, why it has been included, and how it has been or is going to be used.

Research methods

You have learned about primary and secondary research methods and how to generate qualitative and quantitative research data. Now you will have the opportunity to apply a range of these methods and link them to the practical production work you are undertaking in some of your other units.

You will need to decide what mix of research methods and techniques is appropriate for your particular production work. It is often better to undertake some secondary research first so that you can get a greater understanding of your chosen media sector. This should allow you to identify which areas to focus on in more depth in your primary research.

2.1 Secondary research

The secondary research methods you use will depend on what you are trying to find out. Narrow down your secondary sources to ensure that you obtain the right information to support your specific project.

Aim for a balance of qualitative and quantitative research data and information from a range of reliable sources so that you can verify what the research is telling you.

Research log

You need to be well organised and keep a record of the sources you have accessed. The best way of doing this is to keep a log of all the library, Internet and archive searches that you have undertaken while carrying out your research.

Figure 3.2 shows the information trail undertaken by Sarah, a media learner, when researching for one of her own media products.

Note that simply collecting pages of secondary information from the Internet does not constitute valid secondary research. Any information you print off from the Internet or photocopy from books, journals and archives needs to be read and understood, annotated with your own notes and used to inform the production process.

It is important that you clearly understand what the original purpose of the research was, who

commissioned it and when it was conducted. Not every piece of research you find will be reliable or valid.

2.2 Primary research

The secondary research you undertake should always be supplemented and supported by your own primary research. You can use a range of methods and techniques depending on what you are trying to achieve.

As with all research, careful planning is a key first stage.

- Think carefully about what you are trying to find out.
- Decide on an appropriate research technique.
- Choose an appropriate sample to be the focus of the research.
- Be aware of the size, scope and timescale of the task ahead.

Questioning

It is likely that you will use some form of questioning technique for the research tasks that you undertake. You may decide to:

- conduct one-to-one interviews (face-to-face or via telephone or email)
- produce a questionnaire to survey a larger group of people
- organise a focus group or audience panel
- host an Internet forum.

Remember

It is important that you clearly reference any work that you use and take account of any copyright issues.

Research log			
Project: Gathering material for documentary programme on healthy eating			
Date	Source of information	Description of information obtained	Notes
12/5/10	Website: www.eatwell.gov.uk	Information about healthy diet / Eight tips for eating well / Food myths	Good, reliable source of government information. Can be used as captions in final video (copyright issues?)
13/5/10	Website: www.bbc.co.uk/health	What makes a balanced diet / Food needs for different age groups	Reliable source. Age information is useful – we can select right info for our target audience
13/5/10	Book: Romanoff, J. *The Eating Well Healthy in a Hurry Cookbook* (Norton, 2005)	Healthy food recipes	Good recipes but not suitable for our target audience – aimed at an adult audience. Language, terminology and content would not engage our 16–18 primary target audience

Figure 3.2: How do you think Sarah's information trail may be useful later in her project?

Think very carefully about the form and structure of the questions you pose, using both open and closed questions to ensure you obtain the required information.

As a general rule you should start with straightforward **closed questions** that are easy to answer and put people at ease, such as age, gender, occupation and marital status. This will get them responding and will provide basic demographic information so you can check you have covered a representational sample of people, and include more respondents in your research if not.

Closed questions are often answered with 'Yes', 'No' or 'Don't know', or an answer picked from a range of given options. If you use closed questions with tick boxes, it is important to include all of the potential answers. You will need to decide whether to include an 'Other' or 'Don't know' option.

Closed questions and other questions with a limited range of responses can be quick and easy for respondents to answer. They provide quantifiable data which you can represent in the form of graphs, charts and diagrams.

Open questions, where you ask for a more personal response, provide qualitative information that can give more meaningful insights. They often start with the following words: what, why, when, how, who.

Key terms

Closed questions – limiting in terms of the potential answers that can be given.

Open questions – allow the person answering to give their own views and opinions on the subject.

Activity: Producing a simple questionnaire

In small groups, choose a relevant sector of the media industry and decide what media-related information you would like to find out about and what sample of people you are able to survey.

Design and produce a simple questionnaire that includes both open and closed questions to find out the information you want.

Use the questionnaire to carry out your survey.

Briefly discuss the findings with the rest of your group. Did you find any significant information from your survey? Was the data easy to understand? Did any of the results surprise you?

PLTS

Collaborating with others when working on your survey will help develop your skills as a **team worker**.

Functional skills

Producing the questionnaire will help you to develop your **English** skills in writing.

Q1: How old are you?

15 or younger ☐   16–18 ☐   19–21 ☐   22+ ☐

Q2: What gender are you?

Male ☐   Female ☐

Q3: Which of the following television services do you have in your home? (you can tick more than one box)

Terrestrial ☐   Satellite ☐   Cable ☐   Freeview ☐

Q4: Do you have a broadband Internet service at home?

Yes ☐   No ☐   Don't know ☐

Q5: Why did you choose to take a media qualification?

Q6: What three words or phrases best describe your feelings about computer games?

Figure 3.3: Do you think these closed questions and tick boxes cover all the options?

Figure 3.4: Why would the answers to these open questions be difficult to quantify?

Activity: Focus groups

It is a good idea to film and include a recording of any focus group you run in your final portfolio of evidence. How would you plan a focus group? How could you make sure you get the information you want? How could you record, collate, analyse and present the findings?

What sort of information can you get from running a focus group?

Observations

Another form of primary research is observation. Observation visits to media production companies can be a valuable way of developing your knowledge and understanding of the production processes and technology involved. They can also be a useful way of meeting industry practitioners you could interview for your research project.

2.3 Audience research

The profile of the target audience, their preferences and buying patterns are important considerations for any media producer. A lot of time, effort and resource is put into research to better understand audiences.

A number of classifications are used to describe a media audience. Researchers talk about audience **demographics** – by this they mean the way in which an audience can be classified according to a range of different socio-economic and personal factors such as age, gender, ethnicity, social class, occupation, level of education and sexual orientation.

Key term

Demographics – a way of describing a group of people according to factors such as age, gender, ethnicity, occupation, social class and sexual orientation.

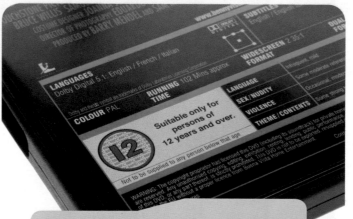

The British Board of Film Classification (bbfc) puts an age category on all films and DVDs available in the UK. Is this an effective way of preventing young people from seeing unsuitable films?

Activity: Planning a visit

Discuss the practical work that you are undertaking with the rest of your group and draw up a list of potential places you could visit to supplement your work.

Decide on the best method of contact to arrange a visit and plan what you are going to do and say. Explain to the organisation what the purpose of your visit is. Ask if you can take some photographs and recordings for your portfolio.

Following the visit, collate and organise your observations and give a short presentation to the rest of the class.

You should offer to share your findings with the organisation that you visited as a courtesy and be open and honest about how you are using the insights they provided you with. This will help you and your school or college to build a professional relationship with them.

Activity: Newspapers and magazines

Age, gender and social class are important considerations for the publishing industry, as they try to target specific newspapers and magazines at a particular audience.

Visit the National Readership Survey (NRS) website (www.nrs.co.uk) and look at the top-line readership for a selection of newspapers and magazines. The readership is analysed according to age, social class and gender.

What does the data tell you?

Produce a short report in which you compare the readership of two different newspapers or magazines. Look at a recent edition of the newspapers or magazines you are studying and see what they have done to target a particular audience. Look at the pictures used, the language and the types of article and stories they feature.

Look at the products and services that are being advertised in them. Do they reflect what the audience profile says?

Table 3.3: Which category do you think that your family fits into?

Social grade	Social status	Chief income earner's occupation
A	Upper middle class	Higher managerial, administrative or professional
B	Middle class	Intermediate managerial, administrative or professional
C1	Lower middle class	Supervisory or clerical and junior managerial, administrative or professional
C2	Skilled working class	Skilled manual workers
D	Working class	Semi-skilled and unskilled manual workers
E	Those at the lowest levels of subsistence	State pensioners, casual or lowest grade workers

Most companies involved with media research and production use a scale that puts people into different categories according to the sort of job they do and the amount of income they have (see Table 3.3). The scale makes some very broad assumptions.

The study of where people live is called **geodemographics** and is important for media producers and advertisers when producing media products for a local or regional audience.

Knowing the profile of the local and regional population and understanding the issues that impact on that community can help a local newspaper and regional radio station provide the right content to appeal to their target audience.

Information about a person's lifestyle, referred to as **psychographics**, is also important to advertisers and media producers as it gives them important clues as to what interests they have, how much disposable income they are likely to have and what type of media products they are likely to be attracted to.

For example, people who have an active lifestyle are likely to be interested in media products that reflect

this, so they might read health-related magazines, watch travel programmes and visit sports-related websites. You can see that advertisers of travel-related products, health foods and sports equipment would be interested in targeting these people with products and that psychographic information about the audience is important in helping them choose the right medium to advertise in.

Key terms

Geodemographics – a way of describing a group of people based on where they live, sometimes organised according to postcode.

Psychographics – a way of describing a group of people based on their attitudes, opinions and lifestyle.

Remember

All commercial media texts are made with a specific audience in mind, and media producers invest a lot of time, effort and money in trying to find out exactly what their target audience want from their media products.

Case study: The Ramblers

The Ramblers is a registered charity that promotes walking and campaigns for greater access to the countryside. In 2009 it launched its 'Get Walking Keep Walking' website to promote the benefits of incorporating regular walking into everyday life, particularly aiming at inactive people and those living in deprived urban areas, and offering a range of resources to encourage people to walk more, including Get Walking packs, maps of good walking routes and advice on improving health and lifestyle through walking.

Simon Barnett, Head of Walking Programmes and Promotions, commented: 'Anyone, from anywhere, who wants to get walking more can find the tools they need on the new Ramblers Get Walking website. Better physical and mental health is the click of a button away.'

1. Why were lifestyle and location important considerations for the designers of the website?

2. How do the images used relate to the target audience?

3. Do some further research into who the Get Walking website is aimed at.

(Source: www.getwalking.org.uk)

Figure 3.5: The Ramblers 'Get Walking Keep Walking' website. Why do you think the designers used a green background for the title?

All media producers want to know as much about their target audience as possible because this information helps them to design and create the sorts of programmes, films, websites, computer games, magazines and newspapers they think the audience wants.

2.4 Market research

As well as looking at audiences, media companies are also interested in the market that their products will have to survive in. This involves looking at what the competition has to offer and comparing similar media products already in the market to see what the commercial opportunities are.

Case study: *Call of Duty*

Computer games company Activision has a good understanding of the market for their war simulation game *Call of Duty* and in 2009 launched the latest version of the game, *Modern Warfare 2*, in the style of a Hollywood movie blockbuster at a lavish event in Leicester Square. The hype surrounding the launch was increased by many UK games retailers opening at midnight to allow customers to buy the product, with over 750,000 registered pre-orders.

The graph below shows that computer games sales have overtaken cinema ticket sales and DVD sales in the UK, and market analysts report that the *Call Of Duty* franchise has sold over 55 million games since its first launch in 2003, generating over $3 billion in retail sales worldwide.

Game, DVD and cinema sales in the UK, £bn

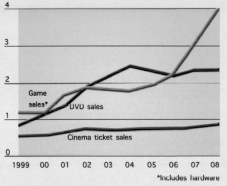

(Source: UK Film Council)

Figure 3.6: What do you think about violent games such as *Call of Duty*?

1. Why do you think the *Call of Duty* games have been so successful?
2. What other games are in this market?
3. What makes *Call of Duty* one of the leading products in this market?

Advertising

Advertising revenue is an important source of income for many commercial media producers and any analysis of the market must include an assessment of what potential revenue is available from advertising.

For example, commercial television companies are very interested in the market information produced by data-gathering agencies such as the Broadcasters' Audience Research Board (BARB), and so are the potential advertisers that want to advertise their products and services within their programmes. As more and more channels become available, the audience becomes more fragmented and advertisers have to work even harder to make sure that they are reaching the right market with their adverts.

Activity: TV sponsorship

Some popular programmes are now sponsored by a company. Look out for any programmes that you watch that are sponsored. Can you identify a clear link between the programme and the company who is providing the sponsorship? Is it easy to understand why this particular company has sponsored the programme?

The government's Department for Culture, Media and Sport is responsible for the rules and regulations that govern broadcasting in the UK, including the ways in which TV companies can generate income revenue. Media analysts estimate that the revenues from product placement, where named products are seen in television programmes, could bring around £72m additional revenue to British commercial television.

Activity: Product placement

Do some research of your own to find out what the current rules say about product placement for British commercial broadcasters.

2.5 Production research

As you learned earlier in this unit, production research is focused on sourcing and generating material for the content of a media product as well as making sure that the resources are in place and the funding is secure to make the product viable.

Creative media productions can be very complex and so production research needs to be comprehensive. Not only will you need to research viable sources of equipment and facilities, you will need to find suitably trained crew and personnel as well as talent to appear in your product. Finding all this is one thing, but you must make sure that it is all in the right place, at the right time, at the right price.

You will of course be planning your own productions in some of your other units and, whichever unit or units you choose to link this one with, the process of gathering material for the content of your media product will be broadly similar and you will need to use both primary and secondary research methods and obtain both quantitative and qualitative information.

2.6 Interpreting results

Having completed your research, you now need to analyse your findings and interpret the results. To do this effectively you need to look at them objectively.

It is easy to misinterpret data or try to make results fit what you expect, or would like them to say.

Look carefully at your results. Are any significant trends emerging? What information is being revealed? Are there anomalies you need to try to understand and explain? Are you surprised by what you have found? Has your viewpoint changed as a result of undertaking the research and what are you now going to do differently?

Did you know?

Media producers will often go to a media agency to recruit talent and production personnel for a specific media project.

Assessment activity 3.2

P2 **M2** **D2** **BTEC**

You now have an opportunity to undertake your own audience, market and production research linked to the practical production work that you are developing in one of your optional units.

1. Decide which practical media production unit you are going to undertake your research for.
2. Devise a coherent strategy and research methodology that will enable you to obtain the relevant information. Your strategy needs to include a plan to undertake audience, market and production research. Your methodology will need to include both primary and secondary research methods to obtain both quantitative and qualitative information.
3. Undertake the planned programme of research.
4. Collate and organise your research material and interpret the results.

Grading tips

For a merit grade, you need to carefully choose and apply a range of relevant research techniques. Your findings will demonstrate a clear understanding of both primary and secondary research methods and the material generated will be accurate, substantial and well focused. Your work will have been approached in a methodical way and carried out with care and thought, and with only occasional assistance.

For a distinction grade, you need to use confidently a full range of relevant and clearly understood techniques and procedures that generate a substantial amount of clearly focused material that has been thoroughly analysed. You must show that you can work independently to professional expectations, demonstrating excellent self-management skills.

PLTS

Asking questions to extend your thinking when trying out alternative ways of researching for your media production will help you to develop your skills as a **creative thinker**.

Functional skills

Collating and storing your research material on a computer will help you to develop your **ICT** skills in managing information storage.

3. Be able to present results of research

You will have completed some substantial pieces of research for this unit and you now have the opportunity to present the results of your research and summarise what you have found.

3.1 Format

You should present the results of your research in the form of a written report and an oral presentation, using illustrations such as graphs and bar charts to show the results in the most appropriate way.

Make sure your oral presentation is recorded so that your mark can be checked by the moderator towards the end of the course. Many job interviews now include giving a presentation to a panel of people, so presenting your results in this way is good practice for you.

Remember

- If you are using computer-based slides to help structure and support your presentation, do not be tempted to use too many visual and sound effects as the audience will easily tire of such gimmicks. They can also distract from your message.
- Think carefully about the contents of each slide. Each one should provide a summary of what you are saying rather than a running commentary. A common mistake is to try to cram too much information on to each slide.
- You can include photographs, graphics, charts and diagrams in your presentation to help get your message across more effectively.

3.2 Content

In your written report and oral presentation make sure you include all the required content:

- an introduction explaining the purpose of your research project – what you were trying to find out and why
- an explanation of the research methods, techniques and procedures that you used
- a summary of the data that you obtained, presented in a form that is easy to understand, for example, graphs, charts and tables
- an analysis of your results and how these affected your thinking and conclusions
- what you propose to do now you have the findings. How will they impact on your media production work? How will you use them? What has changed as a result of your research?
- a summary of your sources, including a bibliography, references, credits and acknowledgements of any copyright material
- appendices containing copies of any additional relevant material, such as interview questions and questionnaires

3.3 Quotation and reference

It is important that you list the sources of information that you have used in an appropriate way and that all quotations and references are clear and unambiguous.

Use a valid and consistent approach for citations and references throughout your work. Your college might have its own guidelines for quotations and referencing.

Did you know?

Many colleges and universities advise learners to use the Harvard system of referencing.

The following guide for bibliographies is based on the Harvard system.

For books, include:

- the author's or editor's name (or names). If more than two authors are credited then it is customary to write the first author's name followed by the words 'et al.'
- the year the book was published
- the title of the book
- the edition number if it is other than the first
- the city the book was published in
- the name of the publisher.

For journals and other articles include:

- the author's name or names

- the year in which the journal was published
- the title of the article
- the title of the journal
- the page number/s of the article in the journal.

For electronic resources, try to include all of the information above (if it is available) and also include:

- the date you accessed the resource
- the electronic address
- the type of electronic resource (for example, discussion forum, web page, etc).

When referencing quotations within the main text you should use a shorter 'author, date, page' style in brackets immediately after the quotation (Baylis et al, 2010, p.67) and give the full details of the book in the main bibliography.

Assessment activity 3.3

P3 M3 D3 **BTEC**

Present the results of the main research studies that you have completed for this unit. Produce a written report and do an oral presentation.

1. Gather all the research material that you have produced and make sure that it is collated, organised and stored securely.
2. Work on the content of your report and presentation, making sure that you cover all of the required aspects.
3. Complete the final report and deliver the final presentation.

Grading tips

For a merit grade, your report and presentation must be carefully delivered and detailed, and reflect a good range of research techniques and methods used. You should use good oral and written skills and use illustrations to provide clear information. The use of quotations and referencing in the report should be good.

For a distinction grade, your report and presentation must show fluency and confidence and you should use a wide range of technical vocabulary with accuracy. The points that you are making must be fully supported by sound argument and the use of clear and wholly relevant illustrations. The use of quotations and referencing in the report should be consistent and precise.

PLTS

Inviting feedback to your presentation and dealing positively with praise, setbacks and criticism will help you become a more **reflective learner**.

Functional skills

Developing the presentation of your research will help you to improve your **ICT** skills in entering, developing and formatting information.

Alison Brant
TV researcher

I currently work as a researcher with a regional TV station. It is my first job in the media sector and has been a good introduction for me as I am getting involved with lots of different activities and meeting lots of people.

If I had to sum up being a researcher in three words I would say 'information, information, and information'! The job is all about finding things out for the production team and I get literally hundreds of requests every week for information on all manner of things. I am always busy and have to be well organised.

At the moment I am working as part of the regional news team and have to research any breaking news story quickly to find out if there is a local angle our viewers might be interested in. If there is I will research the story in more detail so that the producer has a better understanding of what the local issues are and the reporters have some positive leads to follow up.

I like searching on the Internet for information and then contacting people on the phone to get more information and to arrange meetings and interviews. I also do audience surveys from time to time to find out what our viewers think about us, either by asking questions over the phone or using a questionnaire and asking people in the street.

Being a researcher is all about managing information and being a good communicator. Knowing how to get accurate and reliable information quickly is the most important aspect of the job – and then making sure it gets passed on to the right people in time for them to do something with it.

Think about it!

- What areas have you covered in this unit that provide you with the knowledge and skills needed by a researcher working within the creative media industries? Discuss with the rest of your class and then produce a written summary of your key points.
- What further skills might you need to develop to be successful in this role? Write a list and discuss what you have written with the rest of the class.
- What do you think you need to do next to improve your chances of getting a job within the creative media industries?

Just checking

1. Define the two main methods of research used in the creative media industries.
2. List the main techniques that are associated with each method of research.
3. Identify five organisations that provide research data to the media industry and explain what each one provides.
4. What are the three main purposes of research undertaken within the creative media sector?
5. What categories are commonly used to describe and segment a target audience?
6. Why is market research information useful for media producers and advertisers?
7. What is the Harvard system?
8. How would you reference a website in a formal report?

edexcel

Assignment tips

*   Have a go at using all of the different research methods and techniques so that you know what to say in Assessment activity 3.1. You might use books, observation, industrial visits, interviews and Internet searches to find out more about the production processes involved and the technology available to you. You might also use the Internet, magazines, books and archive material to gather information for the actual content of your production. Interviewing people is also a good way of getting information to include in your final media production.

*   Link the research for Assessment activity 3.2 to your work in one of your practical units. This will make the research more meaningful to you and will save you valuable time.

*   Be selective. What information is really important? Do not try to include all your research material in your final portfolio. Quantity is not the same as quality!

*   Present quantitative data in the form of tables, graphs or charts. This can be a better way of showing complex information.

*   Be consistent in your use of quotations, citations and referencing in your final written report.

*   Check your work before it is finally submitted. A well-organised folder that has a logical structure, is clear in what it is trying to say and is well written with no spelling mistakes will make a good impression.

Credit value: 10

4 Creative media production management project

To work successfully when producing media products you need to understand the role of production management. Producing a media product requires a team of people with creative and management skills. They all work together to ensure that the product is developed in the right way and on time. Whether the media product is a radio programme, a DVD, a computer game or a poster for a campaign, someone must ensure that the production process goes smoothly. This involves the pre-production, production and post-production phases of the project.

In this unit you will be able to enhance your skills through the planning and management of a media production. You will do this through the origination and researching of an idea, through to pitching your idea, to managing the production process. You might work on your project individually or as part of a team. If you work in a team you will have to take individual responsibility for the effectiveness of the production process.

Learning outcomes

After completing this unit you should:

1. be able to originate, develop and research an idea for a media product
2. be able to pitch a proposal for a media product
3. be able to manage a production process to create a media product.

Assessment and grading criteria

This table shows you what you must do in order to achieve a **pass**, **merit** or **distinction** grade, and where you can find activities in this book to help you.

To achieve a **pass** grade the evidence must show that you are able to:	To achieve a **merit** grade the evidence must show that, in addition to the pass criteria, you are able to:	To achieve a **distinction** grade the evidence must show that, in addition to the pass and merit criteria, you are able to:
P1 originate, develop and research an idea for a media product working within appropriate conventions and with some assistance **See Assessment activity 4.1, page 65**	**M1** originate, develop and research an idea for a media product showing some imagination and with only occasional assistance **See Assessment activity 4.1, page 65**	**D1** originate, develop and research an idea for a media product showing creativity and flair and working independently to professional expectations **See Assessment activity 4.1, page 65**
P2 pitch a proposal for a media product with some appropriate use of subject terminology and with some assistance **See Assessment activity 4.2, page 68**	**M2** pitch a proposal for a media product competently with generally appropriate use of subject terminology and with only occasional assistance **See Assessment activity 4.2, page 68**	**D2** pitch a proposal for a media product to a near-professional standard consistently using subject terminology correctly and working independently to professional expectations **See Assessment activity 4.2, page 68**
P3 manage a production process to create a media product working within appropriate conventions and with some assistance **See Assessment activity 4.3, page 72**	**M3** manage a production process competently to create a media product to a good technical standard, showing some imagination and with only occasional assistance **See Assessment activity 4.3, page 72**	**D3** manage a production process to near-professional standards to create a media product, showing creativity and flair and working independently to professional expectations **See Assessment activity 4.3, page 72**

How you will be assessed

This unit will be assessed by a number of internal assignments designed to allow you to show your understanding of the unit outcomes. These relate to what you should be able to do after completing this unit. Most of the assignments that you will complete for this unit will relate to the practical production work that you are doing in some of your other units. This means that the production work that you undertake will relate directly to the media products that you are developing and producing within the other practical units of this course.

Your assessments could be in the form of:

- presentations
- case studies
- practical tasks
- written assignments
- production documentation.

Fazal, creative media production student

At the start of the course I had a basic idea of what production work would involve, because I'd done various projects of my own for fun, but I hadn't really had experience of working in a larger production team, or thought about all the planning and coordination that's needed.

For my own projects I could just follow my own ideas and interests and more or less make it up as I went along. But in the professional world you need a properly thought-out plan, and you need to make sure you're creating a product that the client wants, not just the thing that you feel like making.

This unit gave me experience of thinking of ideas in response to a brief, presenting the ideas in a pitch, and then working with a team to make sure that the product got produced on time.

I found that one of the most important skills in production management is allocating the most appropriate role to each person, making sure everyone's skills are used in the best possible way, including admin jobs such as booking equipment as well as creative roles such as drawing a storyboard. Things are not going to run smoothly if you don't play to your strengths.

I also realised how important it is to keep careful records of your production management. That way you can always show how, why and when decisions were made and no one can come back to you and say that they wanted one thing and now you have produced something different.

Over to you!

- Which aspects of production work do you already have experience of?
- What are the differences between working on your own projects and working with a team in response to a brief?
- Which practical units do you think this unit links to?

1. Be able to originate, develop and research an idea for a media product

Marketing

You have been approached by the Head of Marketing at your college to produce a promotional package for the next open evening. They would like a short video, a leaflet and a poster that demonstrate the best features of your college. You have to manage the production of these products. You have been allocated a team of six people to work with you on this project.

- How will you allocate the production of these products to the most appropriate members of the team?
- How will you manage the production process to get the products made in time for the open evening?
- How will you maintain communication with the Head of Marketing?

You need to understand the process you must go through when producing a media product. Look at Figure 4.1 opposite, which identifies the pre-production, production and post-production processes.

This unit requires you to manage the whole process of pre-production (pink), production (blue) and post-production (green). You can see that there are a number of stages you will need to go through when managing the production of your media product. To produce a successful media product you must manage each part of the process in turn, which then leads on to the next. For example, if you do not undertake your research in an appropriate way this might lead to the production of an inappropriate idea, and so on.

Whatever kind of media product you make, the production process and management process will be similar.

1.1 Originate ideas

The first stage of the production process is the origination of appropriate ideas. The case study on the next page is a good example of how this might work in practice.

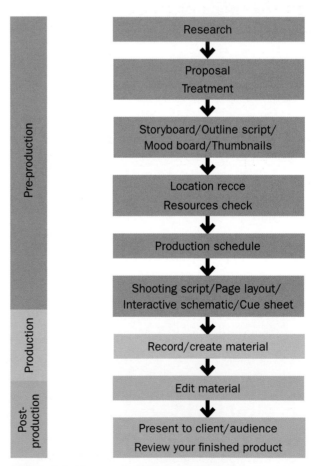

Figure 4.1: The production process: which parts are you most and least confident about managing?

Case study: Originating and selecting ideas in response to a brief

PMH Productions

PMH Productions, an independent production company, was commissioned by a local fashion store to produce a short promotional video for a new range of fair-trade clothes. The video would either be sent to customers on a DVD or streamed on the Internet. The client needed the finished product for a launch event in three months' time.

The producer began by holding a team meeting to brainstorm possible approaches and produced a mind map of initial ideas (see Figure 4.2). The team then undertook some initial research into each idea and assessed each one in terms of cost, practicality and timeframe.

In discussion they rejected the idea of shooting material in Malaysia as this would involve considerable time in setting up and shooting material. They rejected the idea of simply putting lots of still images together in the style of a catalogue because although this would be quick, it would not make best use of the intended DVD or Internet distribution. They decided on a fashion show shot in a local studio with an invited audience, with lots of posters positioned in the

Figure 4.2: When could you use a mind map?

background to provide subliminal images of fair-trade logos and text.

1. What are the advantages of producing a mind map?
2. What factors need to be taken into account when assessing the feasibility of a range of product ideas?

First of all you must think about the medium you intend to use to produce your media product. Will it be a video programme, an audio recording, a website, a computer game, a magazine or a poster? These are just some of the products you might create.

Whatever medium you choose, you will need to plan a process to come up with appropriate ideas, research these ideas and select one idea to take forward to production.

Doing a mind map similar to the one in Figure 4.2 can be a good way of putting all your ideas down and then considering them in terms of resources and time available and your skills in making the product, to help you identify the strongest and most feasible idea. It will allow you to demonstrate not only a range of research skills but also that you have thought creatively about your final product.

1.2 Develop an idea

Once you have chosen your idea and you are sure that it is appropriate, you will need to develop the idea further. You could produce a mood board or a sample script as part of the development process. You may

be able to take some sample shots or create sample material to see how things turn out. You may be able to make a mock-up of your media product or conduct a survey of people's opinions that will help you to develop your idea further.

Remember that you will need to produce evidence of your origination and development of ideas. To do this you must record how you thought of your ideas, how you developed them and the research that you undertook.

1.3 Constraints

You will find that there are always constraints on the way that you plan to produce your media product. Here are some possible constraints.

- **Time** – will you have sufficient time to plan and produce your product?
- **Costs** – will you have sufficient funds to produce the product?
- **Personnel** – will you be able to find the right people for your team and will you be able to get permissions from people appearing in your product?

- **Resources** – do you have the resources to produce the product?
- **Legal and ethical considerations** – will you be able to get permission to use locations? Is anything you want to say or do likely to break the law or be considered unethical?
- **Codes of practice** – are you clear about the codes of practice you must follow as laid down by your area of the media sector (for example, doorstepping interviews, covert filming, age guidelines)?
- **Copyright** – will you be able to ensure that you comply with copyright law, either by using your own materials and copyright-free material or by clearing and paying for rights to use copyright material?

As a production manager it is your role to ensure that any such constraints have been identified at an early stage and addressed before you begin the production process.

Case study: Sophie, student

On one project we found out the hard way how important it is to plan everything carefully from the outset, and to communicate within the team.

Our production manager did not realise that a sequence to be filmed in a school would involve filming children. It was only when the crew arrived at the location that it became clear that this was a problem. We were not allowed to film any of the children without the written permission of their parents or guardians. With better communication and the right planning, this issue could have been sorted out by sending permissions forms in advance.

1. Think about one of your own productions. What constraints will apply?
2. How will you need to plan around these constraints?

1.4 Research an idea

Market research

Carrying out research will help to ensure that your idea is feasible and appropriate.

It is important to consider the audience when planning a media product. You need to think about the age of your audience, their likes and dislikes, their socio-economic grouping and their lifestyle. It would not be sensible to plan to produce a product that alienates the audience you are aiming at.

You may have to take into account the number and type of viewers you expect to look at your product. This might influence the ways in which you construct your product. This would be particularly important if you were considering producing a broadcast programme or a newspaper or magazine. Your client will need to know that they are spending their money wisely and that they will reach their target audience.

When planning a product such as a magazine the producer will need to know what an audience wants and what they are willing to pay. To do this they might undertake market research by asking people from the target audience appropriate questions and then analysing their answers. They may ask a small group of the target audience to attend a focus group where they review a sample of the intended product and answer questions about their opinions. It is unlikely that a producer would proceed with the production and distribution of a product if the feedback from the target audience was unfavourable.

Activity: Audiences and markets

As we have seen in Units 1 and 3, a number of organisations offer information about audiences and markets within the creative media sector. If you have not already, find out about these organisations.

RAJAR Radio Joint Audience Research Limited
www.rajar.co.uk

BARB Broadcasters' Audience Research Board
www.barb.co.uk

ELSPA Entertainment and Leisure Software Publishers Association
www.elspa.com

Content research

In order to identify appropriate style and content for your media product, you will need to undertake careful primary and secondary research.

Primary research might include:

- interviews with intended audiences
- questionnaires to ascertain audience views

- holding a **focus group** to see how people react to your ideas for a media product (a focus group is a group of people drawn from the target audience who are invited to offer ideas and to give opinions about proposed products)
- your own observations of the intended audience.

Secondary research could include:

- looking at existing media products to see how they were made
- using the Internet, magazines or books to see how other people have made media products

- identifying competitors in the marketplace for your media products.

Once you have undertaken your research you need to collate it and use it to inform the production of your media product.

Key term

Focus group – a group of people drawn from the target audience who are invited to assess proposed products.

Assessment activity 4.1

Think about one of the production projects that you are undertaking in your practical option units. Think about the things that interest you. Are you better at producing some types of media products than others? Can you think of an idea that uses your strengths?

Work through the stages of pre-production right up to the point where you have to pitch your idea to a client. Produce a range of documentation that demonstrates that you have:

- thought of a range of ideas
- researched these ideas
- carefully chosen an idea based on resources and your strengths
- developed the idea fully
- considered a wide range of constraints
- researched into audience and content.

Present your documentation in a pre-production file.

This Assessment activity relates to the following grading criteria.

- Originate, develop and research an idea for a media product *working within appropriate conventions.* **P1**
- Originate, develop and research an idea for a media product *showing some imagination.* **M1**
- Originate, develop and research an idea for a media product *showing creativity and flair.* **D1**

Grading tips

For a merit grade, you need to originate, develop and research an idea showing some imagination. You will need to demonstrate that you have considered a range of ideas, provide evidence of your research and development work and demonstrate you understand the constraints on your idea. You must indicate how you researched each idea and list the research materials that you used.

For a distinction grade, you will need to demonstrate your creativity and flair by originating a range of imaginative ideas, thinking 'outside the box' rather than using only mundane, traditional ideas. You will also demonstrate creativity and flair in your development and research with imaginative approaches that are well documented and reflect near-professional standards.

Your pre-production file will grow as you work through this unit. Keep your documentation carefully to ensure that you have all the evidence you need to meet the highest grade. It is not sufficient to simply copy pages from the Internet. You must show that you have used your research in a productive way.

A production diary, either in hard copy or in the form of a weblog (or blog), can be a really useful tool for recording your findings and your thoughts on your researched material.

PLTS

Undertaking your research and choosing the most appropriate idea to develop will help improve your skills as an **independent enquirer**.

Choosing ideas and developing ideas for a media product will help develop your skills as a **creative thinker**.

2. Be able to pitch a proposal for a media product

2.1 Proposal

You have identified your media product, conducted research into content and style and ensured that you have sufficient resources available.

The next stage is to prepare a **proposal** and present this to the client. There are a number of ways to do this in the media industries. You may just send your proposal to the client, either by email or by post. You may be able to **pitch** your proposed idea to the client in a meeting. In this way you can get instant feedback about your proposal. You can pitch your proposal using a presentation format such as PowerPoint®. In this format you can use text, graphics and embedded video and audio. This will allow the client to see just what you are proposing to do.

The proposal is a document that allows you to sell your idea to the client. It should be written in a way that the client will understand and demonstrate that you have the resources, time and competence to produce this media product.

The proposal needs to include:

- sufficient details about your idea to secure your client's interest in taking it further
- supporting facts and figures about the audience
- information about the resources required
- information about the potential costs involved
- information to demonstrate that you can produce the media product within the required timescale.

A proposal has been described as a sales tool – in other words, it is used to whet the appetite of a potential client.

Key terms

Proposal – a document that sells an idea for a media product to a client.

Pitch – a verbal presentation that allows for the expansion of the key points of a proposal.

Functional skills

Writing your proposal will help you to develop your **English** skills in writing.

Case study: The proposal

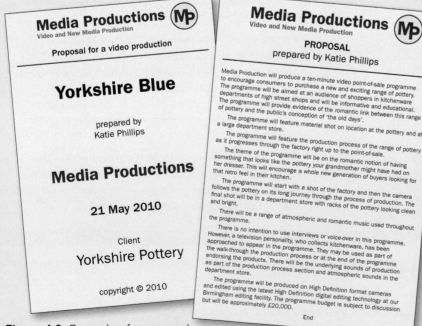

Figure 4.3: Example of a proposal.

This proposal has been used to pitch an idea to the client. It is generally accepted that a short proposal is effective in selling an idea. However, if you need to provide more information, you should do so.

1. Which key factors does your written proposal need to cover?

2. How can you make your proposal capture the client's interest and imagination?

2.2 Pitch

It is common practice in the media industries to deliver your proposal in a face-to-face meeting with a potential client or commissioner – this is called a pitch. It is an opportunity for you to demonstrate to your client the feasibility of your idea. You can also demonstrate how you intend to be creative and enthuse them with your skills and flair.

Format

A typical way of pitching your proposal is to use a presentation format such as PowerPoint® or Keynote. The presentation should be professional and avoid using lots of text on each slide. You could add video or audio clips as well as graphics to illustrate your presentation.

Whichever way you choose to pitch your proposal you should include for assessment:

- presenter's notes
- a handout for the client
- copies of your presentation slides.

Where will you be doing your pitch? Do you need to rearrange the room to suit your presentation?

> **Remember**
>
> Make sure that any technology you are going to use for your pitch is in working order and that you know how to use it. There is nothing more embarrassing than having to fiddle with equipment during your pitch!

Style

You could pitch your proposal in a variety of ways. Try to be as creative as possible, however you choose to do it.

- Maintaining eye contact with the client helps to convince them that you know what you are talking about.

- Using the technical language of your medium confidently will impress the client and show them that they are dealing with a media professional but be careful not to alienate the client by overusing jargon.

- Try to make your pitch as friendly as possible without going too 'over the top'. A client will not want to be patronised.

- Simply reading out your notes will not inspire the client's confidence. Make sure you know the key points you want to include before the pitch starts, and try just to use brief presenter notes as prompts.

- Be prepared for questions! Your tutor will be observing your pitch and might ask you questions to confirm that you really understand what you are going to do. Clients in the industry will usually have questions too, so make sure you have thought everything through and have all the information you might need.

Assessment activity 4.2

You have prepared a proposal and now have to pitch this to a client. To do this you must:

- use an appropriate presentation technique to pitch your idea
- express your idea clearly, ensuring that the information can be understood
- use appropriate media language in your pitch
- sell your idea effectively to the client
- answer any questions they might have.

This Assessment activity relates to the following grading criteria.

- Pitch a proposal for a media product with *some appropriate use of subject terminology.* P2
- Pitch a proposal for a media product *competently with generally correct use of subject terminology.* M2

- Pitch a proposal for a media product to a *near-professional standard consistently using subject terminology correctly.* D2

Grading tips

In order to achieve the highest grades, you must pitch your proposal competently or in a way that demonstrates near-professional standards. This means that your pitch should reflect the ways in which a professional would pitch a proposal.

You must use correct subject terminology in your pitch. This should be appropriate for the medium you have chosen; for example, if you have chosen a print product you could use language such as 'white space' and 'gutters', or for a video product you could use language such as 'camera angles' or 'music bed'.

PLTS

Producing and presenting your pitch will help develop your skills as a **creative thinker** and a **self-manager**.

Functional skills

Presenting your pitch and answering questions about your idea will help you to develop your **English** speaking and listening skills.

3. Be able to manage a production process to create a media product

In this part of the unit you will be planning and managing the production of your media product. It is vital that you understand and manage the production management process in order to ensure that you can produce your media product successfully.

As a production manager you will need accurate records of all your work. A good way to do this is to keep a **production diary**. This might be a book that you fill in every time you make a decision or to note something you need to action. It could also be in the form of an electronic online diary such as Yahoo! Calendar or Google Calendar, or a **blog** (an online software package that allows you to record text, graphics and images via the Internet). Whichever

Key terms

Production diary – a way of recording all the activities undertaken on a day-to-day basis.

Blog (or weblog) – an online software package that allows the user to record text, graphics and images via the Internet.

method you choose, you must keep it up to date and accurate. The activity on blogs on the next page may help you to make up your mind.

As a production manager you will also need to use appropriate documentation to record your actions and communicate with your team.

Activity: Blogs

Find examples of BTEC learner blogs (for example, those created by other learners at your school or college may be hosted on your school, college or course website).

- Can you understand how the production progressed and how and why decisions were made from the information included on the blog? What kind of information is and is not useful in helping you to understand how the project went?

- If you intend to use a blog to document your own production work, what kinds of information do you think will give the best evidence of your work in progress?

Functional skills

Investigating production management techniques will help you to develop your **English** reading skills.

Case study: Paul, interactive media production manager

As a production manager, I keep careful records in a production diary. I also use an online production calendar that all the team can access, whether they work in-house or not. Everyone can then make sure that they are available for particular dates, such as meetings or the pitch to a client.

Once the project has been confirmed, I add schedule dates for the production and post-production of the project.

I am also responsible for maintaining a range of documentation to keep all the team aware of developments. I can send these by email to the team and use them when the team get together for production meetings.

1. What are the advantages of using an online calendar?

2. How will you create your production schedule? Are you familiar with the appropriate software?

3. How will you ensure that the right people are available at the right time during the different stages of production?

3.1 Planning

Early in your production planning you need to identify your team members, allocate appropriate roles according to their skills and hold an initial production meeting with your team. It is important at this stage to ensure that you have agreed all the content of the media product. Go back to your proposal and check that everything you have planned to do is now in place. You also need to ensure that everyone involved is aware of the schedule and of their own commitments and responsibilities in the production. Once you start the production process, it will be difficult to make any major changes to your plans.

Your production meetings will continue throughout the production cycle so that the team can update you on their progress and you can update them on any changes that might be necessary. These meetings should be minuted and copies sent to all the team members. You could also record the production meeting using an audio recorder or a video camcorder.

The production minutes will provide an ongoing picture of how the project is progressing (see an example on the next page). If there are problems with one area of the production this can be highlighted and schedules adjusted accordingly.

Functional skills

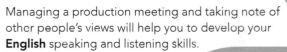

Managing a production meeting and taking note of other people's views will help you to develop your **English** speaking and listening skills.

Did you know?

Producers sometimes make mistakes when casting people for parts in their products. During the making of *Back to the Future* (1985), the producers realised as the filming went ahead that they had miscast the leading role. They went back to their original choice, Michael J. Fox, and persuaded him to join the cast. This meant having to re-shoot footage and reschedule to fit around Michael's television commitments in order to make the film a success.

Minutes

Date: 15 June 2010	Time: 9.30am	Place: Oak Room

Present: Sophie, Ben, Deepak, Brooke

Apologies for absence: Kevin

Minutes recorded by: Sophie Jones

Deepak gave a report describing how he had contacted the managing director of WeRbrides2bee, Gillian Fisher, to ask about the deadline for their next wedding fair. Gillian has invited the group to visit her studio, so they can see some of the behind-the-scenes preparation for a wedding fair.

Brooke has done a lot of research into local wedding planners and was able to report on the equipment that would be needed and the timescales involved.

Ben has contacted local newspaper offices to find out about advertising for wedding-related products. The advertising of the group's final film will be a key part of this project and needs careful research.

Sophie has researched different venues and looked at the kind of creative film work that they might be able to undertake. She has also spoken at length to the media crew to find out what would and would not be possible.

The group agreed to work together to create the best film they can and to combine their talents effectively.

The meeting finished at 10.30am.

Date of next meeting: 14 July 2010.

Figure 4.4: The minutes should record all decisions made and actions agreed. How can you make sure that everyone knows what they have to do next?

Proposed schedules

As you saw in Unit 1, a production schedule will help you to plan and monitor the production process. Most productions will need a detailed schedule which shows exactly when each individual task will be done and flags the key dates that you need to meet from the start of the project to the end. You may have to revise the schedule if you need to make changes to your plan in order to ensure meeting your key dates.

Your production schedule is a vital piece of evidence for the assessment of your planning and production work; therefore you must date and store it carefully, and have it available for assessment.

Logistics

Logistics are an important consideration in any production. The production schedule should include a section identifying all the requirements for personnel, equipment, resources and post-production. This will help the production manager to confirm that everything is in place for the production. Logistics requirements are varied and include anything practical that has to be organised and put in place for any part of the production process. In film and television productions, logistics requirements may include identifying and booking locations, props, talent and any specialist equipment; for radio they may include voice-over artists, music and permissions. Interactive media and games products may require the booking of specialists to create appropriate graphics and sound as well as the necessary hardware and software, while print-based media may require particular assets such as photography, permissions, specialist finishing techniques and so on.

Contingency

You will need to prepare for sudden changes of plan. It may be that the weather is particularly bad when you plan to shoot a scene outdoors or the audio recording you have planned cannot go ahead because of road works outside the location. You may encounter problems with equipment such as battery failure, bulbs blowing or hardware or software malfunctions. You need to have a plan in place to ensure that you can carry on regardless.

To do this you need to produce a contingency plan. This plan will identify potential problems and work out how you will overcome them. It is good practice to do this at an early stage of your planning.

Risk assessment

It is important that you take into consideration the possible risks to yourself, your team and the general public when producing your media product. When you are undertaking a **risk assessment**, you must consider all the hazards you might encounter and take steps to make sure that everyone will be safe. You should use a risk assessment form to identify potential hazards and solutions.

Key term

Risk assessment – the identification of potential risks to staff, the public and equipment in a production.

Activity: What could go wrong?

Think about one of your practical media productions.

- List all the practical problems that could arise and interfere with your production, for example, poor weather, illness, malfunctioning equipment, permissions. Write a contingency plan that identifies the actions you would take for each of the points you identify.

- Consider the range of health and safety risks that your production could pose. What risk assessment activities must you undertake? Produce a risk assessment document that identifies the potential hazards and indicate how you would ensure the safety of your team and the public.

3.2 Production management

An essential part of the management of your project is keeping to time and budget. In order to do this, you will need to monitor progress and keep careful records. These records might be paper-based or electronic, using project management software packages. Whatever system you use, you must monitor:

- the use of resources
- the use of personnel
- time spent in production and post-production
- the ongoing budget
- communication between producer and the team.

If the production is to run smoothly, you will need to be well organised, communicate your plans clearly to your team and make sure you have the necessary permissions and documentation in place. Getting well organised will help you to monitor the progress of your production constantly, so that you can identify problems when they arise and find solutions. You may find the following useful.

Daily planner/call sheet – this provides a plan for the following day of the production and is given to everyone involved.

Staff list – this identifies all the personnel and their roles, mobile telephone numbers and contact email addresses.

Release and consent form – if you are including actors, or filming or photographing people performing in the street, you will need evidence that this person has agreed the use of their image in your production. For children, you will need to get parents/carers to sign the release.

Location release form – to be signed by the owner of any land you want to use to confirm that they have given their permission. Remember that a lot of 'public' spaces, such as parks, are owned by local councils, and you will need to get permission from them.

Remember, if you do not secure all the necessary permissions, you may find at a later stage that you cannot use the material in your final product.

Think about it

As the production manager, you will be managing people.

- What kind of management style will you adopt?
- How will you monitor and manage personal performance?
- How will you monitor and manage team performance?

Did you know?

In 2004 the company 118118 used an image in its advertisements that appeared to be the likeness of David Bedford, a famous athlete in the 1970s. David Bedford complained to the Independent Television Commission that his likeness had been used without his permission. The case went to Ofcom who ruled that the company had breached a rule of the Advertising Standards Code. They could have ordered the company to pull all of their advertisements featuring this image.

3.3 Product

You will need to give your client the opportunity to view your work in progress and ask them for their views while there is still time to respond to their comments. You may want to gather the views of a focus group of people from the target audience before your product is finalised. You can then evaluate the feedback you get and make changes as necessary, remembering to keep careful records of how and why you made any such changes.

You will need to assess how well your media product has met the intentions of your original proposal, and justify any changes that have taken place. Carefully kept records, including an up-to-date production diary or blog, will help you to find the relevant information to identify and explain how and why any changes happened.

Did you know?

Film producers show early versions of their products to an audience to gauge their reactions. If the reactions are negative the producers either re-shoot or re-edit to make the product acceptable to the audience. They know that if the product receives negative feedback from a group that reflects the target audience for the film, that they might make a loss when it is distributed.

PLTS

Managing the production process will help develop your skills as a **team worker**.

Undertaking the role of a production manager will help develop your skills as a **self-manager**.

Assessment activity 4.3

P3 **M3** **D3**   **BTEC**

For the Assessment activity for this element of the unit, you will demonstrate that you can undertake the production and post-production process using your management skills. You need to show that you have managed your work using creativity and flair in the production of an appropriate media product that meets the intentions of your proposal.

You will:

- plan effectively – demonstrating that you can allocate roles, agree content, manage logistics and manage contingency

- manage the production process – demonstrating project management techniques, monitoring and reviewing your work, meeting deadlines and budget, and making modifications where necessary

- review the final product – demonstrating that you have considered the needs of the client and audience, technical and aesthetic qualities of your product and the product's fitness for purpose.

This Assessment activity relates to the following grading criteria.

- Manage a production process to create a media product *working within appropriate conventions and with some assistance.* **P3**

- Manage a production process *competently* to create a media product *to a good technical standard, showing some imagination* and with *only occasional assistance.* **M3**

- Manage a production process to *near-professional standards* to create a media product, *showing creativity and flair* and *working independently to professional expectations.* **D3**

Grading tips

In order to achieve the highest grades, you will have to demonstrate that you have managed the production process to near-professional standards, showing creativity and flair in managing the product.

You must demonstrate that you have been effective in your management role, working independently within appropriate conventions to manage the production process. In other words, you need to demonstrate that you have worked in a similar way to a professional production manager.

Keeping careful records of your work and appropriate documentation will be vital in demonstrating this in your assessment.

Martin works as a production manager at Voiceovers-UK, a voiceover production company that supplies audio assets for a wide variety of media. One publishing client required a large number of foreign language audio files to be supplied in the required file format for inclusion in a complex educational DVD, which was being produced for the publisher by a software company.

'I always monitor our production and post-production processes carefully to ensure that the work we produce matches the brief, as it can be expensive to go back at the end of a project and make changes. On this project the challenges were the sheer volume of files, keeping track of everything, achieving a high level of accuracy for the foreign language teaching product, and working at a distance with both the client and the software company they had commissioned to produce the final DVD.

Although we never met face to face, I communicated with the client regularly. In pre-production there were many discussions by phone and email to clarify the brief, and to establish the technical requirements of the software company. We then agreed the exact details of the audio brief in writing, confirming the script, choice of voice artists and the technological requirements.

During production I invited the client to attend or to dial in remotely and listen in to key recording sessions, so they could comment while it was still relatively easy to make adjustments. If anything seemed wrong or was unclear during the recording, I always checked this straight away with the client so we could solve it on the spot. Getting the voice artists back again another day and having to charge for another day of studio and editing would have made costs soar.

In post-production I provided a "rough cut" of the recorded material for approval, which was then edited to produce the finished files in the format agreed. It was crucial to be well organised and use a clear file-naming convention and to log everything so that everyone could keep track and identify what was what.'

Think about it!

- Why is regular communication with the client so important?
- How would you record discussions and agreements with a remote client?

Just checking

1. Have you originated a range of ideas and then developed one idea for a final product?
2. Do you have clear evidence of your research into the range of ideas and the content of the final agreed idea?
3. Were you able to pitch your idea in an appropriate way and does the proposal you produced match your final product?
4. Do you have sufficient evidence of your management of the production?

If you think that the answer is 'no' to any of the questions, you will need to go back and add extra material to your folder of work for this unit.

edexcel

Assignment tips

- Use your time on the course to try out a range of management techniques and to improve your ability to communicate with a client.

- Try to find an opportunity to work with a professional in your chosen industry to gain insight into the management process.

- Use your practical productions to practise managing your time, not only so you get your work done on time, but also in preparation for working effectively with your future clients.

- Keep careful, thorough records so you can demonstrate all the skills and thought that have gone into your work. An excellent final product will not be enough on its own!

5 Working to a brief in the creative media industries

The aim of this unit is to provide you with a greater understanding of the working practices within the media Industries. In the creative and media sector you are likely to be provided with a brief that outlines what a company wants from a product or service; it is then up to you to fulfil the brief and meet the client's needs.

You will need to become familiar with this way of working and you will need to bring all your creative, technical and interpersonal skills together in order to follow your brief through from inception to completion. You will need to be able to work closely with your client and you should be able to interpret your ideas clearly so that they can be understood by all concerned.

It is likely that this unit will be contextualised within another, practical unit so that you have an actual 'live' production to work on. Which unit you work through will depend on the pathway of study and will be selected by your centre.

Learning outcomes

After completing this unit you should:

1. understand the requirements of working to a brief
2. be able to develop a planned response to a brief
3. be able to apply a response to a brief
4. be able to review work on completion of a brief.

Assessment and grading criteria

This table shows you what you must do in order to achieve a **pass**, **merit** or **distinction** grade, and where you can find activities in this book to help you.

To achieve a **pass** grade the evidence must show that you are able to:	To achieve a **merit** grade the evidence must show that, in addition to the pass criteria, you are able to:	To achieve a **distinction** grade the evidence must show that, in addition to the pass and merit criteria, you are able to:
P1 describe the requirements of working to a brief **See Assessment activity 5.1, page 81**	**M1** explain the requirements of working to a brief with reference to detailed illustrative examples **See Assessment activity 5.1, page 81**	**D1** comprehensively explain the requirements of working to a brief with elucidated examples **See Assessment activity 5.1, page 81**
P2 plan a response to a brief working within appropriate conventions and with some assistance **See Assessment activity 5.2, page 84**	**M2** plan a response to a brief competently showing some imagination and with only occasional assistance **See Assessment activity 5.2, page 84**	**D2** plan a response to a brief to near-professional standards showing creativity and flair and working independently to professional expectations **See Assessment activity 5.2, page 84**
P3 apply a response to a brief working within appropriate conventions and with some assistance **See Assessment activity 5.3, page 86**	**M3** apply a response to a brief competently showing some imagination and with only occasional assistance **See Assessment activity 5.3, page 86**	**D3** apply a response to a brief to near-professional standards showing creativity and flair and working independently to professional expectations **See Assessment activity 5.3, page 86**
P4 comment on own work on completion of a brief with some appropriate use of subject terminology **See Assessment activity 5.4, page 90**	**M4** explain own work on completion of a brief with reference to detailed illustrative examples and with generally correct use of subject terminology **See Assessment activity 5.4, page 90**	**D4** critically evaluate own work on completion of a brief with reference to professional practice, and consistently using subject terminology correctly **See Assessment activity 5.4, page 90**

How you will be assessed

Assessment for this unit will take the form of an ongoing production project in which you will be required to respond to a client brief. You will need to produce all necessary production paperwork and documentation for final assessment as well as a final product. It is very likely that the work required for this unit will be undertaken in other units such as the optional practical production units chosen by your centre. Your tutor will probably track your progress in an integrated assignment, rather than by separate assessment.

Your assessment could take any of the following forms:

- undertaking written work including producing production paperwork

- pitching your ideas to the tutor/client

- presenting a review of your work in either written or oral formats.

Tania, creative media production student

This unit really helped me to understand the ways in which work is commissioned in the creative and media sector and to realise that I need to develop professional working practices in order to meet specified deadlines in line with the client's needs.

Interpreting a brief and understanding client requirements is vitally important. Very often the client isn't available for you to ask them questions so you need to be able to 'read between the lines' in order to come up with ideas that the client will find acceptable.

It is also important to be able to work well as part of a production team and to work with each member's strengths and weaknesses, communicating effectively in order to get the job done. The client isn't interested whether or not you fell out with a member of the group. What they want is results and ideas that will work for their company.

The work I have done has made me realise that I am doing this course in order to get a job. This is my training for the industry and it is important to get a realistic view of what I can expect out there. I really feel that I now understand these working practices a lot better and although it can be quite full on at times it is incredibly rewarding when the client accepts your ideas and you provide them with the finished product.

Over to you!

- Why does Tania say she needs to develop professional working practices?
- Name some of the important skills needed for group work.
- What does Tania say she feels she has learned from this unit?
- What does she find most rewarding?
- What do you want to learn from this unit?

1. Understand the requirements of working to a brief

Working through a brief

During your course your tutor will provide you with a brief similar to the one given below. Your job as part of a production team will be to work through the brief and make a note of the important information that will help you to generate suitable ideas for the client.

Drink culture

Young people are increasingly using alcohol as an important part of their social lives. Many of them see binge drinking as acceptable and part of their lifestyle. Some are encouraged by their peers to consider alcohol as a safe drug that has no long-term effect.

STOP.co.uk is a charity that wants to produce materials to distribute to schools and colleges. They are looking for a range of media products that will inform young people of the dangers of excessive consumption of alcohol and binge drinking. The products will be aimed at young people in the 16–18 age group, identified in recent research as the age when some young people start to indulge in binge drinking. Your media product can be in any style and genre.

Brief: Moving image

Here at STOP.co.uk we are preparing a campaign that encourages young people to consider the effects of consuming excessive amounts of alcohol and binge drinking.

We want you to research, plan and produce a moving image product that will help to communicate our message to young people. The message must be appropriate for the 16–18 age group. We are happy for your moving image product to be in whatever format you think suitable for the target audience. We want it to be relevant to the target audience and we would welcome conventional and unconventional approaches to the subject.

The product you develop could be in a fictional or factual genre, and we do not want to put any restrictions on its style, content or length. However, it must communicate an effective message about the effects of excessive alcohol consumption and binge drinking.

You must include appropriate ideas development, pre-production, production and post-production documentation as well as an evaluation of your work.

- Who is the client in this brief?
- What is their intention?
- Who is the target audience and why?
- Outline what it is you have **specifically** been asked to do.
- How could you begin to approach this topic? Start outlining some initial ideas.

In order for you to respond to a client brief you need to be able to understand what is required of you and what the client wants you to achieve. This is not simply the process of reading the brief and doing what it says but a negotiated interpretation of the client's requirements and their intentions towards their target audience. You need to consider what it is the client is hoping to achieve and how you can best help them to do this.

Remember that just because you think something is a great idea, it does not mean everybody else will agree. Your suggestion has to make sense to the client and the audience, and provide the required response. After all, the client is investing time and money into this project and they will want to see results.

1.1 Structure of briefs

A client brief can take many forms and this will dictate how you should respond to it. For example, a piece of work could be specifically commissioned from you by a company on the basis of your reputation or specialism in a specific field. Alternatively some companies choose to put their work up for tender. This means that you will have to generate some ideas and provide a swift but suitable response to a brief in order to win the contract to provide the work. Your ideas will be considered among those of many other companies and individuals, and you will really have to work hard to sell your ideas and concepts to the client.

There are different ways in which a client brief could be presented to you.

- **Contractual** – the brief is outlined in an employment contract, such as written work for publication.
- **Formal** – a meeting could be organised with the client and they outline their requirements for you.
- **Negotiated** – you might help the client to develop the brief by working collaboratively with them, discussing and agreeing the aims and objectives.
- **Informal** – the client could call you and discuss their requirements over the telephone.
- **Tender** – some briefs are sent to several companies by post or email and you are invited to respond with your ideas, for them to be considered in competition against the ideas from other suppliers.

However the client brief is presented to you, it is the job both of you as an individual and of the whole production team to respond to the client's needs and provide them with suitable ideas. However, for the most part, client briefs will have similar requirements, which should include, but are not limited to:

- an overall outline or proposal
- some background details about the client, for example, company history, work undertaken
- any research that may already have been carried out by the client into their proposed production
- what the client hopes to achieve with the project
- target audience
- an initial or at least basic outline of the proposed budget
- the timescale in which you will have to complete the project.

1.2 Reading a brief

To begin with, you will need to recognise the nature of the client and their demands as implied in the brief. This means, as you have done in the Set up activity, breaking down the content of the brief and outlining for yourself what exactly the client requires of you. Always keep the client's needs foremost in your mind and keep referring back to the brief should you need clarification. Remember that some requirements may not be spelled out explicitly. You may need to interpret what the client really means, though this can have its dangers if you misunderstand what the client is getting at! If you are not sure exactly what the brief means, always go back to the client and clarify anything vague or ambiguous.

Activity: Project brief

Think about a project brief from one of your practical units.

- What are the explicit requirements?
- Are there any implicit requirements?
- Is anything left open to interpretation?

Compare your thoughts with someone else in your group.

- Did you pick up on the same things?
- How could you ensure you have a shared understanding with the client?

Consultation with the client is extremely important, and although not all clients will make that initial face-to-face contact, it is important to ensure that you open a channel of communication with them to ensure that they can feed back to you on your ideas and provide valuable input. That is not to say that you will not have a degree of discretion in interpreting the brief – you are after all being paid for your ideas and creativity – however, you are working for a client, so interim 'check ins' will not do any harm.

Constraints

You will already be aware that all work produced is subject to legal, ethical and regulatory constraints and you need to ensure you are aware of what these constraints are and how you can work within them.

Legal constraints – remember that you are legally obliged to deliver to your client the entire project as laid out in the contract between you. Failure to meet the agreed production requirements within the specified budget and deadlines could be a breach of contract and lose you money, respect and even the entire project, as well as potentially lead to serious legal ramifications.

Ethical constraints – you have to behave ethically throughout the production process. You must keep in mind that you cannot do, say or produce whatever you want, but must consider the thoughts, ideas and opinions of others in all that you do.

Regulatory constraints – each medium is controlled by its own governing body, such as Ofcom, for example, which lays down and enforces the rules and regulations that you have to work by. You need to know what restrictions these governing bodies may place on your production and what the possible consequences may be if you ignore them. Make sure that you are clear about any codes of practice and legislation that apply to your area of work.

Case study: Jonathan Ross and Russell Brand

An example of the importance of abiding by professional guidelines is the scandal in 2008 when Jonathan Ross and Russell Brand made a prank telephone call to the actor Andrew Sachs, which was broadcast on radio. This incident resulted in numerous complaints and an Ofcom investigation. Russell Brand resigned from the BBC, Jonathan Ross was suspended without pay and the BBC was fined £150,000. Members of the production staff involved were also disciplined or asked to leave the company.

1. What professional codes of conduct did the programme producers infringe?
2. Who do you think was responsible for these infringements?
3. Could the Ofcom fines have been avoided?
4. What steps do you think a company could take to avoid these problems occurring in the future?

1.3 Negotiating the brief

You may need to clarify or modify the initial brief with a client, either at the outset of the project or during production.

Negotiating changes to proposed final product

This could happen at the request of either the client or the producer, at any stage, and should be subject to an ongoing review process. There should be a willingness and ability to adapt as and when required. However, you should always ensure that an agreement has been reached with the client before you begin the work for them. You do not want to produce something they are not expecting!

Negotiating changes to the budget

Contingency planning is essential. At least a 10 per cent contingency buffer should be set aside at the beginning of the project to cover any unexpected eventualities. This might not cover everything that could occur but should help keep things on track if problems arise.

Negotiating changes to conditions and fees

You may need to negotiate a change to the conditions of the contract or the fee payable, even the schedule of payments that have been outlined. You must be prepared to discussed these matters with the client and ensure that all necessary amendments have been agreed in writing before undertaking the work.

1.4 Opportunities

You will be working as part of a team and may be required to take on more than one role throughout the project. This offers the potential for developing new skills and broadening your experience. Consider the contributions you can make to the project brief and outline them for yourself, but also identify opportunities within the project where you could learn and develop new skills. Set yourself goals to work towards and be sure to manage your time effectively.

Remember

Regulation of the creative media sector must be considered at all times when undertaking your own production work. The point of your studies is to prepare you for work in your chosen sector and here you will be subject to these constraints on a regular basis. They will affect your ideas, the products you create and your working practices, so do not underestimate the effect they have on media producers as well as audiences.

Assessment activity 5.1

P1 M1 D1 BTEC

For these learning outcomes, you will be required to show your understanding of the requirements of working to a brief within the creative media industries.

Write or record a report that highlights your understanding of the requirements of working to a brief. Include details of the purpose of the brief, any constraints that might affect your work and the skills you will need in order to complete it.

- Be able to *describe* the requirements of working to a brief and demonstrate an understanding of its purpose and constraints as well as the skills required to fulfil it. **P1**

- Be able to *explain* the requirements of working to a brief in more detail by demonstrating an understanding of its purpose and constraints as well as the skills required to fulfil it. Provide detailed illustrative examples to help make your points more relevant. **M1**

- *Fully and comprehensively explain* the requirements of working to a brief by demonstrating a sound understanding of its

purpose and constraints as well as the skills required to fulfil it. Provide targeted and highly relevant examples to make relevant points. **D1**

Grading tips

For a merit grade, you will need to produce a report that reflects a good understanding of all of the requirements of working to a brief. You should use detailed illustrative examples from your own work and experiences as well as those from the industry in order to make your points more relevant.

For a distinction grade, you will need to provide a detailed and well-written report that makes reference throughout to elucidated examples of your own and from the industry in order to illustrate your points. You should show a clear and rounded understanding of the full requirements of working effectively to a brief.

PLTS

Inviting feedback and dealing positively with praise, setbacks and criticism throughout the process of working on a brief will help you become a more **reflective learner**.

Functional skills

Consulting with others to identify suitable opportunities to work to professional briefs and developing a variety of appropriate responses to a professional brief will help you to develop your **English** skills.

2. Be able to develop a planned response to a brief

2.1 Plan

Planning a response to a brief is a step-by-step process that needs thought and consideration. Remember that you are not working for yourself and that you need to consider and respond to the client's needs at all times. The following are some key factors to remember.

- Preparation: plan to meet the requirements of the client throughout.
- Address health and safety issues before beginning production.
- Investigate relevant legislation prior to production.
- Identify team members and agree the roles of the team members. Everybody should know what they are required to do and when. They need to be consistent and reliable at all times.
- Consider working practices, and professional, legal and ethical requirements.

2.2 Timescales

The deadline is one of the most important things to keep in mind. One of the main issues that could affect your project is availability, both of group members and of the client. When planning your response to the brief, you need to ensure the availability of personnel and resources at the time you need them. Can you rely on your team? Make sure they are aware of their responsibilities and commitments and that they understand the importance of reliability and consistency for the production process.

When planning the schedule, you need to build in time to obtain and respond to feedback from the client. You should also establish how to gain access to the client at short notice in case you run into unexpected difficulties and need to agree solutions or negotiate changes swiftly. Remember, you are trying to demonstrate to the client that you have a realistic, workable production plan, have thought through the practical implications of your ideas, are going to show them work in progress and give them the opportunity to respond and influence how the work is developing, and that you can deliver a successful, appropriate production within the timescale and parameters specified.

Working within the timescale

- Set group and individual targets throughout the project to ensure you stay on target to meet the final deadline.
- Plan well in advance! Book equipment and studio time to suit your schedule rather than squeezing it in at the last minute.
- Hold regular update sessions with the client to review progress and agree any changes to the brief or schedule to keep the project on track.
- Keep clear records of any changes agreed with the client (for example, extended deadlines).

2.3 Develop

Once you have considered the basic planning requirements you need to work through the brief and use it to draw out ideas. You can pull out key words from the brief that will be relevant to the production or use methods such as mind-mapping to help you develop your ideas. It can be useful to have an imaginative mind-mapping session, where no ideas are rejected initially, since these sometimes spark off further creative ideas. As explored in Unit 3, Research techniques for the creative media industries, you will need to do some research into similar products, the market and audience. Your findings will feed into your creative thinking.

How can your group best generate creative ideas?

As you saw in Unit 1, Pre-production techniques for the creative media industries, your aim during the development phase is to work through all of your group's ideas together, explore possible problems and solutions and select the strongest idea(s) that best fulfil(s) the brief.

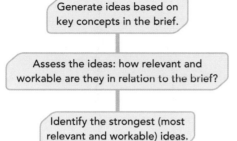

Generate ideas based on key concepts in the brief.

Assess the ideas: how relevant and workable are they in relation to the brief?

Identify the strongest (most relevant and workable) ideas.

What problems might arise with each of these?

What are the potential solutions? Research and evaluate potential solutions against the requirements and constraints.

What further changes would improve the fit to the brief and strengthen the impact of the product?

Select the strongest idea(s) that best fit the brief and present these to the client using appropriate documentation as required.

Develop the preferred idea(s) further in response to the client's feedback.

Figure 5.1: Ideas generation and the process of negotiating the brief.

Remember

- Hold regular meetings to generate, sift and refine your ideas.
- Do not be afraid to go back to the drawing board: you may need to repeat these stages several times.
- Keep dated **minutes** of all discussions and make sure everyone gets a copy so they are aware of the latest thinking.
- Always check back: how relevant and workable is the idea in terms of meeting the brief?
- Keep in touch with the client and negotiate any changes needed. Agree and confirm any decisions in writing before starting production.

Key term

Minutes – notes that record what has been discussed and agreed at a meeting, usually in a succinct or bullet-pointed format.

Case study: David, advertising executive

When we receive a client brief, first we sit down as a team and pick through it to discover exactly what it is the client is asking us to do. It may seem quite obvious in the first instance but it is important to find the finer details and ensure you are meeting the client's requirements at all times.

We begin by looking at key words and phrases and discussing how they are relevant to the production and the product identity. We then go through those phrases and try to think of ways the client could effectively be represented through our production. This can be done as a team or we sometimes go away to develop our own individual ideas and discuss them at a later date.

When we go through our ideas we always ensure that we are constructive in our feedback to each other and that we consider all the viable options before accepting or rejecting an idea and moving on to the next. Again during this process we will constantly be referring to the brief and considering the needs of the client.

Finally we select a few of the best ideas to be developed further and presented to the client, allowing them a choice when it comes to selecting an appropriate platform for their product or service.

1. How do David and his team start the production process?
2. What are they looking for within the brief?
3. Describe the working processes outlined here.
4. How and why do you think they will be effective?
5. What does David say they are constantly considering throughout the process?

Assessment activity 5.2

(P2) (M2) (D2) **BTEC**

When addressing this learning outcome you will be required to plan and develop a response in line with the requirements of the client's brief.

Client brief

You have been provided with a brief by a local company that creates and designs computer games for larger companies.

They are a fairly small concern at the moment but want to increase their visibility among larger potential client companies in the hope of gaining more work.

The company wants to launch a campaign advertising what they do, including details of their best-selling titles. In line with their area of expertise they want this promotion to be interactive and sent out to companies in a relevant format.

- *Plan a response* to the brief by working within appropriate conventions and *with some assistance.* (P2)

- *Plan a response to the brief competently,* showing some imagination and *with only occasional assistance.* (M2)

- *Plan a response to the brief to near-professional standards* showing creativity and flair and *working independently* to professional expectations. (D2)

Grading tips

For a merit grade, you need to respond to the brief by providing a competent range of responses to the client's needs that show some creativity and imagination. You will, for the most part, work on your own but you may occasionally seek support and guidance from others.

For a distinction grade, you need to plan a clear, detailed and creative response to the brief to near-professional standards. You will work independently and efficiently and will consider all aspects of the client's needs and professional conduct.

PLTS

Planning and carrying out research which involves gathering information from written sources will help develop your skills as an **independent enquirer**.

Generating imaginative ideas in response to a brief will help you develop your skills as a **creative thinker**.

Planning and preparing your response independently will help you become a **self-manager**.

Functional skills

Gathering and annotating research from a variety of sources will help you improve your **English** skills.

3. Be able to apply a response to a brief

Your response to the brief should persuade the client that you can put your ideas into practice and make the product they require within the constraints specified.

You will need to act on all of your planning and ideas generation, beginning by working through pre-production, creating the necessary **production documentation** where relevant. All industry sectors have their own different sets of required paperwork to help ensure the production process runs smoothly.

You will then create the product itself and finally edit or finish it ready for presentation to your client.

Key term

Production documentation – all production paperwork from pre-production to post-production.

3.1 Pre-production

Pre-production should take place no matter what medium you are working in, making use of the correct, relevant paperwork. The medium and the brief itself will dictate the paperwork required but whatever documentation you produce it should always be relevant, neat, clear, legible and kept up to date.

All production work will require you to produce a production schedule that outlines what activities will be undertaken by the group, when, where and why. Your schedule should included detailed timescales to ensure that you stay on schedule and are able to meet the client's deadlines.

It is also helpful to keep a production log or diary that details all of the events that took place throughout the production, contains feedback from clients and minutes of meetings and so on. This will keep relevant information in one place where it is easy to refer to. Keeping a thorough record of progress in a production log will also prompt you to carry out ongoing self-monitoring, help you to recognise emerging problems and alert you to the need to adjust the plan as necessary during production. It will also be invaluable at the end of the production when you come to review your work, but do not let it become just a passive record of what went wrong for forensic examination later!

The pre-production paperwork you may need to produce could include:

- schedules
- risk assessments
- permissions, releases and clearances
- **treatments** (the initial outline of a moving image production providing details of scenes, characters and locations)
- scripts
- storyboards
- call sheets
- running orders
- cue sheets
- playlists
- draft layouts
- structure diagrams
- navigation charts
- mood boards
- concept drawings.

Key term

Treatment – the initial outline of a moving image production.

Production log

Week	Work to be undertaken	Completion date
1		
2		
3		
4		
5		
6		
7		
8		
9		
10		
11		
12		

Figure 5.2: What information would it be useful to include in your production log?

3.2 Production

The production phase is the point when you bring all your ideas together and undertake the creative part of the production, whether it is filming or recording, designing print or planning web layouts, or working in some other medium. Whichever medium you are working in, you need to pay attention to timescales and deadlines, and make the best use of your time.

3.3 Post-production

Post-production is where you finish off or 'fine-tune' your product and sort out any minor errors. Remember, if you have not planned properly and organised yourself, there may be nothing you can do to save your project now; and if you have not followed the brief or the basic guidelines and reviewed your work as you have gone along (see next section) you could be in a lot of trouble. Post-production phases are more relevant in some mediums than others but can include the following.

Editing – most usual in audio-visual media, reviewing the recorded footage and placing it into order so that it forms a final product. This can also be done in audio production. Similarly a publishing editor will oversee, edit and approve all print products before publication.

Finishing – often used in photography, where a photograph is 'cleaned up' or made to look in line with the requirements of the production.

Mounting – method used to display photographic or other graphic pieces.

Manipulation – can be done with any digital medium; used to alter or enhance the product in some way.

Transitions and effects – effects are added to television and film products to enhance footage, providing things that were not there during filming. Transitions are placed between scenes and can include fades, wipes and so on.

3.4 Monitoring and reviewing

Keep a close eye on your own and the group's activities throughout and undertake regular progress reviews in order to monitor performance. You must respond to what comes up and revise your plan if necessary. For example, if you are constantly being let down by a member of the team then you could allocate that job to someone else to ensure that it gets done, or even take on that role yourself. That said, be sure to try to divide work equally between you. Do not overload one person just because they are reliable or good at their job.

Keep a working production log that you can refer to alongside your production paperwork, and use it to record progress and make adjustments to ensure that the final product meets all of the client's needs.

Assessment activity 5.3   P3 M3 D3   BTEC

When addressing these learning outcomes you will be required to produce a product in appropriate style, genre and medium in response to the client's requirements as outlined in the brief.

Once you have outlined your ideas and had them approved by the client you need to move forward into the production phase, making use of all relevant production techniques and paperwork, and liaising with the client throughout.

- Be able to produce the product required in the brief by *working within appropriate conventions* and *with some assistance*. **P3**

- Be able to *competently* produce the product required in the brief *showing some imagination* and *with only occasional assistance*. **M3**

- Be able to produce the product required in the brief to a *near-professional standard* by showing *creativity and flair* and *working independently* to professional expectations. **D3**

Grading tips

For a merit grade, you will need to follow your ideas through to the production phase, making competent use of paperwork, equipment and technology to produce the product required by the client, which will show some imagination in its overall style and content. You will work independently, with only occasional assistance.

For a distinction grade, you will need to realise your ideas in order to provide the client with a product that shows creativity and flair and that meets their expectations. You will need to work independently to professional expectations and show that you are able to act professionally throughout.

4. Be able to review work on completion of a brief

The final review of your work could take a number of different formats including a presentation, written report or a *viva voce* (spoken assessment) with your tutor.

4.1 Project management

At the end of your project it is time to reflect back on the entire process and review the performance of the whole team, including yourself, and assess how successfully you have responded to the client's needs as defined in the brief.

4.2 Time management

It is important to remember that deadlines in the creative and media sector exist for a reason. All members of staff, cast and crew are being paid for their time and all of them have to use it productively. For example, overrunning on a film production could cost millions of pounds in wages, location and equipment costs that may never be recouped through later sales. Each production needs to be completed in the required time and within the agreed budget in order to fit its purpose. If it is a commercial product, it needs to be ready to be marketed on time, should be appropriate to the intended audience, and on budget in order to be profitable.

Time management is an important aspect of everyday life and is particularly relevant during the production process as you will often be working to schedules and deadlines.

Activity: Deadlines

List your original scheduled completion dates for all phases of the production.

Next, list the actual completion dates as detailed in your production log or diary.

- How closely do these dates match?
- Did any area of the production overrun and, if so, when and why?
- What were the effects of missing your scheduled deadlines?
- How did you manage your time to ensure any time lost was gained in a later phase?
- What was the impact on how successfully you met the brief?

4.3 Technical competencies and creative abilities

For this you need to look at the competencies of all team members, including yourself. At the beginning of the project you allocated roles and you probably did so by considering the strengths and weaknesses of the team members. It is the same in the creative and media sector: people are hired to do certain jobs because of their skills and abilities and often as a result of the reputation they have built up over the years.

While your team may have played to their strengths, that does not necessarily mean that everything went according to plan. For example, some group members may have had wonderfully creative ideas which later turned out to be unrealistic or unworkable. You may well have experienced such problems along the way, and you need to review these constructively.

4.4 Your contribution to the team

Finally you need to consider your personal contribution to the entire production process and how involved you have been with the work of the group as a whole. For this you will probably need to review your production logs and other paperwork, but mostly you will need to be honest with yourself about what you have done over the past weeks.

Use the activity below to assess the abilities of the group and how well you all used your skills during the production process.

Constraints

You need to consider in detail any legal and regulatory constraints that were placed on your project as a result of the choices you made. These constraints could relate to the chosen genre or medium and could be as simple as observing the watershed for audio-visual productions or as complex as ensuring the correct copyright permissions were obtained in order to use the work of others.

There may also have been financial constraints on your productions; after all, the client will have provided you with a budget to work within as part of the brief. This could have meant that you were not able to access expensive equipment, professional actors or purchase copyright materials. Whatever the budgetary constraints, they too must be reviewed and discussed in terms of their overall effect on the final product, and any impact on realising the agreed brief.

Activity: Evaluating the product

1. **What is the overall technical quality, style and content of the final product? How does this relate to the brief?**

   Here you need to consider what is called the 'aesthetic' of the product. This factor will affect all types of product from print to video as it is concerned with how the product looks and whether it realises the original intentions. You need to reflect on the overall quality of the style and content of the product and consider whether you have added all the necessary elements required for it to fit the brief in your chosen genre.

2. **Does your product look how you intended?**

   If the brief was to produce a glossy magazine and you have actually printed it on dull, matt-finished paper, then your product will not have the look you originally intended it to have.

   Technical qualities are also a consideration. If you have produced a product that lacks technical competence then it is not going to fulfil its purpose. A moving image product that has been badly edited, with poor transitions and jumpy sound will neither look nor sound good and it will fail to get the message across as the audience will be too busy concentrating on the errors to pay attention to the content.

   Use the checklist below to help you to review your product. Be prepared to make some harsh judgements if you have to, and always keep in mind how your production compares with the brief you were following. Think about:

   - the overall finish of the product
   - how well you have worked to – and met – the requirements of the brief
   - the intended and actual look of the product
   - the intended and actual technical quality of the finished piece
   - factors that contributed to changes in the final product
   - the effect those changes have had on the product.

4.5 Responding to the client's feedback

One of the most important sources of feedback is the client (or your tutor, who is likely to be acting as your client). They commissioned your product in the first place and therefore what they think of it is of the utmost importance! Make sure that you are open to this feedback.

Reacting to feedback is not just about attributing praise or blame, or making excuses. It is an important opportunity to learn from your experience and may even give you a chance to address and put right any final concerns the client may still have. No matter what the client says, you need to respond to their feedback reflectively and in a way that will inspire them with confidence in your professionalism, so as to increase the chance of them coming back to you for future productions.

What kind of feedback would you find helpful? What would be the best way of getting this feedback?

Think about it

Think about the feedback from the client in relation to the brief.

- Does the client's feedback indicate that there were problems with how you understood or interpreted the brief?
- What would you look to clarify in a brief in the future to avoid similar problems?
- What are the advantages and pitfalls of working to a client's brief rather than purely from your own creativity?

Annotate the feedback you have received to help you identify key points that you need to respond to, can still address, or can learn from.

Comments from others

It is always vital to get feedback from others as well as conducting your own review. This is because others are not as close to the project as you are and are more likely to see any faults or errors or to pick up on details you may have overlooked.

The product's audience is always a good way to start and there are different ways of getting them to review and feed back on your product. A method often used in the film industry is test screening, where an audience is shown the film and asked to respond to what they see and how they feel about it. This feedback can then be analysed and changes made to the film, if necessary.

For your productions it is likely that you will obtain feedback from your peers (members of your class). They are likely to be readily available for you to ask, and may also fit the profile of your intended target audience, so their feedback will be relevant and helpful. You may want to talk to them informally, hold a focus group, or get them to respond in writing (for example, using a questionnaire, either with space for answers to direct questions or tick-box evaluations). You need to choose the method that you think is most likely to give you honest, useful responses.

Case study: Reacting to feedback

John, marketing executive

At first I found it really hard to take feedback. When you've spent weeks working on something, the last thing you want to hear is someone picking holes in it, especially if it's something you're pleased with.

It wasn't until I was asked to give my feedback on someone else's production that I found how frustrating it was to have things to say and not be listened to. I realised I really could pick up on things that the production team hadn't noticed, because I wasn't involved like they were, but they just didn't want to know. That experience made

me feel differently about getting feedback on my own work. Now I try to be open to what people say without taking criticism personally. It can be hard, but I have to keep reminding myself that I might learn something useful!

I think it's important to try not to get defensive or upset. In the working world it just wouldn't be professional to react like that.

1. What is the difference between criticism and feedback?

2. How and why do you think feedback could be helpful to your production work?

Assessment activity 5.4

P4 M4 D4 **BTEC**

When addressing these learning outcomes, you will be required to conduct and present a review of your work, looking at all of the areas outlined and responding to the feedback and critique of others.

Now your work has been completed and submitted to the client you need to review the entire production process, your response to the client and the brief provided, and the feedback obtained from the client and the target audience.

- Once you have completed the brief, *comment* on your own work making *some appropriate use of subject terminology.* **P4**

- Once you have completed the brief, *explain* your own work with reference to *detailed illustrative examples* and with *generally correct use of subject terminology.* **M4**

- Once you have completed the brief, *critically evaluate* your own work with reference to your own professional practice, and *consistently using subject terminology correctly.* **D4**

Grading tips

For a merit grade, you will need to show that you are able to reflect on your work, making some critical comments and referring to detailed examples of your own work, as well as the work of others, to illustrate your points. You will generally use subject terminology correctly.

For a distinction grade, you will need to provide a good, all-round critical analysis of your product and working practices using relevant and targeted examples of your own work and the work of others. You will consistently use subject terminology correctly.

PLTS

Reviewing progress and evaluating experiences, and learning to inform future progress when evaluating others' work on completing a brief, will help you become a **reflective learner**.

Functional skills

Planning and interpreting data gained from an audience will help you improve your **Mathematics** skills.

I have been working as a freelance writer for many years now and mostly produce work for the academic field. When a publisher decides that they want a specific product, they contact me with an outline of their requirements and schedule and ask if I can help.

If I agree, I then get a detailed brief with all the project requirements: how much I am expected to write, and an outline of the content and layout, so that I know what to cover and how my manuscript should look. It also specifies the number and kind of images, the design and text structure required, and what details or sketches I must provide for photographers, artists and others to produce illustrations and clear rights for any quotations or other copyright material.

I also receive information about the intended readership, such as the age range, so that I can use an appropriate style of language.

Most importantly, the brief gives the deadlines that I must adhere to. I usually have to deliver several drafts (usually first draft, second draft and final copy) so the publisher can give their feedback at each stage, ensure that the work is developing as they require, and is on schedule. Lots of other people are booked to design, edit, typeset, illustrate and print the work, so if I'm late with my writing, there can be considerable knock-on practical and cost implications for the publisher.

I also get contractual information with the brief, including details of royalties or fees, and when and how these will be paid.

If I feel a change needs to be made to the brief, for example, an extra photograph, I have to negotiate that with the client. Every part of the content costs money, and extra photographs can amount to a lot when you consider a large production, so all changes and additions must be justified.

The brief can be complicated, with lots of information in several different forms, and sometimes we need a briefing meeting to make sure we all have the same understanding of what is required and who is doing what. Keeping in touch is essential throughout the process to make sure things stay on track.

Think about it!

- How does the commissioning process start out?
- What sorts of details are given in the brief?
- What do you think are the most important considerations to keep in mind and why?
- Why are deadlines important?
- What sorts of things need to be negotiated with the client and why?
- What sort of justifications do you think there could be for changing the content or presentation of a piece of work?

Just checking

1. Name four ways that a client brief might be structured.
2. Define the following: legal, ethical and regulatory constraints.
3. Why is it important to keep referring back to the original brief?
4. What sort of things might need amending within a brief and why?
5. What sort of production paperwork might you be required to produce? Think of what would be relevant to the medium you are studying.
6. What is the point of the review process?
7. What sort of things do you think you may be able to learn from the review process?

edexcel

Assignment tips

- Plan your report carefully before producing it. Research relevant points and topics thoroughly and outline what you want to say and why it is relevant.

- Refer to the guidance in the student case study and Set up activity to help you to respond to the client brief so that you can pick out relevant information to help you to generate appropriate ideas.

- Make good use of production paperwork to ensure your project runs smoothly and stays within the required timescale.

- Conduct detailed and ongoing progress reviews, not just of yourself but of the entire team, and make sure that problems are dealt with and changes made accordingly.

- When reviewing your work, be sure to take a step back and be subjective about your own contributions, providing a critical analysis of the overall production as well as the processes.

6 Critical approaches to creative media products

The creative and media sector is perhaps one of the most changeable industries in modern society, being subject to the demands of new and emerging technologies and the changing patterns of consumption within a diverse and multicultural population.

The creative and media sector not only has to adapt to changing tastes and interests but is often responsible for instigating those changes in the first place. In order to make your products appeal to an audience, you need to understand that audience and how they will react to the products that are constructed for them. To do this it is important to look at and reflect upon the products made by other media professionals and think about them critically. Taking a 'critical' approach in this context means taking a considered view, evaluating key features and strengths as well as weaknesses, not just picking holes and making negative comments.

The relationship between media producers and the audience is dynamic; that is, both sides have an effect on the other, so it is important to explore how producers think about and target specific audiences, looking at how products are constructed, or 'encoded', by the producer and how they are deconstructed, or 'decoded', by the audience. You will need to learn to 'read' or analyse media products using current and appropriate analytical techniques.

Learning outcomes

After completing this unit you should:

1. understand how media producers define audiences for their products
2. understand how media producers create products for specific audiences
3. understand how media audiences respond to media products
4. be able to develop responses to media products.

Assessment and grading criteria

This table shows you what you must do in order to achieve a **pass**, **merit** or **distinction** grade, and where you can find activities in this book to help you.

To achieve a **pass** grade the evidence must show that you are able to:	To achieve a **merit** grade the evidence must show that, in addition to the pass criteria, you are able to:	To achieve a **distinction** grade the evidence must show that, in addition to the pass and merit criteria, you are able to:
P1 describe how media producers define audiences with some appropriate use of subject terminology **See Assessment activity 6.1, page 99**	**M1** explain how media producers define audiences with reference to detailed illustrative examples and with generally correct use of subject terminology **See Assessment activity 6.1, page 99**	**D1** comprehensively explain how media producers define audiences with elucidated examples and consistently using subject terminology correctly **See Assessment activity 6.1, page 99**
P2 describe how media producers create products for specific audiences with some appropriate use of subject terminology **See Assessment activity 6.2, page 102**	**M2** explain how media producers create products for specific audiences with reference to detailed illustrative examples and with generally correct use of subject terminology **See Assessment activity 6.2, page 102**	**D2** comprehensively explain how media producers create products for audiences with elucidated examples and consistently using subject terminology correctly **See Assessment activity 6.2, page 102**
P3 describe how media audiences respond to media products with some appropriate use of subject terminology **See Assessment activity 6.3, page 104**	**M3** explain how media audiences respond to media products with reference to detailed illustrative examples and with generally correct use of subject terminology **See Assessment activity 6.3, page 104**	**D3** comprehensively explain how media audiences respond to media products with elucidated examples and consistently using subject terminology correctly **See Assessment activity 6.3, page 104**
P4 present a descriptive response to a media product with some appropriate use of subject terminology **See Assessment activity 6.4, page 108**	**M4** present a discussion of a media product with reference to detailed illustrative examples and with generally correct use of subject terminology **See Assessment activity 6.4, page 108**	**D4** present an analysis of a media product with supporting arguments and elucidated examples, and consistently using subject terminology correctly **See Assessment activity 6.4, page 108**

How you will be assessed

Assessment for this unit could take the form of research projects, case studies or even field work in order to investigate the various topics being studied. You will need to produce project folders, reports and assignments or any other relevant documentation requested by the tutor for final assessment. It is likely that the topics studied for this unit will be integrated within other units chosen by your centre in order to contextualise them. Your tutor will probably track your progress in a series of separate assessment pieces that allow you to highlight your knowledge and understanding of the topics you are studying.

Your assessment could take any of the following forms:

- written report or case studies
- *viva voce* discussion with tutors
- field research.

Tim, creative media production student

I was quite surprised to find how much time and effort media producers put into the construction of their products. Of course I knew that a director didn't just get a camera person and some actors and shout 'shoot', I knew there was a process, but I just didn't realise how involved that process was.

Codes and conventions were the biggest eye opener for me. I hadn't realised that these had always existed in the TV programmes or films that I had watched and that I was aware of them without really being aware of them. I suppose after so many years of viewing you get used to the way things are, the accepted way of doing things and you just take that to be the 'norm', not realising that there are a set of rules and structures that are followed to make things fit their respective 'conventions'.

I found the work on critical approaches fascinating and I really do feel that it has helped me with my production work. I now take more time to think about who I am creating a product for and why. What do I want my audience to think, feel or walk away from my product with? I'm also sure that it has changed the way I will view media products forever! I am now much more analytical about the products I consume and aware of the techniques they're using on me, and how they're manipulating my reactions. I sometimes really annoy my family with the comments I make when we're watching telly! I can't help it, I just notice things more now!

Over to you!

- What are codes and conventions?
- Why do you think media products follow these codes and conventions?
- How does Tim think the Critical approaches unit has helped him?

1. Understand how media producers define audiences for their products

Set up

Audience research agencies

Media production is costly, sometimes extremely costly, and producers need to be sure that they will make back their investment, with interest.

Media companies fund audience research agencies which classify and profile audiences in order to help the industry stay in touch with changing tastes and ensure that they are targeting their products correctly.

Two such agencies are BARB (Broadcasters' Audience Research Board), which is involved in audience data for television broadcasters, and RAJAR (Radio Joint Audience Research Limited). As we have seen in earlier units, both of these agencies collect and collate audience data and monitor trends. They report what is most popular and what is losing popularity and pass on their findings to their respective industries; this way producers can decide to rethink their programming based on current audience demands.

Revisit the websites of BARB and RAJAR:

www.barb.co.uk

www.rajar.co.uk

- How does each agency describe itself and what it does? Write a brief outline of each.
- Who does each agency work for and how are they funded?
- What reasons do they give for collecting audience figures?
- How relevant do you think their work is to media producers?
- Do you think they are also beneficial to the consumer?

Consumers covered by BARB.

Consumers covered by RAJAR.

1.1 Defining audiences

Media producers spend a lot of time and effort on defining the audience for their product. They want their product to be successful and profitable and therefore they need to ensure that they are targeting their product to the right audience and that the audience will respond in the desired way to it. There are many considerations to take into account when profiling an audience and research is essential to this process. Both quantitative and qualitative research methods are used in order to gain a full understanding of the audience.

Quantitative audience research

As highlighted in Unit 3, quantitative research involves collecting facts and information that can be counted, producing numerical and statistical data. This section will put quantitative research methods into context for you and help you to realise how important this kind of data is to media producers.

BARB and RAJAR are two of the leading agencies from whom media producers can obtain this sort of information. The data will inform programming schedules and affects the types of products that producers decide to make.

These agencies use different methodologies in order to collect their data. However, they do ensure as wide a coverage as possible and look at the tastes of all sections of the viewing and listening audience from a range of different ages and backgrounds. This gives broadcasters as wide and diverse a view as possible and helps them gain a better understanding of their target audience.

Qualitative audience research

Qualitative audience research was also covered in Unit 3. This type of research is based on opinions, attitudes and preferences rather than hard facts and figures. It is important to look at the different ways in which media producers carry out such research.

Focus groups are extremely popular as they allow the producer to gain direct feedback from a small, distinctly targeted group of individuals.

Questionnaires also allow for specific targeting of certain sectors of the audience and means that very precise and targeted questions can be asked.

Face-to-face interviews, while time consuming, are also beneficial as they allow for the interviewer to gauge the response and reaction of the interviewee to the questions being asked.

Audience profiling

Audience profiling is where media producers make assumptions about an audience and their likely consumption or preferences, based on many social and economic factors that contribute to their tastes, their understanding of the world around them and their possible leisure activities. The following are a range of factors that can contribute to these profiles.

Socio-economic status

This relates to somebody's class, for example, upper, middle or working class, which is also related to how much they earn. As a general rule the more you earn, the higher up the scale you are. However, there are exceptions to every rule and there are some rather poor 'upper class' people and some very wealthy people who will always consider themselves 'working class'.

Table 3.3 in Unit 3 shows the broadly recognised socio-economic classifications that advertisers use.

Psychographics

This is more of a psychological profile of a consumer based on how they see themselves in relation to everybody else. Wealth often has some bearing on this. Some examples of psychographic groupings are:

- succeeders
- aspirers
- carers
- main-streamers
- individualists.

Geodemographics/Regional identity

As the name suggests, this is to do with the way that people identify themselves in relation to nationality or geography, such as northern/southern, Scottish not British, Londoner or Cockney.

Age

The age group that people associate themselves with could be defined on questionnaires as an age range, such as 15–25, or as a descriptive grouping, such as teenager, young adult, middle aged, senior citizen.

Gender

Although gender-related audience preferences are not always clear-cut, male and female viewers are generally assumed to have different interests, such as sport and action movies for men and fashion and romantic comedies for women.

Sexual orientation

The sexuality of a group of people, whether heterosexual or homosexual, can be related to consumer preferences. In recent years there has been much talk about the strength of the 'pink pound' as more companies market their products to suit specific tastes of the gay community.

Race or ethnicity

Race and ethnicity can be defined in many different ways and are not always directly related to skin colour. People may prefer to define themselves in relation to geographic factors, for example, Mediterranean, Australian, African, American, Jamaican and Bangladeshi, as well as religious identities, for example, Jewish.

Mainstream

The mainstream is the generally accepted norm or the way things usually are. It reflects the current conventional way of thinking and the tastes and ideas of the majority.

Alternative

The alternative is anything 'other' than the mainstream; an alternative to it. There is no ultimate definition of what is alternative as it can be anything that deviates away from mainstream ideals.

Niche

'Niche' literally means a small crevice in a rock or recess in a wall, and it implies the idea of a special place where something small and valuable can be put. In everyday speech it refers to a small and often exclusive market. A media producer might choose to target a niche market because although they will sell lower quantities, an exclusive product can command high prices, producing a higher profit from what they do sell. Exclusive niche products are often targeted at the rich and famous.

Activity: Profile your class!

The members of your class are likely to include a range of people of different genders, cultures and tastes. Although it is likely that you will all share a broadly common age range it is also likely that you will have very different likes and dislikes.

Over the years, teen culture has been defined in many ways, according to age, musical tastes and dress preferences, and sometimes even race or gender, for example, Teddy Boys, Rockers, Mods and punks.

More common youth culture groups today might include Emo, Indie, Ravers, Gangsta and so on. Again, many of these classifications can be related to musical tastes but can also be related to the type of clothes people wear, their hairstyles and even a tendency towards body piercing.

- As a group, have a go at profiling several volunteers from your class by looking at their mannerisms, the way they dress and how they 'style' themselves. In the first instance you will be relying on a form of stereotyping and making assumptions about these people and their consumption habits.

- Once you have outlined your profiles, ask the volunteers some questions to see if you can get a more detailed picture of them and their interests and tastes.

- Try to link your questions to some of the profiling factors outlined above and see if you can find things that link as well as separate people.

- What have you found to be the most unifying factor between the people you profiled (for example, age, race, gender)?

- When did your profiles start to narrow down and become more defined?

- What did you find difficult about this activity?

Assessment activity 6.1

P1 M1 D1   :BTEC

You have applied for a job as a researcher with a local media company and they want to see how well you understand the importance of defining audiences in the media industry.

They have asked you to produce a report that looks at how audiences are defined by media producers and shows that you understand audience research and classification.

This Assessment activity relates to the following grading criteria.

- Describe how media producers define audiences with some appropriate use of subject terminology. **P1**

- Explain how media producers define audiences with reference to detailed illustrative examples and with generally correct use of subject terminology. **M1**

- Comprehensively explain how media producers define audiences with elucidated examples and consistently using subject terminology correctly. **D1**

Grading tips

When addressing these learning outcomes, you will be required to show your understanding of how media producers define audiences for their products within the creative and media industries.

For a merit grade, you will need to produce a report that clearly explains different ways in which media producers can define audiences. You will use suitable examples that illustrate your points and will use the correct subject terminology for the techniques that you describe. This will show that you understand these terms.

For a distinction grade, you will need to produce a full and comprehensive report on how media producers define audiences. This means that you will cover all the important techniques in some detail, in a well-organised report. You will use extremely well planned and targeted examples to explain the importance and relevance to media producers of the techniques that you describe. You will use the appropriate subject terminology confidently and accurately throughout your report.

PLTS

Organising time and resources and prioritising actions when researching for a written report will help develop your skills as a **self-manager**.

Functional skills

Writing reports and applying research methods will help you improve your **ICT** skills.

2. Understand how media producers create products for specific audiences

2.1 Addressing audiences

Media producers construct their products to appeal to a specific audience. They have done their research, they know their market and they have a defined audience in mind from the beginning. Media producers construct their products in different ways; here are some of the elements they keep in mind.

Selection of content

What is going to go into the product to make it effective and appeal to the target audience? Most products will probably have words in some form or other and these can be targeted to relate to certain age groups, genders and so on. Similarly images can be used to appeal to people with particular tastes. All products contain words, images or a mixture of both and these are carefully selected to widen or narrow the appeal of a product.

The use of sound in some products is extremely important. Sound can often be used to set a scene, reflect a mood or even provide a link to another scene. There is such a vast range of musical tastes in society that it is hard to find something to appeal to everybody, but the flip side of this is that it can be used to great effect to catch the attention of a specific target audience.

Print products often feature a range of colours and fonts. This too is done in order to appeal to a specific audience. It is known that different age groups and genders respond differently to different colours and styles of text.

Construction of content

The content of a product is based on its narrative structure, which is the story being told or the point being made. This has a huge effect on the content as it has to convey what you are trying to represent. If you choose arbitrary content that does not fully relate to the narrative, you are likely to confuse and lose your audience.

In print products, narrative and content are closely related to layout. This is defined by carefully selecting and placing the written content and making it visually appealing to the reader using different fonts, colours and pictures.

The construction of content, or how a media product is put together, is often related to accepted 'codes and conventions'. These are common elements that are used to help us to feel familiar with a product and find it easy to consume. There are many types of codes such as linguistic, visual, audio, symbolic and technical.

Activity: Identifying codes and conventions

If you switch on an unfamiliar television programme, how quickly can you tell what sort of programme it is? For example, how would you recognise that a programme is a situation comedy (sitcom)?

The list below shows the main elements or codes and conventions of a sitcom genre. You can see that there are many easily identifiable elements that you are probably familiar with, although you may not have realised it.

Sitcom codes and conventions:

- limited number of characters
- exaggerated characteristics of characters; 'types'
- limited sets
- catchy theme tune (often introducing all the characters)
- canned laughter
- use of catchphrases
- linear narrative that uses equilibrium, disruption (from which the comedy derives) and then returns to equilibrium
- set around a small social group, for example, family, friends, work.

Now have a go at identifying the codes and conventions of the following genres:

- television soap opera
- tabloid newspaper front page
- horror movie.

Remember, every product from television and film to radio and print operates within a range of identifiable conventions, although what these are may change over time.

2.2 Audience feedback

Audience feedback is essential to media producers as it allows them to assess and understand the ways in which the audience will respond or have responded to their product. Some examples of sources of feedback are outlined below.

Focus groups – as mentioned in Unit 3, focus groups are useful to gain feedback on a product from a specific and highly targeted segment of your chosen target audience.

Audience panels – audience panels are made up of members of the public who are invited to comment on existing products, providing their views and opinions on all areas. Their feedback is then sifted and collated for relevance.

Trialing and testing – this involves making a one-off 'tester' of a product and then putting it on the market for the public to view, read, listen to or try out. The reaction to the product is then gauged by the producer. If it is positive, the product will continue to be made. If it is negative, it will be dropped in favour of something else.

Reviews – these are often written by professional reviewers but can also be found on a number of personal blogs and websites. These allow producers to gauge reactions to a particular product and may provide an insight into the popularity of a particular genre, for example.

Complaints – complaints are perhaps the worst kind of feedback, since they may indicate that you are doing things wrong or have upset someone's sensibilities. Complaints should be taken seriously and addressed carefully, not just dismissed out of hand. If many complaints are received, then products may need to be drastically reviewed or might even be pulled altogether. In certain circumstances, complaints may require an apology or other form of redress from the producer, or may even be referred to a regulating body for resolution.

Case study: Testing

Test screenings are used by television and film producers in order to gauge the audience's response to the overall production. The product itself may have been through a rough but probably not a final edit and can be subject to change depending on the response of the audience. Often film or television producers will have already filmed alternative scenes or endings ready for such an eventuality; it would be very costly to re-open a production once all the filming had taken place and the actors had moved on to different projects. Some films that have famously been changed as a result of test screenings are *Bladerunner* (1982), *Titanic* (1997) and *Mary Poppins* (1964).

In the games industry, testers who fit the profile of the target audience are employed to play games that have been newly designed and are due for market release. These testers provide the company with precise and detailed feedback on the game play experience. This feedback can inform possible changes to the final product.

1. Find out more about how other kinds of media products are tested or piloted commercially (for example, magazines, advertisements, television and radio programmes).

2. How could you test your own productions? How could you build in time and resource to respond to the feedback?

Assessment activity 6.2

Produce case studies of two different products, showing your understanding of how these products were constructed with the audience in mind. The products you choose can be from any medium or genre, produced by small or large companies; the choice is yours.

Use your knowledge of audience profiling to identify the target markets for each product. Identify specific elements of each product that would appeal to their target audience.

Grading tips

When addressing these learning outcomes, you will be required to show an understanding of how media producers create products for specific audiences.

For a merit grade, you will need to explain how the media producers who created each of your chosen products appealed to a specified audience which you are able to identify. You will need to use detailed examples to illustrate your points, with generally correct use of subject terminology.

For a distinction grade, you will need to produce case studies that comprehensively explain how the media producers have created each of your chosen products to appeal to a specified audience which you are able to identify. This means you will cover all the important relevant aspects. You will use highly targeted and detailed examples to illustrate your points clearly and effectively, and consistently use subject terminology correctly.

PLTS

Analysing and evaluating information, and judging its relevance and value when analysing media products for research, will help develop your skills as an **independent enquirer**.

Functional skills

Researching information for assignment reports improves your **English** skills.

3. Understand how media audiences respond to media products

Audiences react to – or read – media texts in many different ways and some of the reasons for this have already been outlined in Section 1. Audience response is a significant academic field of study and many theories and discussions revolve around this topic.

3.1 Audience theory

'Audience theory' is often used in media production and is related to a number of academic theories about how products are consumed by the audience and how active or interactive that consumption is. Some of these theories can be difficult to interpret at times as they require a sound and detailed understanding of audiences and the creative and media sector as a whole. Some of the better-known and regularly used theories are briefly outlined here.

Hypodermic needle model – this theory is based on the idea that the audience are **passive consumers**. This means that they consume media products without question, accepting the dominant ideology. The producer encodes a product with an intended message and that message is then directly received and fully accepted by the consumer.

Uses and gratifications theory – this theory gives the audience a little more power and sees them more as **active consumers**. Here, people are not helpless consumers of mass media; rather, they are able to use the media to gain certain gratifications, such as laughter, interaction, information and so on. In other words, the audience questions and analyses media texts rather than just consuming them.

Reception study – in this theory, the audience is again seen as *active*. The theory suggests that every media text has a meaning which is not obvious or transparent but hidden within the text itself. In order to understand the meaning of a text, an audience must actively extract that meaning from it. How they interpret this meaning will be affected by their individual cultural background and life experiences.

Key terms

Passive consumers – the audience accept what the text contains.

Active consumers – the audience is able to read and interpret media texts for themselves.

3.2 Effects debates

The effects that media products have on an audience have also been the subject of much debate. In particular, the need to protect and safeguard the more vulnerable members of society, such as children, is often a matter of heated discussion. Some of the debates are outlined here.

Effects of exposure to explicit sexual or violent content – there is an argument that the audience, especially children, should be protected from exposure to violent and explicit materials because they can be unduly influenced by them. This argument presupposes that the audience is passive and not able to discern between right and wrong, and that they will therefore react to the text and possibly act out its content.

Effects of advertising – this debate focuses on advertising as a very powerful media tool which aims to persuade us to purchase certain products and services by claiming that we need the products or that the products will make our lives better. Again this approach assumes that the audience is passive and will be pressurised to purchase products and services

by the advertisers. This is accepted with regard to children, and advertising aimed at them is tightly regulated.

Censorship debates – censorship debates centre on the idea of passive and active consumption of media texts and our ability to decode the content of these texts and make rational decisions for ourselves. Some people believe that audiences should be protected from certain things and that the best way to do this is to censor it in the first place, thus taking away the choice from the consumer.

Activity: Effects

- Which of these arguments do you find the most convincing?
- What do you think about the concept of passive and active audiences?
- How often do you actively read media texts?
- What are the negative and positive sides to censorship?
- What alternatives are there to censoring media content?
- Are there any existing alternatives within the creative and media sector?

3.3 Responses

The way in which we respond to a text is linked to the way in which we 'read' it. Some of the different theories about how audiences read texts have already been outlined; here are some others.

Oppositional reading – this means that the audience disagrees with the message within the text and actively decides to reject it. This can be a considered process by which the reader has taken on board all of the information and decided to reject the message as a result, or it could be an emotional reaction based on previously or strongly held beliefs and lived experiences.

Negotiated reading – on the whole, negotiated readings are more considered. For the most part the view or message is agreed with by the audience. However, it may be slightly altered, again depending on the way in which that information is filtered by the reader, based on their own personal experiences and opinions.

Dominant reading – in a dominant reading, the message is fully accepted by the audience as they find the ideas or dominant ideology consistent with their own.

Other types of responses include the following.

Participatory – this theory suggests that in this modern age we are more likely to be directly involved in the creation of media texts rather than just consuming them. For example, we are able to become involved in the media we consume by appearing on reality television programmes, voting on outcomes, participating in interactive media online or creating our own websites and blogs.

Cultural competence – according to this theory, because we can communicate with people globally through modern technology such as the Internet, we are becoming more 'culturally competent'. This means that we are better able to access, understand, interact and communicate with other cultures.

Fan culture – this is a new and emerging theory that fans are actively having an influence on – and input into – media production in modern society; fans are now seen as a valuable commodity to media producers.

Remember

When referring to these theories, remember that:

- a 'text' can be any media product that contains a narrative or meaning
- 'reading' means the way in which we assimilate or interpret any kind of text.

Assessment activity 6.3

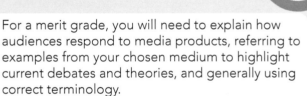

Look at some of the computer games currently available on the market and at what they contain. Many different genres for different age groups are easily accessed in the shops or online. Find a game that is targeted at a 16+ audience. Analyse the content in terms of how it could be interpreted by the consumer, especially if that consumer was younger than the intended target audience. Apply the 'effects' debates outlined above where relevant.

Grading tips

When addressing this learning outcome, you will be required to show an understanding of how media audiences respond to media products.

For a merit grade, you will need to explain how audiences respond to media products, referring to examples from your chosen medium to highlight current debates and theories, and generally using correct terminology.

For a distinction grade, you will need to clearly and comprehensively explain audience responses. This means you will explain all of the essential points clearly. You will apply the appropriate media theories to a range of well-chosen and targeted examples, and use correct terminology throughout.

PLTS

Organising time and resources and prioritising actions when researching for a written report on media products will help you become a **self-manager**.

Functional skills

Researching information for assignment reports improves your **English** skills.

4. Be able to develop responses to media products

4.1 Critical approaches

In this section you will need to apply your knowledge of critical approaches to the analysis of a media product or text. This is known as a content or textual analysis. You will be required to search out, identify and show your understanding of the ideas outlined in this section, applying critical approaches to your content analysis and looking at some of the key elements of construction that can be broken down.

4.2 Genre

'**Genre**' is a French word which literally means 'kind', 'sort' or 'type'. In media, genre often refers to categories such as comedy, horror, documentary, fantasy, sci-fi and so on. All media products, or 'texts', will fit into a specific genre according to different factors such as the following.

Production technology – products can be made using different technologies for different mediums, for example, film, video, audio, print, digital.

Distribution method – media can be distributed in many different ways such as television, cinema, radio, Internet, CD, iPod, mobile phone, home computer and hand-held console. A film may have been made with a certain technology, but it can be distributed on DVD and the Internet as well as at the cinema.

Generic codes and conventions – these are the accepted or standard ways of producing products within a certain genre, as outlined in Section 2. Codes and conventions are concerned with things such as content and style, symbolic and cultural codes, what certain things mean to different people from different backgrounds and technical codes such as the use of lighting and camera angles.

Changes over time – as time goes by, audiences change. For example, there could be ideological shifts as a result of cultural and economic change which will result in a change in what is acceptable or thought of as interesting, relevant or funny.

There are also other factors that can affect the classification of genre of a product or text. For instance, a **parody**, or **spoof**, of an existing product or genre is a form of imitation which is often done in a comic or satirical way, poking fun at the original. Examples are *Meet the Spartans* (2008), which was a

spoof of the film *300* (2006), and *Scary Movie* (2000), a spoof of such horror films as *Scream* (1996).

Another example is **pastiche**. This is a copy of a genre, usually done respectfully, but sometimes seen as an inferior way of exploiting other people's good ideas without giving full credit to the source. In cinematography pastiche is where a film maker uses the same style, lighting and camera angles as another film maker that they admire, as a homage to their work.

> ### Key terms
> **Genre** – literally means a 'kind', 'sort' or 'type'.
> **Parody/spoof** – a send-up that pokes fun at a genre.
> **Pastiche** – a copy of a genre.

4.3 Narrative structures

The 'narrative' is the storyline of a media text. The 'storyline' in this context does not necessarily mean a fictional story; it can equally mean the unfolding argument or presentation of information in a non-fiction text. There are many different ways of telling a story, some conventional and others more unconventional.

A **single strand narrative** is when one story is told from start to finish. There is usually a particular point, moral or otherwise, that the producer is trying to make or get the audience to engage with.

Most single strand fiction narratives follow a set format of equilibrium > disruption > equilibrium. This means that the story opens with everything as it should be, then something happens to cause disruption to the norm and this is the point from which the 'action' will start; then the narrative will end with equilibrium restored, either back the way things were originally, or of a new kind.

In contrast to this there are also **multi-strand narratives** that tell two or more stories alongside each other. These stories can often cross over each other or offer an alternative 'reality'. A good example of this is the format of many television advertisements, which mix a fictional narrative acted as a short drama with a product information narrative, often presented as a voiceover to differentiate it from the fictional line.

Activity: Multi-strand narratives

Can you think of other examples of multi-strand narratives in a range of media products? Think about film, television, radio, print-based materials, games and interactive media. Try to find examples of both fiction and non-fiction genres.

Narratives usually have a beginning, a middle and an ending. A **closed narrative** means that the story starts in a certain place (see linear narrative, below) and will be resolved at the end, giving the impression that there is nothing more to add; things are as they should be and that is that. This narrative form is commonly used in film making.

An **open narrative** does not really have a clear beginning or end. For example, a soap opera is a continuous narrative based on the lives of the characters within it, and the viewer drops in and out of their lives. Often cliff-hangers are used as a means of encouraging viewers to engage with the programme again and again, but there is rarely a complete resolution or climax to a storyline.

Finally, narratives can be referred to as **linear** or **non-linear**. These descriptions are closely linked to the structures. Figure 6.1 below shows how these narrative structures work.

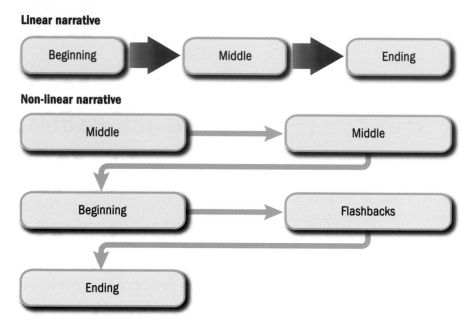

Figure 6.1: Can you think of examples of texts in any media format with linear and non-linear narratives?

Examples of narrative types

Semiotic analysis is a means of analysing texts through signs or signification and decoding their meaning. Often semiotic readings are based on the cultural capital of the individual.

An **enigma** (or puzzle) is a device often used in narratives. The producer of the text creates a 'riddle' that needs to be decoded and interpreted by the reader.

4.4 Representation

'Representation' relates to the way in which people or characters are represented in a text. Some representations can be negative, depicting individuals, social groups or even social issues in a bad light. They can also be positive, showing things in such a way as to make the audience feel inclined towards them. How these representations are used will depend on the viewpoint of the person producing the text and what they want the audience to believe.

Stereotyping is an effective means of representing characters as it is linked to the way a society tends to see groups or individuals and allows us to categorise people according to their tastes, consumption, age, gender, way of dressing and so on, as previously outlined. We associate certain character traits with particular stereotypes; we make assumptions about them and the way they may act. When they are placed in media texts, stereotypes are easy for us to recognise and comprehend.

Activity: Identifying stereotypes

Stereotypes differ from culture to culture. They are easy to identify from the way they look or their character traits, which media producers often exaggerate, especially in comedies, to make the character funny to the audience and easier to relate to.

Below are pictures of four different stereotypes that we can recognise in our society. See if you can identify each one and make a note of the character traits that they would conventionally have, to fit your chosen stereotype.

- Can you think of any more common stereotypical character types?

- Why are they important to media producers?

- Do you think stereotypes are positive or negative?

- Can you think of any other ways in which we categorise each other?

Assessment activity 6.4

Pick a product from a medium of your choice and conduct a content analysis on it. You will need to identify the genre and codes and conventions, then look in detail at the content, discussing all of the elements of construction such as narrative structure, **mise-en-scène**, representation and so on. The literal translation from French of mise-en-scène is 'putting on stage' – it means creating a setting for a scene in a production on stage or screen by the placement of props, sets, actors, lighting and so on.

Grading tips

When addressing this learning outcome, you will be required to develop responses to media products.

For a merit grade, you will need to review a media product by discussing the content in detail and using examples from the text to illustrate your

points. You will need to deconstruct rather than describe the text. This means you need to break it down into its different parts and explain which elements contribute to the product. You will need to use the correct subject terminology fairly accurately.

For a distinction grade, you will need to analyse a media product by critically discussing the content, using highly relevant examples from the text to support and clarify your points. You will need to present a consistent and accurate deconstruction of the text, which means that you will take the text apart to identify the different components of its structure, and will explain and discuss these accurately, showing a good understanding of the theoretical approaches you use. You will need to use the correct subject terminology confidently and accurately throughout.

PLTS

Analysing and evaluating information, and judging its relevance and value when analysing media products, will help develop your skills as an **independent enquirer**.

Functional skills

Exploring, extracting and assessing the relevance of information websites improve your **ICT** skills.

Key term

Mise-en-scène – the literal translation from French is 'putting on stage'; it means creating a setting for a scene in a production on stage or screen.

Kieran Clark
Researcher

When the company I work for decides to make a new product, it is important to conduct research into audience tastes and consumption in order to understand how well that product will be received.

If we were making a new reality TV show, for example, we would need to know how popular these types of shows are with current audiences to see whether they are still interested or are suffering from reality fatigue! Television programmes cost a lot of money to make – there is the studio, cast, crew and equipment to be paid for – so producers need to be sure that they are not spending money out that they will never get back.

One of the places I would go to in order to find out audience viewing figures is BARB. We receive regular updates on audience viewing trends and use them to work out what types of programmes are most popular. We can also see if there is a gap in the market for a specific genre of programme that is not currently being produced.

Various kinds of send-ups, particularly of the documentary format, have been popular in recent years but it gets to a point where even the spoof itself becomes so familiar that it just enters the mainstream and doesn't feel so edgy and exciting any more. So then the hunt is on for new ideas that the audience will find fresh and exciting again. Producers are constantly looking for new ways to surprise the audience, whether by finding a new way to play with familiar conventions, or something that breaks with the norms completely.

Think about it!

- At what stage of production does audience research begin?
- Where does Kieran say he gathers information from?
- How does this information help with decisions?
- How can an understanding of the existing conventions of a medium contribute to the development of new ideas?

Just checking

1. How do media producers define audiences?
2. Why do they do it?
3. Name some of the ways media producers select and construct content for their products.
4. How can media producers gain audience feedback?
5. How and why is audience feedback so important?
6. Outline three major media theories that have been discussed in this unit.
7. Which of these theories make the most sense to you?
8. What can you gain by undertaking a content analysis of a product?

edexcel :::

Assignment tips

- When writing reports, always conduct detailed and thorough research beforehand and produce annotated notes to work from.

- Building an argument or discussions can sometimes be rather complicated. It is always best to decide what your standpoint or opinion is going to be first and then sketch out a plan of how to make your main arguments.

- Media theories can often be hard to understand. To help break them down, look for different interpretations of these theories until you find one you can engage with. Extract from each one the key points of information that will help you produce your report. Do not forget to acknowledge and reference any sources that you use or quote from.

- When conducting textual analysis you should always make notes of relevant factors in a media product. You should review your media product more than once to ensure you have a more detailed understanding for your reading of the 'text'.

7 Understanding the creative media sector

The media industries are one of the largest growth business areas both in the UK and throughout the world as new technologies are constantly created and used by a mass audience. Job roles within the creative media sector are wide ranging and diverse and offer opportunities to use a number of personal, technical and creative skills. This unit will offer an insight into the different creative media industries, and you will learn how the creative media sector is structured and funded and how ownership and control of these industries can affect production output.

However, the creative media sector is subject to ongoing, and often substantial, regulation that affects the products and working practices of all those involved in production. Legal and ethical issues are a consideration for all media companies and although there have been moves towards deregulation in recent years there will always be a need for media producers to consider the appropriateness of the content of their products.

You will gain an insight into – and understanding of – employment opportunities and job roles in a creative media industry relevant to your studies. You will be able to start thinking about how you can become skilled and multi-skilled through investigating and engaging in opportunities for training and professional development. You will also have the opportunity to begin creating your own professional career development materials in a range of formats used within the creative media sector.

Learning outcomes

After completing this unit you should:

1. understand the structure and ownership of the media sector
2. understand ethical and legal constraints within the media sector
3. understand the regulation of the media sector
4. know about employment opportunities and job roles in the media sector
5. be able to prepare personal career development material.

Assessment and grading criteria

This table shows you what you must do in order to achieve a **pass**, **merit** or **distinction** grade, and where you can find activities in this book to help you.

To achieve a **pass** grade the evidence must show that you are able to:	To achieve a **merit** grade the evidence must show that, in addition to the pass criteria, you are able to:	To achieve a **distinction** grade the evidence must show that, in addition to the pass and merit criteria, you are able to:
P1 describe the structure and ownership of the media sector **See Assessment activity 7.1, page 119**	**M1** explain the structure and ownership of the media sector with reference to detailed illustrative examples **See Assessment activity 7.1, page 119**	**D1** comprehensively explain the structure and ownership of the media sector with reference to elucidated examples **See Assessment activity 7.1, page 119**
P2 describe ethical and legal constraints within the media sector **See Assessment activity 7.2, page 122**	**M2** explain ethical and legal constraints within the media sector with reference to detailed illustrative examples **See Assessment activity 7.2, page 122**	**D2** comprehensively explain ethical and legal constraints within the media sector with reference to elucidated examples **See Assessment activity 7.2, page 122**
P3 describe the regulation of the media sector **See Assessment activity 7.3, page 126**	**M3** explain the regulatory issues affecting the media sector with reference to detailed illustrative examples **See Assessment activity 7.3, page 126**	**D3** comprehensively explain the regulatory issues affecting the media sector with reference to elucidated examples **See Assessment activity 7.3, page 126**
P4 describe employment opportunities and job roles in the media sector **See Assessment activity 7.4, page 129**	**M4** explain employment opportunities and job roles in the media sector with reference to detailed illustrative examples **See Assessment activity 7.4, page 129**	**D4** comprehensively explain employment opportunities and job roles in the media sector with reference to elucidated examples **See Assessment activity 7.4, page 129**
P5 prepare personal career development material using basic formal language **See Assessment activity 7.5, page 132**	**M5** prepare carefully produced personal career development material using generally correct formal language **See Assessment activity 7.5, page 132**	**D5** prepare personal career development material to a quality that reflects near-professional standards, consistently using correct formal language **See Assessment activity 7.5, page 132**

How you will be assessed

Assessment for this unit can take a variety of forms, from portfolios and diaries to written reports. You will need to place your studies into some context and your tutor may find it necessary to link your studies to your practical production work. All necessary documentation will need to be submitted for final assessment which may well include a final product in the form of a CD, showreel or portfolio. Your tutor may choose to track your progress in a single integrated assignment, rather than by separate assessments.

Your assessments could be in the form of:

- presentations
- case studies
- written assignments
- portfolios
- diaries
- practical productions.

Bethany, creative media production student

After finishing my GCSEs at school I decided that I wanted to work in the creative media sector and began looking for work, any work that could get me in the front door. It turned out that this was not as straightforward as it seemed and even though I was prepared to work for free, I lacked a lot of the skills and knowledge I needed to get a job in my chosen field.

I decided that I should think about doing more training and chose the National Diploma course at my local college. I needed skills and knowledge and I needed to find out more about the industry I wanted to work in. At least that way when I went to interviews I had something to offer and knew what I was talking about.

I'm not saying that I would never have got a job without doing this course, but I do think it would have been a much longer and more difficult process, especially working my way up to a job that I was really happy in and was something I really wanted to do. Not only that, but the college had links to local creative media businesses and I was able to get some work experience which helped me decide whether or not I was making the right career choice.

I work part-time volunteering at the hospital radio station now; I help run the station and get involved with production and scheduling. I am learning new skills all the time and I am building up a pretty impressive CV which should help me get paid work when I have finished my studies.

Over to you!

- Why did Bethany find it hard to get work straight out of school?
- What do you think Bethany gained from this course?
- How will Bethany's updated CV help her gain work in the future?

1. Understand the structure and ownership of the media sector

The creative media sector in the UK

The UK's creative content industries have for many years punched above their weight globally. One third of television format sales around the world originate with British production companies. The creative centres of many global CGI, advertising, games, publishing, design or other creative knowledge-economy businesses are based in the UK. The transition to digital is, however, overturning old business models much faster than new ones come into their place. Look at the Digital Britain Report 2009, which you can find at www.culture.gov.uk/what_we_do/broadcasting/6216.aspx

- What is the purpose of this report?
- What does it tell you about the growth of digital communications within the creative media sector in the UK?
- Who is responsible for compiling this report and why?

The creative media industries in the UK are among the strongest in the world. The sector has grown rapidly in recent years to the point where it employs more people than any other industry in the UK. Estimates from the publishing industry are around 200,000, while the Digital Britain report states that over 300,000 people work in creative media and that the sector is still growing. Developments over the last 25 years have taken place across the sector as a result of digital technology and one of the features of the sector is that change continues to happen. Successful companies in the UK have produced media products with great content: ideas for characters, storylines, formats for new programmes or performing talent. At the same time, this sector has been very effective in the way it has developed ways of using digital technology. However, this is a very competitive world: being successful one year does not guarantee success next year!

1.1 Sector

The creative media sector includes a wide range of industries, each employing large numbers of people in a variety of creative and technical roles (and sometimes with roles overlapping and individuals working in more than one industry):

- film (27,800)
- television (55,800)
- publishing (200,000)
- interactive media (40,000)
- games (10,000)
- radio (22,000)
- photo-imaging (44,000)
- advertising (17,000)
- animation (4,700).

What do these industries have in common? They use words, sounds and images to communicate with mass audiences, and require the creativity of people with ideas for content which will appeal to audiences, as well as the technical skills of staff who can operate the equipment to make the media products. Like other industry sectors, the creative media industries also employ people who can organise, manage and run the companies which create the productions. Not all jobs are focused on the use of digital technology.

The sector is made up of companies of all sizes. Many tiny companies with two or three staff work successfully in media production alongside global companies and giant organisations such as the BBC. At the same time many of the jobs in the sector are carried out by freelance self-employed people.

Working in the sector can require an understanding of the range of different companies and their varying skills needs. Smaller companies need staff with creative, technical and professional skills. For example, in a small web development company, some of the staff will be involved in marketing, and someone in the company will need to manage the production, organising schedules and overseeing budgets. Another role will be meeting clients which will involve interpersonal skills and the ability to negotiate. These roles run alongside the creative and technical skills needed for the production itself and often all the roles are carried out by a small team of staff. In bigger companies these tasks would be carried out by different specialists.

Most staff in media production companies spend a significant amount of time in an office environment.

1.2 Structure and ownership

There are at least three different models of production, according to the size, set-up and funding of the production organisation, as outlined below.

Small company productions

Many creative media companies earn money by producing work for clients. Typically a client would be another company which requires a website, printed material or a DVD, for example. This accounts for a huge amount of employment in the sector.

For a web project produced by a small company, the sequence of events might go like this:

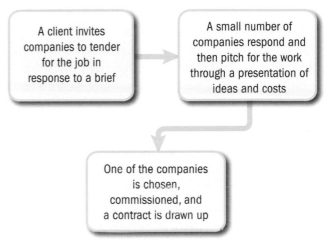

Figure 7.1: Usually a client 'hires' a production company after going through the commissioning process.

Once the supplier has been chosen and commissioned, the following stages take place:

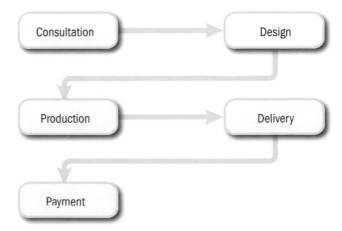

Figure 7.2: These are the main stages in a small company production.

As part of your course, you will work on assignments for which you will take the role of the production company/producer responding to a brief. These are likely to be either similar to industry briefs or 'live' briefs with a real client and an audience for your work.

Broadcast television and radio productions

Broadcast television and radio have different models of funding. The BBC receives its income from the licence fee while commercial broadcasters are funded by advertising. While the production sequence of events is similar to that outlined above for small company productions, the BBC commissioning process is constrained by certain organisational requirements. These ensure appropriate use of the licence fee to fulfil its public service broadcast obligations, while commercial broadcasters have an imperative to satisfy the advertisers who fund their output by paying for advertising slots on their networks. Advertisers want to reach the largest possible audiences, which naturally has an effect on the programming.

Major creative productions

In industries such as film, games and sound recording, the usual production model involves at least one large company putting up funding. For example, a Hollywood studio or a global music company would put money into a film or recording of a new album. Projects on this scale often involve multi-million pound budgets and some long-term planning.

All three models have certain factors in common. A typical project, large or small, would involve concept, development, design, project management, sound and/or images. Ideas which will appeal to the audience or client are at the centre of all productions. All projects will follow similar methods to develop these ideas and produce a final product, and all will need careful management of the production to ensure it keeps to budget and schedule.

Activity: Where does the money come from?

1. Choose two creative media industries and identify which of the following methods of income generation apply to each.
   - retail sales
   - downloads
   - advertisers
   - sponsorship
   - BBC licence fee
   - commissions from clients
   - cinema box office
   - CD and DVD sales
   - DVD rental
   - television subscriptions
   - merchandise
   - licensing: images of characters in films, use of 'intellectual property'.

2. Choose a media product made by a UK company. Find out the name of the company who made it and discover:
   - what else they have made
   - how many people they employ (full-time and freelance)
   - where they are based
   - where their income is derived from.

Case study: Realtime Worlds

Founded in 2002, Realtime Worlds is Scotland's largest independent video games developer. Its main development base is in Dundee where it employs 200 people. The home office is in Colorado, USA.

The company describes itself as a 'software technology company specialising in the entertainment sector'. They have created some of the world's best-selling video games, including *Crackdown*, and the franchises *Lemmings* and *Grand Theft Auto* (estimated 70 million unit sales worldwide). Realtime Worlds is a major competitor in the area of new and emerging digital media production and offers opportunities for creative and innovative games design and IT specialists to work in this sector.

1. Go to the Realtime Worlds website **www.realtimeworlds.com** and investigate the structure and ownership of the company.

2. Outline the products and services provided by the company.

3. What employment opportunities do the company offer and where?

Indies and the Internet

The Internet offers ways for film makers, musicians and radio producers to reach audiences which don't involve the major companies. Small independent companies or new bands, for example, no longer have to wait until they have the backing of a conglomerate or major broadcaster. Internet radio is one example of this, and another is the use of MySpace by the band Arctic Monkeys in 2005.

Franchises and formats

A successful film can produce income not simply though the box office, television or DVD sales, but through licensing other companies to use the name, logos and characters of the film in a computer game, a television spin-off or 'the book of the film'.

At the same time, the creators of a television game show can earn a significant amount of money by allowing, at a price, television companies in other countries to make their own version of the game show. Celador, the company which originated *Who Wants to be a Millionaire?*, continues to receive income through versions of the show produced around the world.

Activity: Company structures

Find three examples of each of the following situations:

- an independent company taken over by a conglomerate
- independent companies or artists using the Internet to reach audiences
- a franchise or format generating income for its creators.

Case study: Global Radio

Global Radio is a UK-based company that owns some of the top commercial radio stations in the UK. Currently listening figures stand in excess of 18.5 million across their range of stations, with income being made through sales of commercial advertising space to local and national companies.

The company's stations include Heart, Classic FM, 95.8 Capital FM and Galaxy.

In 2009 commercial radio stations had an overall market share of 42.4 per cent of the UK's listening audience, allowing them to reach a substantial part of the country on behalf of their advertisers. The market for advertising revenue is very competitive.

1. What is the difference between commercial radio and public service broadcasters such as the BBC?

2. What is a commercial broadcaster's main source of income?

3. Look into commercial broadcasters in your local area. How do they ensure a stable listenership?

Key issues

Convergence

The umbrella term 'creative media' encompasses a wide range of industries including television, film, radio, sound recording, print-based media and publishing, interactive media and games, advertising and others. In the past the more traditional industries have each had their own production processes and practices, but with the emergence of new media and new industries within the creative media sector the boundaries have become blurred, as processes, audiences and markets increasingly merge. This merging is known as 'convergence'.

Competition and salary levels

In order to win the contract for a production or to maximise profit, companies are constantly under pressure to produce work for less money. If their costs are too high at the pitching stage, it is unlikely that they will get the work. Sometimes the people commissioning the work simply do not have the budget to pay more. One option for media companies is to pay staff less or to employ fewer staff. This can have a negative effect on quality of production as well as employment levels.

Monopolies and competition between companies

Media audiences, like most consumers, are seen to benefit from competition between companies as this keeps the quality high and the costs down. If one company dominates an industry, competition has effectively ended and we have a monopoly. Audiences could then be restricted in choice of what is available to them and at the same time the company could charge more since they no longer need to worry about audiences switching to a competitor. Regulations in the UK (see later in the unit) currently limit the proportion of an industry which one company is allowed to own.

Multi-skilling or specialism?

The pressure for companies to make media productions more cheaply has encouraged some organisations to develop multi-skilled staff. These are people who have been trained to undertake a range of different tasks, for example, to shoot photographs, design layouts and produce web pages. Sometimes presenters edit their own content or a researcher may be trained so that they can also act as sound recordist.

Some digital equipment has become very easy to use and less expensive than in the past. Employees in all sorts of roles can use a video camera to shoot footage for a website, for example. This means that fewer people need to be employed, saving costs.

However, many people believe that if you do not use skilled specialists, then the quality of productions goes down. Having a video camera and knowing how to operate it does not guarantee a professional-looking video. Major productions, where the quality is key, continue to use specialists in key roles.

The advertising 'cake'

In the past, the money from advertising was a significant source of income for newspapers, magazines and commercial (that is, non-BBC) radio and television. In 1990 most people in the UK received a maximum of five television channels. More recently, the number of television channels and radio stations has increased dramatically. The amount spent on advertising has remained the same but it is now shared between many more companies. If the same-sized cake is shared out between more people, the slices will be smaller and so companies relying on advertising have been having a difficult time. In television there is further competition from digital media which is becoming more attractive to advertisers. For example, more money is spent advertising on Google than on ITV.

Conglomerates, takeovers and subsidiaries

These terms relate to the way that an increasing amount of work in the industry is done by a small number of giant companies. Many small independent companies in the UK have found success across the media. Sometimes these companies produce work which competes with major companies. The majors might then 'buy out' the independent company, leaving the owners wealthy, while the company becomes a subsidiary of the major company. The smaller companies often keep their name, and sometimes their staff and logo as well, but lose their independence. A major company owning a number of smaller companies is known as a conglomerate, such as the Sony Corporation, which owns subsidiaries including Columbia Pictures.

Assessment activity 7.1

For this unit you will need to build a portfolio of evidence that shows your understanding of the creative media sector.

To begin with you need to create a section for your portfolio that identifies and investigates:

- relevant examples of changes in the organisational structures and ownership of a creative media sector relevant to your studies
- the size, shape and patterns of ownership within the sector
- the impact of ownership on production and distribution.

Grading tips

For a merit grade, you will need to be able to clearly explain the structure and ownership of the chosen media sector using a range of detailed illustrative examples throughout.

For a distinction grade, you will need to provide a comprehensive explanation of the structure and ownership of the chosen media sector, using a range of elucidated examples throughout.

PLTS

Analysing the media industries for research and investigating media ownership will help develop your skills as an **independent enquirer**.

Functional skills

Researching media industry information, collating gathered information and presenting findings will help you to develop your **ICT** skills.

2. Understand ethical and legal constraints within the media sector

2.1 Ethical constraints

Working within ethical constraints is an important part of professional practice. This means being aware of people's sensitivities, treating people with respect and courtesy, and working responsibly within the bounds of professional standards in the sector. This is an enormous area which is difficult to pin down, and the creative media industries have developed various codes of practice which help define such issues and provide guidelines on working professionally in a range of situations and contexts (see, for example, the BBC activity).

Media producers sometimes court publicity by pushing the boundaries of taste and legality. Values about what is acceptable do change over time and producers constantly have to make judgement calls balancing taste, shock and sales. Some examples include:

- intruding on individual privacy: deciding whether it is legitimately in the public interest or whether the intrusion is simply 'interesting' to the public
- running premium rate phone competitions
- presenting an individual or their views as representative of an entire group of people (for example, representation of gender or religious beliefs)

Activity: The BBC

The BBC website provides guidelines for suppliers across all their media: television, radio, online and publishing. The BBC Trust monitors compliance with these guidelines and publishes press releases and details of complaints, appeals and their outcomes.

1. Find the BBC's editorial guidelines and online services guidelines by searching for 'editorial guidelines' at www.bbc.co.uk

   - What are the main areas that these guidelines cover?
   - Why is there a need for the BBC to publish these guidelines?

2. Search for 'breaches of editorial guidelines' on the BBC website and explore a range of these.

   - What were the issues?
   - What were the findings of the BBC Trust?
   - What were the consequences for those who were judged to have breached the guidelines?

- using hidden microphones or long lens cameras: when is it acceptable to record people without their knowledge?

- interviewing vulnerable people, such as the children of people in the public eye, or people in hospital: is this exploitative?

- using 'off the record' information that was given confidentially

- making a creative media product that may offend or insult any user, viewer or listener, particularly if it refers to a minority or specific group of people.

While some areas, such as discrimination, are covered by law, other ethical issues are not so easy to define and producers need to be guided by their industry's professional codes of practice. Failure to comply with a professional code of practice can have serious

implications for a producer, ranging from legal action to being removed from supplier tender invitation lists, loss of reputation and loss of business.

2.2 Legal constraints

In addition to self-regulating industry codes of practice, a wide range of legislation controls the creative media industries.

For any production, everyone involved needs to consider the relevant legal issues and be aware of their responsibilities within the law. This applies equally to producers, their employees and even to learners and people on work experience.

The following areas of law, among others, commonly apply to creative media production work.

Can you think of examples in the news where freedom of expression has collided with the right to privacy?

Table 7.1: Areas of law that apply to creative media production work.

Libel law	You can be sued for damages if you publish or broadcast things about a person which are untrue and damage their reputation (defame them).
Discrimination legislation	Discrimination on grounds of race, gender and age are illegal. This is likely to be a consideration when employing staff, cast and crew and in the way that individuals and groups are depicted in any creative media product, factual or fictional.
Obscenity	Lawyers may be needed to check whether a production breaks obscenity law. This can depend on factors such as the age range of the audience, the time a production is broadcast and where and how it is produced, released or published.
Data protection	Storing certain information about people without their permission is illegal. Any records you hold about a person can be accessed by them under the Freedom of Information Act. On the other hand, information obtained, for example, in the course of journalism may be covered by the Official Secrets Act, which means it cannot be made public. In other contexts, suppliers may in the course of their work gain access to information which is covered by a confidentiality clause in their contract, which prevents them from disclosing the details to any other company or person.

Did you know?

The European Convention on Human Rights protects freedom of expression, while the Human Rights Act 1998 protects the right to privacy.

Intellectual property and copyright

You would understandably be annoyed if you saw work that you had created being used by someone else without your agreement. You, like many others, might well view this as theft of your property and feel inclined to pursue the matter in court.

If you have worked to produce something such as a photograph, a script or a piece of artwork, it is your intellectual property (IP). If other people want to use your IP, then they have to obtain your permission and pay you the amount agreed for a specified type of use. Media producers at all levels must avoid using someone else's work in a production without permission, whether it is music that is wanted for a soundtrack, photographs used as stills in a production, or any other piece of IP.

Copyright protects the rights of the creators of music, sound recordings, images, photographs, films, broadcasts and written work to control use of their material by other people. However, copyright does not protect ideas, or such things as names or titles. It protects the way the idea is expressed in a specific piece of work, but it does not protect the idea itself.

The Internet has made IP a huge issue. It is very hard to find out if your work is being used and sometimes even harder to find the people who are responsible. YouTube is well known for the unauthorised use of copyright material, for example, when people use recorded music as soundtracks for the productions and home-made clips they post on YouTube. Large companies who own the IP for a range of media such as televised football, Hollywood movies and the recorded music industry employ teams of lawyers to watch for unauthorised use, but it is a huge task!

Activity: Copyright and intellectual property

The following organisations will give you more information about copyright and intellectual property.

- Intellectual Property Office (www.ipo.gov.uk) – the official government body responsible for granting Intellectual Property (IP) rights in the UK.
- Pact (www.pact.co.uk) – the UK trade association representing and promoting the commercial interests of independent feature film, television, digital, children's and animation production companies.
- Skillset (www.skillset.org) – the Sector Skills Council for Creative Media.

Visit the websites of these organisations.

1. Produce six bullet points which summarise advice for producers wanting to use either an existing music track or a well-known photograph in a production.
2. Produce a six bullet-point summary of advice for people wanting to prevent unauthorised use of a production they have made.

Case study: Tom, creative media student

Legal issues

I had always thought that sampling someone else's music was OK. I have heard loads of tracks that sampled music or lyrics by other artists and thought it was just a standard thing that happened in the music industry.

What I didn't realise is that you have to make sure you get the right copyright clearance from the artists and production companies to use samples of their music in your own work. We looked at some famous cases like Vanilla Ice using Queen's and David Bowie's *Under Pressure* at the start of his hit song *Ice Ice Baby*. He didn't license or credit the original. That caused a huge uproar and he was threatened with legal action.

There are a lot of discussions over issues of sampling tracks and there are schools of thought who consider this practice 'theft' and others that consider it 'homage'. Whichever way you feel about it, you had better be sure you have permission before you start using other people's work and not try passing it off as your own!

Assessment activity 7.2

(P2) (M2) (D2) **BTEC**

For the second section of your portfolio you need to show your understanding of ethical and legal constraints within a creative media sector relevant to your studies.

Create a section for your portfolio that identifies and investigates:

- details of relevant constraints that might affect your practical production work
- explanations of how and why particular legislation and ethical considerations need to be taken into account
- details of 'real' occasions when regulators have

become involved with your chosen creative media sector and what the outcomes were.

Grading tips

For a merit grade, you will need to be able to explain ethical and legal constraints within the chosen media sector relevant to your studies and provide detailed illustrative examples.

For a distinction grade, you will need to be able to provide a comprehensive explanation of the ethical and legal constraints within the chosen media sector relevant to your studies, providing highly relevant, elucidated examples.

PLTS

Researching legal, ethical and regulatory issues in the media industry will help develop your skills as an **independent enquirer**.

Functional skills

Researching information for reports will help you to develop your **English** skills.

3. Understand the regulation of the media sector

3.1 Regulatory and professional bodies

A large number of **statutory** and industry organisations regulate the creative media industries. The major ones are described in Table 7.2.

Key term

Statutory – having the force of law.

Table 7.2: Regulatory organisations in the creative media industries.

Advertising Standards Authority (ASA)	The UK's independent regulator of advertising across all media, including television, Internet, sales promotions and direct marketing	www.asa.org.uk
British Academy of Film and Television Arts (BAFTA)	Supports, develops and promotes the film, television and video games industries	www.bafta.org
British Board of Film Classification (bbfc)	The independent regulator of the film and video industry in the UK; classifies films and videos in terms of age suitability	www.bbfc.co.uk
British Interactive Media Association (BIMA)	The industry association representing the interactive media and digital content sectors	www.bima.co.uk
British Video Association	The trade body that represents the interests of publishers and rights owners of video home entertainment	www.bva.org.uk
Film Distributors' Association (FDA)	The trade body for theatrical film distributors in the UK – the companies that release films for UK cinema audiences	www.launchingfilms.com
The Independent Games Developers' Association (TIGA)	The trade association representing the UK's games industry	www.tiga.org
International Visual Communications Association (IVCA)	The independent not-for-profit membership organisation representing the creators and commissioners of film, video, digital and live events for the corporate and public sectors	www.ivca.org
Mobile Entertainment Forum (MEF)	The global voice of the mobile entertainment industry	www.m-e-f.org
Office of Communications (Ofcom)	The communications regulator; regulates television and radio, fixed line telecoms and mobiles, plus the airwaves over which wireless devices operate	www.ofcom.org.uk
Pan European Game Information (PEGI)	Provides age ratings for computer games using a system recognised across Europe	www.pegi.info
Performing Rights Society for Music (PRS for Music)	Brings together two royalty collection societies: MCPS and PRS; collects and pays royalties to its members when their music is recorded onto any format and distributed to the public, performed or played in public, broadcast or made publicly available online	www.prsformusic.com

Table 7.2: continued

Press Complaints Commission (PCC)	An independent self-regulatory body which deals with complaints about the editorial content of newspapers and magazines and their websites	www.pcc.org.uk
RadioCentre	The merger of the Radio Advertising Bureau (RAB) and the Commercial Radio Companies Association (CRCA); supports the commercial radio industry	www.radiocentre.org
UK Web Design Association	Encourages and promotes industry standards within the British web design and new media sector	www.ukwda.org
Video Standards Council (VSC)	Oversees a Code of Practice designed to promote high standards within the video game and computer games industry	www.videostandards.org.uk
World Wide Web Consortium (W3C)	An international community that develops standards to ensure the long-term growth of the Web, including accessibility standards, to make web content accessible to a wider range of people with disabilities, as well as to make web content more accessible to users in general	www.w3.org

Activity: The regulators

Select the websites of five of the regulators listed above and answer the following questions.

1. Which media sectors does each body regulate?

2. How does each body enforce its regulatory powers?

3. What are the consequences of not adhering to the regulator's rules and codes of practice?

Case study: Louise, computer games developer

When I am coming up with ideas and planning the content of a new video game, I always have to keep in mind the target audience and exactly who will be playing the game when it is released onto the market.

Current regulations play a big part in this and I always have to consider whether or not the content of the game is suitable for the player. I tend to try and think about this in terms of genre. If I am looking at creating a 'shoot 'em up, *Grand Theft Auto*' type of game then the audience is going to be around 18+ and the content can be a little more violent and risky.

However, if I was working on a game for a company like Disney, I could be looking at an audience of anywhere between 3 and 15, depending on the

theme, and so I would have to ensure the content was appropriate and would be suitable for younger players, not only in terms of game play but use of language and violence, and so on. After all, if the game wasn't appropriate it either wouldn't get taken up by the company or if it was released the company could face complaints and legal action.

1. Put yourself in the position of a production company in an industry that interests you. List the factors you would need to consider in order to avoid complaints or legal action.

2. Consider how younger audiences are covered by regulations and what approaches companies might take to create exciting games which also meet the regulator's requirements.

3.2 Regulatory issues

There are many organisations involved in the regulation of the creative media sector and each is involved, to one degree or another, in considering the rights and interests of producers and consumers alike. Some of the issues affecting the creative media sector are related to ownership and control; who owns what and how much of it. Some relate to the rights of consumers and the ability to draw a fine line between protection and censorship. Others are related to intellectual property and the right of media producers to expect fair payment and recognition for their work.

Activity: Identifying issues

Here are some of the key issues affecting media producers and consumers:

- media ownership and monopoly
- consumer choice
- censorship and taste and decency
- protecting under-18s.

Which of the organisations that you have looked into are involved in these issues? Answer the following questions.

1. What is a monopoly?
2. Why is it important to ensure that no single media producer in the UK has a monopoly?
3. Why is consumer choice important?
4. What is censorship?
5. Why do some people think there is a fine line between censorship and protecting the public interest?
6. Why should under-18s be subject to particular consideration by regulators?

Piracy

Piracy is a particularly relevant issue in today's society, especially given the substantial availability of products such as music and films that can be downloaded from the Internet. There are different ways to download materials, some legal and others illegal; it is this illegal downloading that is considered piracy.

Although it is sometimes downplayed by consumers, the fact remains that piracy is theft. Producers of media products lose out and this will ultimately have an effect on the consumer in the long run, possibly resulting in tighter controls, regulations being more rigorously enforced, and higher prices for original products.

Protection of intellectual property

Protection of intellectual property is also related to piracy issues and involves ensuring that media producers are given due consideration and receive recognition and payment for their work. For more information on intellectual property and copyright, see Unit 1, Pre-production techniques for the creative media industries.

Impartiality, accuracy and fairness

As consumers we are entitled not to be lied to by media producers. We have a right to expect that the information we receive is accurate and truthful, and that there is a level of impartiality to it.

You will have been taught already that there are many different kinds of truth and that a media text will always contain the opinion or viewpoint of the 'author'. In a diverse, multicultural society there are many views and opinions held by different groups and individuals. However, it is important for media producers to ensure that they provide fair and accurate information and that, for example, news producers provide factual impartial information and not commentary that is littered with bias or personal opinion.

Assessment activity 7.3

P3 M3 D3 ⋮BTEC

For the third section of your portfolio you need to show your understanding of the regulation of the media sector relevant to your studies.

Create a section for your portfolio that identifies and investigates:

- a reflection of your understanding of regulatory issues and the work of regulatory bodies
- details of the extent to which regulatory bodies are effective
- consideration of the issues of censorship and self-censorship
- the possible constraints of regulation on creative media production.

Grading tips

For a merit grade, you will need to be able to clearly explain the regulation of – and the role of – regulatory bodies in the media sectors relevant to your studies, and provide a range of detailed illustrative examples.

For a distinction grade, you will need to be able to provide a comprehensive explanation of the regulation of – and the role of – regulatory bodies in the media sectors relevant to your studies, and provide an extensive range of elucidated examples.

PLTS

Evaluating report writing will help develop your skills as a **reflective learner**.

Functional skills

Exploring, extracting and assessing the relevance of information about regulation on websites will help you to develop your **ICT** skills.

4. Know about employment opportunities and job roles in the media sector

4.1 Employment opportunities and 4.2 Job roles

The creative media industries are very competitive and jobs tend to involve hard work with long hours.

However, the sector is very wide ranging and in some of the creative media industries, people may be based more in offices working on longer-term contracts. For the industry or industries that you are interested in, you will need to know about the range of jobs available.

Activity: Job roles in the creative media industries

Creative roles, technical roles and production management roles can often overlap, and the same job title can mean different things in different industries. Some of the most common job roles include:

animator	information architect
artist	journalist
designer	mixer
developer	modeller
director	presenter
editor	producer
engineer	production assistant
programmer	project manager
runner	sales and marketing manager
researcher	scriptwriter.

- Investigate what is involved in the job roles relevant to your chosen industry.
- Identify which jobs are entry-level posts in the industry you are interested in.
- Which jobs are you most interested in for the longer term?
- Are the jobs that you are interested in likely to be short-term freelance contracts or long-term employed posts?

The websites of the industry bodies listed in Table 7.2 will help you with this activity, along with those listed in the 'Industry publications and organisations' box on page 128.

Having identified broadly the sorts of roles that might interest you, you need to do some more detailed research about the jobs that come up in your industry for this kind of work. Looking into this will help you think more about the path you would like to take once you leave school or college. This process will also help to prepare you for making your university choices if you wish to take that route.

Activity: Looking for work

Select a range of job roles which interest you. Then find a selection of job advertisements and application packs for each one, using the websites of the organisations listed in Table 7.1 and those in the 'Industry publications and organisations' box on the next page.

For each job, make notes summarising:

- where you found the job advertisement
- what the job involves
- the skills, qualifications and experience needed
- where the job is based
- the rate of pay
- the terms of employment: whether it is a permanent job or a short-term freelance contract
- what you need to do to apply: whether it asks for a portfolio, a showreel or a CV.

Organise the advertisements and job specifications you have found into a portfolio, using your notes as a cover sheet for each one. Add to this over time.

4.3 Professional development and 4.4 Professional behaviour

Whatever the roles you are interested in, there will be a range of creative, technical and project management skills that you need to develop and be confident of using. While your studies will prepare you for this, there is no substitute for practical experience.

If you are seriously committed to working in the creative media sector, you will need to get hands-on experience by finding opportunities to job shadow, getting work experience placements, or by working, probably voluntarily, in any capacity you can at a creative media production company. You need to be ready to watch, listen and learn as much as possible in real industry environments. Not only will this build your knowledge and understanding of your chosen industry, but it will also help you make your first professional contacts in the industry, which may be vital to you when you are starting out and applying for your first paid job.

A number of personal skills are required by people who work successfully in the media industries, and are just as important when you are looking for work experience opportunities. These include:

- reliability
- punctuality
- courtesy
- ability to work as a team member
- ability to use initiative
- ability to take direction
- ability to work under pressure
- ability to meet deadlines.

Showing a prospective employer that you have these qualities will be an important task when you apply for a job or placement in the industry.

Activity: Assess your own skills

Spend some time thinking about areas in which you have skills and those you need to develop.

1. Which creative and technical skills do you need to develop for the job roles you are interested in?

2. Which personal skills do you need to develop?

You might also think about identifying your stronger areas and looking for employment which involves those types of skills.

Case study: Anna, freelance graphic designer

Being freelance means you are self-employed, working on a series of short-term contracts. It's flexible, but not secure. You are always looking for the next job and keeping an ear to the ground to try to hear about upcoming projects.

It's important to make and maintain contacts who might be able to offer you work in the future. And you need to build up a reputation that's going to make you the person that everyone wants on their job – not just good at doing the actual physical work technically and creatively, but also being reliable, professional, flexible and good to work with. Relationships count for a lot in this industry.

Of course it doesn't always work out and you have to cope with disappointment when you don't get a job you've been hoping to land, but you can't take

it personally and just have to find the next thing. Not knowing what you're going to be working on next can be nerve-racking, but on the positive side you have the chance to work on a wide, exciting range of projects.

There are various practical things you need to sort out when you work freelance, such as being responsible for your own tax and pension arrangements.

1. Why are relationships so important when working freelance?

2. Do you feel you would be well suited to working freelance? What would you enjoy and what would you find difficult?

Industry publications and organisations

The following are useful sources of information on careers, job opportunities, industry events such as trade shows and conferences and training opportunities in the creative media sector.

The Bookseller – www.thebookseller.com

BBC – www.bbc.co.uk/jobs

British Printing Industries Federation (BPIF) – www.britishprint.com

Broadcast magazine – http://info.broadcastnow.co.uk

Creative Review – www.creativereview.co.uk (visual communications)

Develop – www.develop-online.net (game design, coding, art, sound and business)

Edge – www.edge-online.com (global game industry network)

Entertainment and Leisure Software Publishers Association – www.elspa.com

Grapevine Jobs – www.grapevinejobs.com (jobs in broadcast and media)

The Guardian newspaper – www.guardian.co.uk (Media section, Mondays)

Journalism – www.journalism.co.uk

Mandy's – www.mandy.com (film and television production resources)

Media UK – www.mediauk.com

Media Week Online – www.mediaweekjobs.co.uk

New Media Age – www.nma.co.uk

Periodical Publishers Association – www.ppa.co.uk

PrintWeek jobs – www.printweek.com

Production Base – www.productionbase.co.uk (film, television and commercials network)

Shooting People – https://shootingpeople.org (a forum on film making)

Skillset – www.skillset.org (the Sector Skills Council for Creative Media)

UK Music Jobs – http://uk.music-jobs.com

Getting the most out of work experience

You will get the most out of any industry visits or work experience opportunities if you think beforehand about what you want to learn from them.

How can you get work experience?

You need to ask! You could approach someone:

- you have met through your course

- working in a role that interests you at a company you have researched

- you have met during a college industry visit

- you met on an earlier work experience placement

- that a personal friend, relative or colleague can introduce you to: put out 'feelers' to find out if anyone you know has any contacts in the industry.

Depending on your industry, you may also be able to find brief paid or unpaid work opportunities advertised, such as on low-budget film productions or as a demonstrator at a trade fair.

If none of these options are possible, search for career case studies online. Skillset is a good place to start.

What to find out when you get there

Find out as much as you can about the experience of the person or people you are working with or job-shadowing.

- How did they start in the industry?
- What qualifications and experience did they have?
- What training did they receive?
- What does their job role involve?
- What skills and qualities are needed for their job?
- What kind of contract do they have?
- What do they find most enjoyable and most difficult about their job and about the way they work?

What else can you get out of work experience?

Remember, everyone you meet on work experience is a potential contact for the future. Do your best to form a good relationship with them, make a positive impression in terms of reliability, courtesy, professional behaviour and common sense, and make sure you know how to contact them again in the future.

Remember also to check back on your personal skills assessment. Look out for any opportunities in your work placement to build on the skills that you identified as needing development.

Assessment activity 7.4

P4 M4 D4   **BTEC**

For the penultimate section of your portfolio, you need to show your understanding of employment opportunities and job roles in the creative media sector. In order to provide some focus for your work it would be advisable to concentrate on the particular sector in which you hope to gain employment in the future.

Create a section for your portfolio that identifies and investigates: employment opportunities and job roles in two relevant industries, to include:

- details of how some job roles can overlap and interconnect
- details of how job roles can evolve and develop over time
- notes on the need to update knowledge and skills constantly

- descriptions of different opportunities for professional development.

Grading tips

For a merit grade, you will need to be able to clearly explain employment opportunities and job roles in the media sector and provide a range of detailed illustrative examples.

For a distinction grade, you will need to be able to provide a comprehensive explanation of employment opportunities and job roles in the media sector and provide an extensive range of elucidated examples.

PLTS

Managing time and resources to produce written reports, dealing with and meeting deadlines effectively, and seeking advice and support when needed will help develop your skills as a **self-manager**.

Functional skills

Writing reports using a variety of research methods will help you to develop your **ICT** skills.

5. Be able to prepare personal career development material

If you are applying for a job in the creative media sector, you will need to be well prepared in advance. You will need to work on:

- a CV
- a showreel or portfolio
- interview practice
- letters of application
- research before applying for jobs.

5.1 Career development material

You are likely to need a CV (short for the Latin 'Curriculum Vitae') when you apply for jobs in many industries. This is where you'll need to present yourself, your experience and your skills in a really positive, professional way to possible future employers.

Your CV will need to be well presented and contain relevant and interesting information. As you go through your course, think about gathering 'evidence' of your commitment to your chosen area, your experience and your skills. Every production you make, each work experience opportunity, or even visits to companies or exhibitions, could be an item on your CV which will make your job application stronger.

What goes into a CV?

CVs usually include these headings:

- name
- address, telephone, email
- educational history and qualifications
- key areas of study during a course
- areas of skills and equipment training
- employment history and work placements
- production credits: video, print, audio (should link to showreel, demo or portfolio)
- other interests and experience
- referee details: their name and contact details and a note of their relationship with you (for example, tutor, employer).

It is important to customise your basic CV to whatever job you are applying for, to highlight and emphasise your most relevant skills and experience. Do not give too much space to other less relevant information.

Remember: keep your CV concise – two sides of A4 is enough – relevant, and true!

CV presentation

CVs need to be clear, well presented and accurate to make a positive impression on your prospective employers about your design skills, attention to detail, and ability to work with accuracy. It is good to have a PDF version of your CV to put on websites or to enclose with an email.

References

Usually at the end of a CV, you list some people who will give you references. Someone who receives a job application from you can contact these people for their opinion about your skills, your experience and your suitability. Your referee should be able to comment on the basis of work you have produced or how you coped in a work-related situation. Friends and family are not suitable to give references as they are seen as likely to be biased in your favour.

Always check in advance that people are prepared to act as referees before listing them on your CV. Suitable referees might include:

- a tutor at your college
- an employer or mentor from work experience or a part-time job
- someone who has seen the work you produced on your course, for example, a client
- a personal referee: this could be someone who works in your community, such as a youth worker.

Producing a portfolio, showreel or demo

What would be the best way to showcase your work? Whichever creative media industry you want to enter, your prospective employers will want to see evidence of what you can do. You need to prepare a professional-looking sample of your work in an appropriate format for your industry, such as a showreel, a physical or digital portfolio, recorded demo or website or wiki that demonstrates your skills. Aim to show your full range of skills in your portfolio as well as work produced for a range of purposes and clients.

The way in which you produce this will show a lot about your professional expertise so you need to make it as professional as possible, ensuring that you choose strong examples, assemble them competently, and pay careful attention to details such as labelling, titles, captions, navigation and so on. And remember to credit yourself! It is essential to include information about your role in each production and, of course, your full contact details.

Showreels

For a DVD showreel of video work, select the appropriate productions and the sequences you wish to include. Aim for a consistent style, preferably with linking audio sequences. The compilation should be as watchable as possible. If in doubt, keep it short. Edit the showreel onto DVD but also make a compressed version which will work on a website.

Make decisions around the running order, editing, audio and the wording of the graphics, selecting font, colour and style.

Audio demos

For radio work or sound recording, include as wide a range of material as possible, including, for example, speech, music, soundtracks, dialogue, sound effects, games music, and demonstrating both studio and location work. Make sure you provide full details about each clip: your role, the purpose and running time of your clips, information about your role in the production, your course and your contact details and links to any related websites such as a MySpace page. You can do this in the form of carefully produced professional-looking sleeve notes or screen graphics.

Digital portfolios

If your work is interactive, create a digital portfolio that includes a wide selection of projects (for example, websites, wiki, interactive CD or DVD). Label each sample clearly, paying attention to details such as navigation, and making absolutely sure that everything works exactly how it should. Make sure your contact details and information about your role in each production are clear and easy to find.

Print portfolios

Print portfolios and sketchbooks will be appropriate for some kinds of employment, while a selection of

images of your work on a website, USB stick or CD might be useful if you need to send examples of your work. Name each piece of work clearly, labelling it accurately with details of your role in the production and your contact details, using carefully chosen fonts and colours. This is all part of the presentation process and will say a lot about your creative flair and ability to communicate visually, as well as about your organisational skills.

5.2 Presentation for employment

The way you present yourself as well as your work will have an impact on your prospective employer. Don't make the mistake of thinking that the creative media sector is going to be a creative, laidback working environment where anything goes. It is important to be able to show your creativity and original thinking, but it's also important to show that you can work professionally in a competitive, fast-moving industry.

Presenting yourself for interview as a smart, polite and punctual person is always a good start. Interviews can be nerve-racking for anyone but the key is to build your confidence through careful preparation and practice.

Mock interviews can improve your performance in the real thing.

Case study: Amicie, interactive media student

I was very nervous about going for job interviews and something I found useful on my college course was having the chance to practise for these in mock interviews. Rehearsals are good! You can't practise the real interview, but you can feel more confident if you've already had a go at being interviewed in role play.

I had to find details of a real job that I was interested in, complete an application and give a copy of the job description to the college so that the interviewer could think of some relevant questions. For the first one I did, it was a tutor that did the interview with me. I had to do a short presentation about my experience and skills, showing my demo disc, and then it was the formal questions. I was really nervous and the presentation didn't go all that well. But at least it was only a practice, not the 'real thing'. It wasn't much fun at the time but it was useful to show me what I needed to work on. The whole thing went much better for my second mock interview, which

was with a visiting media professional, and that really did build my confidence.

Doing mock interviews has helped me to look at job specifications carefully and think about how I can show that I've got what they are asking for. It's not enough just to claim you can do things – you have to be able to give good examples that demonstrate you really can. Let's just say I reworked my demo disc quite a lot after doing that first mock interview!

1. What sort of preparation do you need to do for an interview?

2. How easy would you find it to use your showreel, demo or portfolio to demonstrate specific skills in an interview? Is there anything you need to change?

3. Can you arrange to have a mock interview with a member of staff at your college or with a media professional?

Assessment activity 7.5

P5 M5 D5 BTEC

By now you will probably have an idea about your career choices and which area of the creative media sector you would like to work in. You must now update your portfolio.

Prepare the following ready for a job application in your chosen field. To do this you will need to look for a 'live' advertisement from a relevant website so that you have a better idea of which of your skills and qualifications to highlight in your application. Be sure to include:

* a letter of application and completed application form for a specific job from your portfolio of job specs; make sure you give clear evidence of how you fit the job description and person specification
* a showreel, portfolio, demo or website, on CD or DVD
* your CV.

Grading tips

For a merit grade, you will need to produce career development materials that competently advertise your skills and qualifications to a prospective employer. You should generally be able to make appropriate use of the correct formal language, both written and verbal, throughout.

For a distinction grade, you will need to prepare career development materials to a near-professional standard that will effectively advertise your skills and qualifications to a prospective employer. You should be able to make consistent and accurate use of the correct formal language, both written and verbal, throughout.

PLTS

Inviting feedback and dealing positively with praise, setbacks and criticism throughout the process of creating career development materials will help develop your skills as a **reflective learner**.

Functional skills

Writing CVs and other career development materials will help you to develop your **English** skills.

Emily Shields

Series producer of television documentaries

I started out as a researcher at the BBC. Most people start as either researchers or runners, then work their way up. Then I joined an independent production company called RDF where I stayed for five years and became a director. I left RDF in 2005 to go freelance and started series producing after I had my first child.

I am responsible for overseeing the production of a series, from the point at which it is commissioned through to delivery to the channel. Television production is roughly divided into three phases: pre-production, filming (production) and editing (post-production). What I do depends on where we are in the schedule.

During pre-production I work closely with the directors and assistant producers working on each programme in the series to make sure their research is heading in the right direction and that the overall narrative of the series makes sense – that they are interviewing the right people and asking the right questions!

During filming I am on hand to deal with any queries and questions from the directors who are out filming. I aim to provide reassurance when things go wrong and encouragement when things go right.

During the edit I supervise all the edits, make sure the programmes make sense as a series and often oversee the voiceover record and final editing.

You need to be a good communicator and team player, and able to see quickly what it's worth spending the budget on – and what it's not.

I like the variety. Working with interesting people and seeing the series take shape under your guidance is very rewarding.

Compliance is a hot issue now; meeting all the regulations. When a broadcaster is guilty of breaking rules, it's always big news. Sometimes the lawyers at channels drive you mad – but they are only doing their job – to make sure we don't end up in the headlines!

Think about it!

- What qualities are needed to work in creative media production?
- What would you find challenging about working in creative media production?
- What would you find most satisfying?

Just checking

1. How well do you think the UK is placed to take part in the ongoing growth of the creative media sector?
2. Can you provide some examples of businesses that are producing exciting and innovative media products?
3. What is meant by the term 'overlapping of job roles'?
4. Can you provide some examples of job roles that do overlap?
5. Briefly outline some of the ways the creative media sector is funded.
6. What does the term 'multi-skilling' mean and how does it differ from specialisation?
7. How and why is there a difference between legal and ethical constraints?
8. Can you name five of the main regulators in the creative media sector and identify what the role and function is of each one?
9. Outline some of the key personal skills required to work in the creative media sector.
10. List some methods you could use to create effective career development materials.

edexcel

Assignment tips

- When conducting research into creative media industries, annotate your work effectively to ensure you extract information relevant to your needs.

- When building a portfolio of evidence be sure to include an index so the reader can easily find work in their relevant sections.

- A bibliography should also be included and should reference books and industry journals as well as websites that have been used for research purposes.

- If you are producing your portfolio electronically, be sure to back up your work consistently to avoid losing essential information.

- When working on production units, always consider whether the materials or footage you create could be used in a showreel to highlight your skills.

Television and film

Television and film production is varied, exciting and creative. The television industry has grown, with more channels than ever before, and audiences are using the media in new ways. Some programmes and films have large crews and big budgets while others are made very cheaply. Watching video online has become common, leading to a growing market in corporate video productions for businesses of all kinds. Non-broadcast video has much smaller budgets than television and film but there is plenty of work in this field and many people start their production careers in this area.

In the Television and film pathway you will learn the skills to make a range of productions, working through research and planning stages to shooting and editing video and sound. You will also explore the structure of the industry, looking at how the industry is organised, the job roles and skills needed by those who work in it.

Everything we see on the television or cinema screen is the result of much planning and hard work. It is also the result of decisions related to money, time and audience numbers, and a range of legal obligations and ethical judgement calls. You will need to understand these factors, and to look at the regulatory frameworks within which the industry has to operate.

Studying the Television and film pathway will allow you to develop your knowledge and understanding of the industry and the production techniques and technologies that it uses. The pathway includes two specialist mandatory units: Unit 8, Understanding the television and film industries and Unit 16, Film and video editing techniques.

This chapter is designed to give you an overview of the television and film industries and the types of skills you will need for this pathway. You will find details of the learning outcomes and the assessment and grading criteria for the Television and film pathway on pages 250–252.

Clare, media student on the Television and film pathway

I've learnt so much on this course, and I've really enjoyed it. I feel I know much more now about how things get made for television or the cinema. Understanding more about the industry and the job roles and doing my own practical projects has helped me to work out what I'm most interested in, and that's editing. I'd say that editing has been one of the best things I've learnt on the course.

Looking at how the editing works in films and TV programmes taught me a lot. I realised that just because I could use the editing software, that didn't mean I was a good editor. I now understand that editing is like telling a story to an audience: it's about what you show them and when.

Another big lesson has been about the professional side of editing. If you aren't organised and you don't set up folders and clip names carefully, the whole thing takes much longer. On my final project, which was a drama, I discovered that using lots of crazy effects and transitions looked great at first but actually they were distracting to the audience, so I decided not to use most of them. I also got better at using the script to check the strengths and weaknesses of footage: are there any technical problems? Is there enough coverage or is more shooting needed? There are so many things to think about, but that's what I enjoy: putting it all together and getting a great result that people actually want to watch.

Over to you!

- Which parts of the course are you most excited about?
- What do you hope to get out of the course?

Who controls what we see and hear on the screen?

This section of the chapter is relevant to Unit 8, LO1.

Set up

Producing commercials

Think of a television commercial that everyone in your group has seen. Discuss and list the main features and content of the commercial, and discuss what techniques and job roles would have been involved in its production. Try to relate these to specific elements of the commercial.

- Which aspect of the production would you be most interested in being involved with?
- Which aspects of the production do you feel you already have some insight into, and which elements do you want to know more about?

To answer the question of who controls what we see and hear on screen, you will need to know the answers to these key questions.

- Where does the money for productions come from?
- Who are the 'main players' in the television and film industry?
- Who owns them?

Where does the money come from?

Television

The television industry receives income from a number of sources:

- the BBC licence fee is paid by all UK households that receive television (see the case study on the next page)
- subscription: paid monthly by satellite or cable subscription customers, for example, Sky, Virgin
- pay per view: some big sporting or music events are available for a one-off fee paid by the customer to a satellite broadcaster or for an online 'webcast'
- sponsorship: you will be familiar with the company logos and branded sequences before and after many commercial television programmes (not the BBC)
- advertising: television commercials

- product placement: companies pay the production company to include their product in the film (such as a soft drink or a car), rather than a product made by one of their competitors. Until recently this applied only to film.

Did you know?

In the USA, companies have paid as much as $1m to screen an advertisement during commercial breaks in American football's Super Bowl. The cost is so high because there is a watching audience of 100 million people!

Film

Film making is expensive. A UK film costing £3 million to produce is considered 'low budget'. The money typically comes from:

- distributors who buy the rights to films before they start production
- private investors hoping to share in any profits the film might make
- development funds, for example, the UK Film Council.

If a film is made by a major studio, as with 20th Century Fox and *Avatar* (2009), then the studio will put up the money themselves.

Case study: The BBC and the licence fee

The BBC is the original 'Public Service Broadcaster'. Public Service Broadcasting (PSB) aims primarily to benefit the audience, whereas a commercial broadcaster aims to make a profit. Generally entertainment programmes attract large, profitable audiences, while educational and factual programmes usually have smaller audiences. PSB aims to ensure the provision of beneficial programmes that might not be profitable.

The BBC is funded by a licence fee which reflects its PSB role to 'inform, educate and entertain' without worrying about making money. It provides services including 8 national television channels, 10 national radio stations, 40 local radio stations and a website.

The licence fee

The licence fee is a big topic of debate. Here are some of the key points.

- Other channels choose to broadcast PSB-type programmes, but do not receive any of the licence fee.
- The BBC is the only broadcaster that can cater for some minority audiences.

- The BBC's commercial arm, BBC Worldwide, sells programmes abroad and publishes books, DVDs and merchandise. It competes with commercial channels but has protected income from the licence fee. Its profits are invested back into new BBC programmes and services.
- Even if people only watch non-BBC channels, they still need a licence.
- Not having to secure advertising revenue arguably enables the BBC to be impartial. They don't have to worry about upsetting a client who might withdraw their advertising.
- You can watch BBC programmes through iPlayer, and receive radio, without a licence.
- Many believe that the BBC's high quality programming and news coverage would be damaged if its funding system was changed.

1. Is the licence fee good value for money?
2. Is it fair that everyone who watches television has to pay it?
3. What do you think would happen if people could opt in or out?

On a profitable film (about two in every ten films released), there can be massive returns on the investment; for example, each *Lord of the Rings* film initially cost Warner Bros. around $90m to produce and $60m to distribute, but brought in over $800m each at the box office.

A film with a great script, good direction and with brilliant acting will not necessarily be a successful film financially. The marketing of a film can make all the difference to how many people see it at the cinema, on DVD or on television.

Once they are released, films and related products generate income through:

- the box office
- DVD sales and rental
- television sales worldwide
- pay television channels
- record companies who pay a proportion of income from the soundtrack CD
- computer games companies who pay to use the film as a basis for the game
- merchandise, for example, hats, T-shirts, mugs

- licensing: images of characters in films, use of 'intellectual property'
- books of the film: income coming from publishers
- product placement. as with television.

Activity: Film profits

Choose a feature film released in the UK in the last ten years. Find out the budget for the film, and the box office income. Was there any other form of income? Was this film released on DVD? Did it release a soundtrack? Once all costs had been taken into consideration, how much money did the film actually make?

The Internet Movie Database website (www.imdb.com) may be useful for this research.

PLTS

Researching information independently will help develop your skills as an **independent enquirer**.

Case study: The language of the film business

Globalisation and conglomerates

An increasing amount of work in the industry is done by a small number of giant companies. These 'conglomerates' buy up and take over smaller companies. The smaller companies often keep their name, and sometimes their staff and logo, but are then 'subsidiaries' of the conglomerate; for example Columbia Pictures is a subsidiary of the Sony Corporation. Many film studios are based in Hollywood, but the conglomerates that own them have headquarters and other subsidiaries around the world, and work on a 'global' basis which makes it difficult for smaller production companies to compete with them.

Horizontal integration

This is when one company owns a range of companies that can work simultaneously on the same project, which makes good business sense. For example, the film *The Bodyguard* (1992) and Whitney Houston's hit single from the film broke records for both the film division (Warner Bros.) and the music division (Warner Music) of the media conglomerate Time Warner.

Synergy

This means 'working together' on two or more coordinated media marketing projects to greater effect than if the same resources were spent on separate campaigns. In horizontally integrated companies, the music and film divisions increasingly work together, as in *The Bodyguard* example above. The film *Titanic* (1997), on the other hand, involved an alliance between distributors Paramount (in the USA) and 20th Century Fox (operating worldwide) along with Sony, who produced the Celine Dion hit from the soundtrack.

Vertical integration

The three stages of a film's life are **production**, **distribution** and **exhibition**. The production finance is based on the deals made with the distributor, in advance. Usually, the producers receive more money as a film becomes more successful. Distribution companies own the rights to a film and publicise it in order to attract the highest possible paying audiences to the film. They also make and deliver the prints or files for projection in each cinema. Exhibition is the business of showing films to audiences. The box office takings are shared with the distributor on a percentage basis, different for each film. Box office returns for a film are carefully recorded and published weekly.

If a conglomerate owns companies at all three of these stages of a film's life, this is known as vertical integration. Vertical integration is when one organisation owns: (a) the company which made the film, (b) the distributors and (c) some of the cinemas in which the film is shown. This is often seen as giving unfair advantage to the films made by the company, as it does not provide fair competition.

1. What are the business advantages of horizontal integration?
2. How does vertical integration affect business competitors?
3. Think of – and investigate – a media conglomerate. How many subsidiaries do they own, and what range of businesses do these include?

Key terms

Production – where films are developed and made.

Distribution – distribution companies own the rights to a film and publicise it; they also make and deliver the prints or files for projection in each cinema.

Exhibition – the business of showing films to audiences; what cinemas and cinema chains do.

The main players in British television

UK television programmes are made by terrestrial broadcasters, satellite and cable broadcasters and by independent production companies. Terrestrial involves television coming through transmitters, the old fashioned way.

The BBC is probably the best known of these; its structure and purpose has already been described.

What has been happening at ITV?

Much of the future of ITV is linked to the world of multi-channel television and the way people increasingly spend their leisure time playing computer games or using the Internet, rather than watching television programmes at the time of broadcast. Reduced audiences reduce the amount that can be charged for advertising during programmes. Other impacts of this trend include:

- fewer programmes made at television production centres in UK cities
- merging of regional news production so that the area covered is larger, needing fewer separate programmes and therefore fewer staff
- a continued decline in share price
- continuing discussion over ownership.

Other major terrestrial television broadcasters in the UK include Channel 4, Channel 5, BSkyB and Virgin.

Channel 4:

- commissions independent companies to make programmes rather than produce them itself
- is funded by advertising
- spent £400 million on new programming in 2008 (working with 312 production companies)
- made a profit for the first time in 2008 (E4 and the other digital channels have grown).

Channel 5:

- commissions independent companies to make programmes rather than produce them itself
- was launched in 1997
- is owned by RTL (Luxembourg); RTL is 90 per cent owned by Bertelsmann, a German-based media conglomerate.

BSkyB:

- is 38 per cent owned by News Corporation, the company founded by media giant Rupert Murdoch
- bought a 17.9 per cent stake in ITV in 2006.

Virgin:

- is owned by Virgin Media Television
- channels include LIVING, LIVING2, Bravo, Bravo 2, Challenge, Trouble and Virgin1.

Activity: Super indies

When an independent production company has been commissioned by a broadcaster to produce a programme or a series, its logo is usually displayed with the end credits. Many independent production companies have been taken over by larger companies known as 'super indies', such as:

- IMG Media – Tiger Aspect Productions, Darlow Smithson Productions, Tigress Productions
- All3Media UK – North One, Objective, Maverick, Lion, Company, Cactus, Bentley, Lime.

Find out the names of the production companies owned by the following super indies:

- Endemol UK
- RDF Media Group.

The main players in the film industry

Film industry companies work in production, distribution and exhibition. There are around 400 permanent companies in the UK film industry, with others created for a specific film. Approximately 43 per cent of these are in production, 13 per cent in distribution and the remaining 44 per cent are exhibition companies.

The UK

The UK industry makes independent feature films, as well as co-productions partnering the international film industry. Many successful British films have been distributed by a global distributor linked to a studio, such as *Slumdog Millionaire* (2008) which was distributed by Fox Searchlight.

In 2008, UK production activity was £578 million, down from £753 million in 2007. Films made in the UK with money from the USA included *Mamma Mia!*, *The Dark Knight* and *Quantum of Solace*.

Activity: The British film industry

Now take a look at the British film industry in a little more detail. You can carry out some research on the Internet or in trade journals and magazines. *Empire* is a good source of information and is very popular with film fanatics.

- How many films were released in Britain last year?

Choose one film made by a British company and find out:

- the budget and box office income for the film
- which company made it and how many people they employ
- which other films they have made, if any.

Worldwide

Many conglomerates own companies in a range of industries. This expansion of the conglomerates is a key element in your understanding of ownership in the television and film industries.

Table 1: Media conglomerates.

Studio	Owned by	Who also own
Warner Bros.	Time Warner	CNN New Line Cinema AOL (the Internet provider) Home Box Office
Paramount	Viacom	MTV Blockbuster
20th Century Fox	News International	BSkyB *The Times* Mushroom Records Star television
Columbia	Sony	hardware Sony Music
Universal	Vivendi	Canal+ Seagrams Connex trains

Professional organisations

The British film and television industries are supported by a range of organisations. These will be useful sources for your research and for information about employment opportunities.

The **British Film Institute** (BFI) supports cinemas, festivals, publications and educational resources about film; and runs the UK's biggest film archive (www.bfi.org.uk).

The **Broadcasters' Audience Research Board** (BARB) provides the official statistics for weekly UK television audiences used throughout the industry (www.barb.co.uk).

Skillset (the Sector Skills Council for Creative Media) supports skills and training in the UK creative media industries (www.skillset.org).

The **UK Film Council** develops and supports film in Britain at all levels. It provides funding for Skillset (www.ukfilmcouncil.org.uk).

Activity: Television ratings

The number of viewers a television programme attracts is very important. If the ratings are lower than expected, a television programme is unlikely to be back for another series. Audience size is often linked to what advertisers will pay for a slot in a particular programme.

- Look at the BARB website and find the programme ratings for last week. How do the top-rated programmes compare with your own viewing preferences?

- What do you think happens to programmes which have very low or very high ratings?

- How does BARB measure television programme audiences?

Working in the television and film industries

This section of the chapter is relevant to Unit 8, LO2 and LO5.

Who works in film and television?

Film

There are many job roles and areas of work within the film industry. If you are hoping to gain employment in this industry you need to know where those opportunities lie. Statistics published by Skillset show that around 30,200 people work in the film industry in the UK. The majority (59 per cent) are in exhibition (cinemas), with a third (37 per cent) in production and the remaining 4 per cent in distribution. About 89 per cent of film production crew are freelancers, and 41 per cent of the workforce are women. Around 6 per cent of people in the film industry are from a Black, Asian or Minority Ethnic (BAME) background.

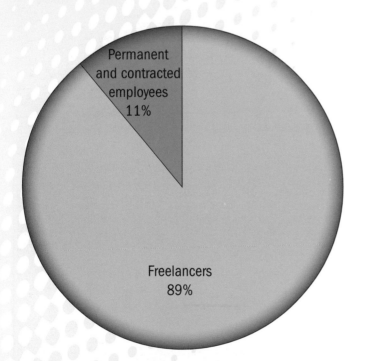

Figure 1: Why do you think such a high percentage of film production crew are freelancers?

Television

Skillset's Employment Census 2009 estimates that 50,100 people work in television, around three in ten of whom are freelance (28 per cent). However, this varies according to the type of work. In independent production companies 44 per cent are freelancers, compared to 19 per cent in terrestrial television and 11 per cent in cable and satellite television companies. Women make up 41 per cent of the television workforce, ethnic minorities 9 per cent.

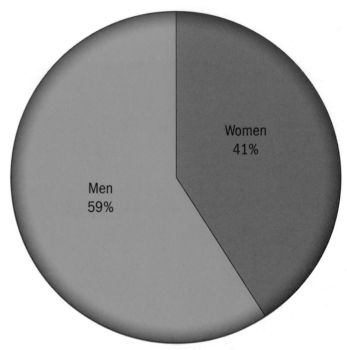

Figure 2: Why do you think that a relatively low percentage of women work in the television industry?

Many more people work in the wider media industries, sometimes using similar skills; for example, editing video for websites can relate to editing for television and film.

Job roles and contracts

Jobs in the television and film industries span creative and technical roles. Below are some of the most common job roles.

Table 2: Job roles in the television and film industries.

Runner	Responsible for a huge range of jobs, usually quite straightforward, such as stopping traffic during production and fetching items from props; requires complete reliability and the ability to use initiative and follow instructions precisely. The main entry point to the film industry.
Researcher	Often develops ideas for television programmes, finding information or contacts to meet the programme's requirements, for the producers to decide next steps. An entry route into television.
Editor	Responsible for completing the production as a sequence of shots made from the rushes, dialogue, sound effects and graphics.
Director	The driving artistic force behind the production. Directs both the crew and cast or presenters as to how they want a section to look or scene to be played. Typically directs actors or participants and shot composition, alongside casting, script editing, and working with the editor.
Floor manager	Liaison between the director and the studio floor; manages the studio, cast, crew, audience and all safety and fire precautions.
Location manager	Responsible for finding, selecting and finalising locations.
Director of photography (DP) or cinematographer	Responsible for the process of filming a scene as the director intends it to look. The role includes choosing cameras, lenses and the type of film stock to be used. DPs also design and select the lighting, and work with the director on shot composition.
Camera operator	Operates the camera to the specifications required by the director. Freelance camera operators often provide their own camera on a small-scale shoot.
Sound designer	In charge of the whole film soundtrack; responsible for designing and overseeing or creating all the audio elements.
Sound editor	Performs editing on the soundtrack.
Sound mixer	The audio engineer who performs the sound mix in post-production.
Sound recordist	Responsible for operating the audio recording equipment on a set.
Producer	In charge of a media production in all matters except for the creative efforts of the director; makes a production happen; responsible for raising finance and hiring key crew members, including the director.
Executive producer	Responsible for the overall production; might handle financial, business and legal matters.
Line producer	Responsible for managing and coordinating the production; managing human, technical and financial resources efficiently.
Designer	Responsible for the art department which designs and builds sets, as well as the work of the props, costume, hair and make-up specialists.

Other areas, such as transport, catering and construction, which the general public does not always associate with film making, are each essential to the television and film industry.

Activity: Applying for jobs in the industry

- What kind of contract are people in each of the job roles in Table 2 usually employed under?

- Find job advertisements for a selection of roles that interest you. What skills and qualifications are needed?

- Write an application letter for one of them.

You may find the following websites useful.

Broadcast magazine: http://info.broadcastnow.co.uk

The UK Film Council: www.ukfilmcouncil.org.uk

Skillset (the Sector Skills Council for Creative Media): www.skillset.org

A forum on filmmaking; Shooting People: https://shootingpeople.org

PLTS

Researching roles and contractual details will help develop your skills as an **independent enquirer**.

Preparing your own career development materials will help develop your skills as a **reflective learner**.

Activity: Specialism and multi-skilling in television

The pressure for companies to produce television more cheaply has encouraged some organisations to develop multi-skilled staff, who fulfil more than one job role, such as shooting and editing material, presenting and editing a piece, or acting as both researcher and sound recordist. As digital equipment has become light and easy to use, very small crews are possible. This, combined with multi-skilling, means that fewer people need to be employed, saving costs.

However, some argue that if you don't use skilled specialists, the quality of productions goes down. Major drama productions, where the quality is key, continue to use specialists in key roles.

Make a mindmap showing the advantages and disadvantages of using multi-skilled staff in television and film production.

Getting into the television and film industry
Getting started

You will need to be proactive to find a way to break into the television or film industry, and find opportunities to gain work experience, arrange visits and develop contacts. You could:

- ask to visit a company in a branch of the industry which interests you

- ask someone you have met through your course if they can offer work experience or an industry visit

- keep in touch with any organisation where you have had work experience, for any further opportunities

- do unpaid work experience at a local company

- offer your services at charity events or local events.

Activity: Gaining experience

Many people begin their careers by working unpaid on a low-budget production, or at a local company. This can be a good way to gain experience and make contacts.

Find out about a range of paid and unpaid work opportunities on the following websites.

BBC: www.bbc.co.uk/jobs (includes radio, television and BBC Worldwide)

The Grapevine: www.grapevinejobs.com (jobs in broadcast and media)

Mandy's: www.mandy.com (film and television production resources)

What one-off local events might offer you an opportunity for work experience?

Case study: Rufus, media student

I was lucky enough to get two days' work experience during the filming of an episode of a BBC series. I was on the set with the sound department. Often I simply observed and learned from the cast and crew who were kind enough to share their knowledge of the industry. I was able to work as a sound assistant at certain points. The first sound assistant took me under his wing and told me how he got into the industry. He advised me to get as many placements as I could and, above all, always to be reliable.

1. What would you hope to get out of work experience and how can you make the most of any such opportunity?
2. What questions would you ask of anyone working in the industry?
3. How can you demonstrate reliability?

Showreels

When you apply for work or a placement, you will need a showreel which contains a selection of your best work. It will demonstrate to prospective employers, clients and interviewers your professional expertise in editing and graphics, so it should be professionally presented, showing a range of your productions and skills. The showreel should run for about five to eight minutes, containing clips or complete pieces if they are no more than about two minutes. If in doubt, keep it short.

Aim for a consistent style, preferably with linking audio sequences. Edit the showreel on to DVD and make a compressed version which will work on a website. You could also provide a link to a MySpace page or similar.

Use graphics at the start to introduce yourself and the course on which the work was produced. Linking graphics (inter titles) between each piece should give the title, genre and date of the work, and your role. At the end, provide contact details and your website address, if you have one.

PLTS

Developing your showreel will help develop you skills as a **creative thinker** and a **self-manager**.

Activity: Analysing your skills

Imagine you are looking for work in your chosen field. You will need to analyse the skills you already have that would help you gain that dream job. You also need to think of an effective way to 'advertise' yourself, highlighting the skills and attributes you can offer.

- What skills do you already have, and how do you hope to develop them further?
- Produce a showreel, portfolio or personal website.

PLTS

Assessing your skills development needs will help develop your skills as a **reflective learner**.

Case study: What makes a good CV?

Greg Browning, television producer, offers his views.

Style
I run a creative company so how things look is important to me. It's hard to read a CV if it's visually offensive. Keep it very simple, wonderfully neat and, above all, clear. Avoid over styling (it just distracts from the information I am trying to find).

Precision
A CV should be concise. Two sides of A4 is usually enough. Outline your previous roles, what you were actually doing rather than the job title. A short, sharp personal statement gives me a sense of your career direction. Finally, grammar matters. Get it right!

Unique
Every CV should be tailored to the job that you are applying for. If you are applying for an edit assistant's job, then I mainly want to know about your editing experience.

Sparkle
Once I'm satisfied you can do the job and are worth interviewing, I'm looking for something about your personality. The creative industries are largely very people driven and you will almost certainly need to be a good team player, a hard worker and passionate about your career. I want to feel that a CV is infused with your character.

1. Produce (or revise) your CV in the light of this advice.
2. Try creating different versions aimed at different job roles.

Producing a television or film sequence

This section of the chapter is relevant to Unit 8, LO3, and Unit 16, LO1, LO2 and LO3.

Editing as part of the production process

Pre-production, production and post-production in the film and television context involve the stages outlined below.

Pre-production

- Ideas generation and research
- Allocation of roles
- Decide format for output: DVD, online, HD
- Create proposal/treatment
- Pitch ideas and gain client response (amend as required)
- Devise script
- Produce storyboard
- Location recce/casting/props/costume/crew
- Risk assessment
- Budget and contingency planning
- Production schedule/shooting schedule
- Book equipment, actors, interviewees, crew

Production

- Location/studio shooting
- Review and log footage prior to editing
- Reshoot footage as and if required (as per contingency)

Post-production

- Use the script to make a timeline of the desired scenes with brief descriptions
- Consider the themes, audience and look; running time will determine how much you can include
- Make an edit decision list; upload selected sequences
- Edit a rough cut
- Work on changes agreed with director or client
- Lay down main audio tracks
- Rhythm and pace: vary the length of shots to create interest and match the soundtrack
- Work on the transitions between shots
- Audio mixing
- Graphics and titles
- Final cut of the film

Figure 3: The stages of the production process.

This section of the chapter gives an overview of just the editing part of the process, since this is the focus of your specialist mandatory unit: Unit 16, Film and video editing techniques.

What is editing?

Editing is the creative and technical process of building up filmed sequences from the footage captured. In all productions, the editor needs a sense of rhythm and timing in story telling, imagination, and an understanding of how editing conventions create narrative, as well as patience, attention to detail, organisational skills and technical skills in the use of editing applications such as Final Cut and Premiere.

In the early days of cinema a single camera followed the action. Later came the idea that the audience might see the action from different points of view. In a car chase, for example, we might see events from the chasing driver's point of view, the rear-view mirror of the driver being chased, a helicopter shot showing both cars, a camera on a car bonnet showing the drivers' faces, and one placed in the passenger seat. The editor can edit these points of view together, controlling time and place, making the sequence last 20 seconds or 5 minutes, and making the audience feel different emotions, and sympathise with one character or another.

Editing can take audiences to different times using flashbacks and flashforwards, and to different places, with the characters first in one setting and moments later in another. This is not perceived as unrealistic, but simply a convention of telling stories on screen.

Editing is about deciding to leave in or cut out material. Good editing withholds information until the right moment, giving the audience information as they need it, without spoiling the ending. An event such as a football match can be reduced to highlights of just a few minutes. Sometimes it is easy to identify the important bits. At other times, your decisions are bound up with issues of representation.

Can what we see on the screen ever be 'the truth'?

Editing conventions

Audiences are familiar with many editing conventions which achieve particular effects. For example, when a scene fades to black, and then fades up again, we understand that time has passed. Some of the most common and most useful techniques are discussed below.

Continuity editing

This seamless editing style shows the action from several points of view in an unrealistic timescale. You might see a person walk towards a door, a close-up of their hand turning the handle, followed by a shot of the door opening in the next room. Such sequences are usually cut so that the timing fits our expectations of how long events last. One unrealistic convention that we accept is the number of points of view from which we see the action. We also need each shot to be from a distinctly different angle from the previous shot, otherwise we get a 'jump cut' which disrupts the continuity effect.

The '180-degree rule' or 'crossing the line'

In a shot where two people are talking, imagine a line running between them. You can film from anywhere you like, as long as the camera stays on the same side of this line. If you 'cross the line', the people appear to have switched places. A good example of this is a football match. You would place the cameras to ensure that the teams look as if they are playing in the same direction in all the shots in a sequence.

Cutaways

In a scene with two characters talking the editor may 'cut away' from their dialogue to a shot of a prop, such as a clock, to point out something significant to the audience.

The Kuleshov effect

In the 1920s Russian film maker Lev Kuleshov investigated how audiences make sense of what they see on screen. In one experiment, he spliced together shots that had been taken in different places at different times. The audience members created whole narratives by making connections in their minds between the shots. For example, if they saw a shot of an actor looking into the distance, and then a shot of a building, they understood that the actor was looking at a building. This showed that film makers could use shots taken miles apart and imply that they were in the same place.

Montage

Kuleshov's theory is linked to 'montage' editing, where a sequence of shots create a meaning without being linked to a timescale. The shots could, for example, create a 'day in the life' of a character compressed down to 30 seconds. Often montages are linked to a soundtrack which either fits or clashes with the images.

Cutting to the beat

Often music soundtracks are laid down first, then clips are trimmed on the timeline to fit the music. 'Cutting to the beat' is very common in music videos but is also used in television and film. Look out for examples where something on the soundtrack 'motivates' an edit. For example, we see two people talking, we hear a door opening, and cut to a shot of the door.

Pip Heywood
Film editor

As an editor the main thing you are doing is telling a story. This is true of drama and documentary. Your first task is to draw the story into a whole, and the way you edit needs to enhance this. The content of the film should dictate the style you use.

For a music video, style is obviously important. You can have a lot of fun with the special effects tools. But if you're making a film about a city, why have the clouds whizz by in a time-lapse if it has nothing to do with the story? It's just distracting.

I don't spend a lot of time labelling or re-arranging all the footage before I start an edit. I start cutting very early. If there's a long interview, or a bunch of landscape shots, I'll clip bits onto the timeline as a sequence straight away, and then have a bin of first cuts labelled 'landscapes', or 'Joe's interview first selects'. When you cut you start to know the footage and immediately start having an editor's relationship with the material. Also, with 'match frame' and 'find bin', you can, at any time, refer back to the original footage to see what else is there. And you've saved yourself hours of tedious labelling at the beginning!

It's important to set yourself deadlines, and work really hard to meet them. If you don't, you'll go on hour after hour being too close to the film. Put something together and then stop and view it. You're trying to see it as a viewer who watches it only once will see it, so you need to stand back.

A film often works much better if it's allowed to 'breathe'. Don't be afraid to linger on a shot, have some space between the words. The viewer needs time to absorb the story – it's all about the story.

Think about it!

- What are the advantages of cutting and sorting your footage at the earliest stages?

- Think of one of your own practical productions. Does it need more room to 'breathe'? Are there any distracting effects that you would consider editing out?

Activity: Using an appropriate output

At the end of an edit, you will need to export your production according to the end use of the piece. Will the production be on DVD which will require high quality, or HD which will be even higher? On the other hand, videos used on the Internet need to be small files which can be downloaded quickly by the viewer, and quality is not so important as having a small 'compressed' file.

Investigate how image quality, file type and file size are connected. What kind of output is appropriate for each different kind of end use?

The law, contracts and ethical issues

For any production, you need to consider the relevant legal, contractual and ethical issues. If a production company fails to follow good practice, it could break the law or a code of practice by mistake, and could end up in court. Producers, their crew and even learners and people on work experience need to be aware of the legal and ethical obligations that apply to their work.

Legal issues

The following areas of law, among others, commonly apply to film and television production work.

Libel law – you can be sued for damages if you publish things about a person which are untrue and damage their reputation (defame them).

Discrimination legislation – discrimination on grounds of race, gender and age are illegal. This is likely to be a consideration when employing staff, cast and crew and when individuals, groups and related issues are depicted on screen.

Obscenity – lawyers may be needed to check whether a production breaks obscenity law. This can depend on factors like the age range of the audience and the time a production is broadcast.

Data protection – storing certain information about people without their permission is illegal and there are rules about what you can use it for. Any records you hold about a person can be accessed by them.

Codes of practice and regulators

Codes of practice are not actually part of the law. They exist usually to protect the consumer or the citizen and have a powerful role in television and film. Significant regulators and their codes of practice for UK television and film include the following.

The **Office of Communications (Ofcom)** is Britain's media regulator. Ofcom's Broadcasting Code sets standards for British broadcasting (www.ofcom.org.uk).

The **BBC** has its own Code of Practice, and also issues its own production guidelines for the programmes it commissions (www.bbc.co.uk).

The **British Board of Film Classification (bbfc)** is an independent body which classifies films and videos in terms of age suitability (www.bbfc.co.uk).

Activity: Regulation

1. Look at the principal summaries for Ofcom's Broadcasting Code guidelines on each of the following topics:
   - protecting the under-18s
   - harm and offence
   - crime
   - religion
   - due impartiality and due accuracy
   - fairness
   - privacy
   - sponsorship.
2. Use the bbfc website to look at recent classification decisions for three feature films. What are the reasons for the ratings given?

Ethical issues

Ethical issues arise everywhere, from protecting sources in journalism to running television competitions, and sometimes overlap with legal issues and codes of practice. Doing the wrong thing could easily land you or your company in trouble. Examples include:

- intruding on individual privacy – when might it be in the public interest?
- running premium rate telephone votes and competitions

- presenting an individual or their views as representative of an entire group of people
- using hidden cameras and microphones – when is it acceptable to record people without their knowledge?
- interviewing vulnerable people, such as children or people in hospital
- using information given in confidence.

What issues would you need to consider if you were planning to film in a school?

Copyright

Copyright issues were discussed in Unit 1, Pre-production techniques for the creative media industries. As a reminder, media producers at all levels need to avoid ending up in legal dispute by using someone else's work in a production without permission. If you want to use copyright material in your productions, you must seek permission and pay any fees required.

Activity: Intellectual property (IP)

The Internet has made intellectual property (IP) a huge issue, for example the unauthorised use of copyright material on YouTube and illegal video downloads.

- What is the current situation with YouTube and/or video downloads and the protection of the IP of television and film makers?
- Research and produce a six bullet-point summary of advice for people wanting to prevent unauthorised screening of a video they have made.

Contracts

As well as being aware of legal issues relating to professional practice in the film and television industry, you need to be aware of legal agreements that relate to your own terms of employment in the form of contracts. If you are offered any contract, read it carefully. You need to be clear about:

- what you are being asked to do
- when you will be required to work
- what payment you will receive
- what is included and what is not.

The professional organisations listed below may be able to offer advice on contracts in the film and television industries.

The Broadcasting Entertainment Cinematograph and Theatre Union (BECTU) is the trade union for people working in broadcasting, film and interactive media. It represents permanently employed, contract and freelance workers (www.bectu.org.uk).

The **Intellectual Property Office** provides information on copyright and other forms of IP protection (www.ipo.gov.uk).

Pact is the UK trade association representing and promoting the commercial interests of independent feature film, television, digital, children's and animation media companies (www.pact.co.uk).

Skillset is the Sector Skills Council for Creative Media (www.skillset.org).

Activity: Contracts

A contract of employment will typically have 'small print'. You will need to scrutinise any clauses (short paragraphs) to check you understand the implications of what you are signing.

Confidentiality clauses and exclusivity clauses are common in film and television industry contracts. Find out what these mean.

PLTS

Describing contractual, ethical and legal obligations using appropriate subject terminology will help develop your skills as an **independent enquirer**.

What checks does your school or college's health and safety policy require for your practical productions?

Developing technologies in television and film

This section of the chapter is relevant to Unit 8, LO4.

Once there was a clear division between such media platforms as television, computers and mobile phones. Now they overlap more and more.

In the 1970s there were just three television channels. If you missed a programme, you missed it, unless it was repeated. Video recorders, introduced in the 1980s, enabled people to record programmes to watch when they wanted. By the early 1990s there were five channels and BSkyB had just started.

You can now watch television and film on a number of platforms: terrestrial television, cable, satellite, DVD, digital television, recorded on DVD or Sky Plus, on a home computer, or on a mobile phone. Many people also interact with a programme or film by telephone voting, playing online games or contacting websites and discussion forums. An important concept for production companies and broadcasters is '360-degree commissioning', where a broadcaster no longer simply commissions a new programme, but also looks for ways to use this new 'content' across a range of platforms.

Since 2006, developments in technology have been good for:

- Google™
- pirates
- major studios
- talent – actors or presenters who have appeared in a range of formats
- BSkyB
- companies who produce content which appeals to audiences.

However, they have been difficult for:

- traditional television channels (especially ITV, C4, Five)
- the British film industry
- newspapers, especially in their print form
- regulators: it's much harder to police a multi-platform world.

Activity: Technological advances

Find reasons why developments in technology have been good for some companies but bad for others.

Did you know?

The impact of digital technology on television and film

- There are over 400 television channels available in the UK.
- There are over nine million Freeview connections.
- Digital television is available in 86 per cent of homes.
- PVRs are available in 20 per cent of homes.
- Fifty-seven per cent of homes have broadband.

The future

'Push and pull' viewing: old style television schedules relied on 'pushing' programmes at you. Going online and choosing content to watch is an example of 'pulling'.

It is predicted that the UK population will be online for four hours a day in the future, but many will still watch network television.

Lee Stephens

Director

Action Image Productions (www.actionimageproductions.com) is an independent video production company offering clients a range of services from concept development, scripting and filming to editing and motion graphics.

Each day is different due to the variety of work: one day we may be out filming and directing for a client, the next could be sitting at one of the edit stations. While not as glamorous, running a business requires lots of other activities, like client meetings, general administration or accounts!

This industry tends to work at a freelance level, and for any production we will hire in extra people with skills we need on a production. These could include camera crew, sound engineers, voice-overs, editors or production assistants through to actors and production managers.

I came into this role following a long-standing interest and passion for media. I'd spent some years in management in big companies. About five years ago I decided to leave the corporate world and set up my own company. The company has grown and I've never looked back.

I totally love what I do and I'm not afraid to put in more effort than I get paid for. I aim to deliver a production which the client loves and if possible to exceed their expectations. Being your own boss or being responsible for others can be lonely and stressful sometimes but there are many good moments.

The career route I recommend is to work your way up and find opportunities to get experience. Training is a great way to get skills and understanding, but also make a great showreel and get references from your work placements. I would always prefer to employ individuals who have demonstrable skills and enthusiasm.

Think about it!

- What do you think you would most enjoy about working in the film and television industry?
- What do you think you would find stressful or challenging?
- Do you feel you would be well suited to working in the industry?

Just checking

1. What are the pros and cons of a multi-skilled workforce?
2. What legal and ethical issues would apply to broadcasting a television talent show involving an audience telephone vote?
3. What makes a good showreel?
4. Do you know how to:
   - import footage?
   - label it and organise bins?
   - cut and trim sequences and clips?
   - produce on-screen text?
   - work with on-screen graphics?
   - edit and sync soundtracks?
   - use effects?
   - export an edit in different formats?

edexcel :::

Assignment tips

- Use the technical vocabulary of the industry appropriately and confidently in your assignments.

- Make sure any written work is neat and methodical, and check carefully for any errors.

- Use carefully chosen examples to justify, illustrate and explain the points you make in your written work. If you hope to achieve the highest grades, it is not enough simply to mention an example. You need to explain the relevance of your examples and use them to support your points, and demonstrate that you have carefully researched and understood the issues.

- Keep a thorough log of your practical production work, including any changes you make, and why. The highest grades will be awarded for reflective work showing the ability to make well-judged decisions. You will need to explain your decisions, demonstrating an excellent understanding of the relevant technical and professional issues.

- Present your practical work as professionally as possible. The highest grades will be awarded for work that shows flair, creativity and the ability to work independently at near-professional standards.

Radio

The radio industry is a vibrant and expanding area of the media, comprising four main sectors: national (public) radio (the BBC), independent radio (commercial), not-for-profit radio (community, student and hospital radio) and independent radio programme production companies that make radio programmes to commission. The BBC and commercial stations operate at national, regional and local levels.

Job roles in the radio industry include presenter, contributor, continuity announcer, newsreader, journalist, technician, producer, editor, commercial sales, network controller, station manager and many more.

This chapter provides an overview which will support your work on the two mandatory radio industry pathway units: Unit 9, Understanding the radio industry and Unit 17, Audio production processes and techniques.

The first section of this chapter provides an introduction to the UK radio industry. The next section looks at working in radio and helps you to prepare for your radio career. This section also introduces the legal and ethical constraints with which broadcasters and producers of radio programmes must comply. The focus is then on programme making. This will help you to develop your knowledge and understanding of the important processes and areas of technology and technical production skills that are used in radio programme making. The last section outlines the developing technologies that bring radio to its audiences.

This chapter is designed to give you an overview of the radio industry and the types of skills you will need for this pathway. You will find details of the learning outcomes and the assessment and grading criteria for the Radio pathway on pages 253–255. Unit 17 is mandatory for both the Radio and Sound recording pathways, so you may also find it useful to look at the Sound recording pathway.

Chris, getting started in radio

After studying a BTEC National Diploma in Media Production, I went on to become a radio broadcaster working in mainstream radio.

As a student, I was really keen to find a way into the radio industry. I arranged a visit to my local hospital station, and offered to do anything for them for free so I could get a foothold and get known. Getting involved with that, I realised that there are a whole lot of other jobs, besides being a presenter, that I find very interesting.

As I listened to a wide range of stations and programmes to find out what they broadcast, I discovered there's much more to radio than just being a 'jock' and playing music.

Getting to know about the radio industry as a whole, and not just the part that I was first interested in, really helped me later on when I applied for my first job and when I moved from one station to another.

Over to you!

- What aspects of the Radio pathway are you most interested in?
- Which other areas of radio would you like to know more about?

The UK radio industry

This section of the chapter is relevant to Unit 9, LO1.

Set up

UK radio stations

How many radio stations can you think of?

Make a list and then try to categorise them under the following headings:

- BBC local
- BBC national
- commercial local
- commercial national.

Who owns the UK radio industry?

The UK radio industry is very tightly regulated in its structure and output. This section outlines the structure of the UK radio industry, the range of job roles, how the radio industry is regulated, changing radio technology and how to prepare for employment in the industry.

Commercial (independent) radio

You will recognise independent or commercial radio by the advertisements which take up a significant part of the time, as much as 12 minutes in every hour. The income from selling advertising space, or 'air time', is used to pay the station's staffing and running costs, and to generate profits for its owners and shareholders. Commercial radio stations also have to pay the government for their broadcasting licence, usually millions of pounds each year according to their income. Licences are awarded every five years by Ofcom, the media regulator. It is illegal to broadcast over the airwaves without a licence.

National public radio

Otherwise known as the BBC, this was the first and continues to be the biggest mass media radio form in the world. Starting in 1922 as the British Broadcasting Company, it became a Corporation by royal charter in 1927. It is an autonomous public corporation independent of private or government influence, run by a trust and managed by a director general. The BBC is financed primarily from a government 'tax' in the form of a licence fee paid by all households that receive, by whatever means (terrestrial, satellite or cable), any television signals (whether broadcast by the BBC or not) for viewing or recording at the scheduled time of transmission. Other income comes from a direct government grant (for the World Service) and income from commercial business media sales and services both in the UK and abroad. BBC radio programmes are made partly in house and partly by approved independent radio production companies.

Not-for-profit radio

Many small radio stations operate on a not-for-profit basis. Many hospitals have their own radio station. Your school, college or university may have a student radio station. Community radio is the fastest rising group of small-scale radio stations, with over 250 stations licensed by Ofcom in 2009. They are operated by volunteers and can only use advertising to generate income if this does not affect a commercial station in the same area.

Activity: Comparing commercial, national and not-for-profit radio stations

Listen to programmes on a range of commercial radio, national public radio and not-for-profit radio stations and answer the questions below. You will need to consult *The Radio Listeners' Guide* to research some of your answers.

- Which type of radio station uses advertising?
- Which stations just played music?
- Which stations used mainly speech?
- What was the difference between news bulletins on each station?
- How many years has each station been on air?
- Has any station changed its name?
- Which parent company owns each station?
- Does the parent company have interests in other media, such as television, newspapers, mobile phones?
- How is each radio station financed?

Independent radio programme production companies

Independent radio programme production companies are commissioned by their radio station clients to make programmes to order. The BBC has been by far the largest client of such independents, and invites approved independent companies to tender for the production of many of its radio programmes, especially drama and documentary. The target audience, duration, budget and broadcast date is usually fixed by the commissioner, but the initial research to establish style, content and cost is completed by the independent production companies, who then pitch their ideas and compete for the commission. As intelligent speech radio becomes more widespread and the monopoly held by BBC Radio 4 on such content is challenged, there is likely to be more high speech content programming and commissioning in the commercial radio sector.

Some independent radio production companies specialise in producing jingles for commercial radio stations and radio advertisements, which are commissioned by a wide range of businesses.

Activity: Independent production companies

Log on to the BBC website and find the network radio commissioning pages.

- Check out the commissioning process for two or three network radio stations.
- Locate the lists of independent production companies approved to make BBC radio programmes.
- Obtain a copy of the *Radio Times*. How many independent production companies can you find in the radio programme listings?
- Listen for the name of any independent production company in the credits at the end of radio programmes, particularly on BBC Radio 4.

PLTS

Researching organisation in the industry will help develop your skills as an **independent enquirer**.

Working in the radio industry

This section of the chapter is relevant to Unit 9, LO2 and LO5.

There are many job roles in the radio industry. They include news reporter, interviewer, researcher, script writer, presenter, radio journalist, producer, studio assistant, programme scheduler, commercial trafficker, audio/sound engineer, editor, station manager, air time salesperson, community training and volunteer support.

Theo Angelis
Independent radio station presenter

I studied the BTEC National Diploma in Media Production and developed a passion for playing dance music on radio. While I was studying I started helping out at my local commercial radio station on a Saturday afternoon. I got to know the staff and had the chance to edit the sports commentary and do other odd jobs.

When I finished my BTEC course I volunteered to work for nothing at the station, and learned all I could about presenting. One day the presenter of one of the programmes was ill, so I volunteered to stand in. The rest is history and now I'm a DJ presenter at a national commercial radio station.

Being a presenter can involve working very unsociable hours: late nights, early mornings, Saturdays and Sundays and even Christmas Day, so don't decide to do this unless you are prepared to work when all your friends are having fun! You must also like the music because you will be playing it all the time. You also have to answer emails from listeners, prepare your links between music tracks and carry out additional admin tasks as well.

Think about it!

- What kind of administrative tasks does the presenter have to do?
- Share ideas with your group.

Working practices vary according to the type of job you want to do. All jobs in radio can involve working unsociable, irregular hours. Some require a range of skills, while others are dedicated to one task. Employment contracts can vary considerably. Details are outlined in the job description, person specification and terms and conditions of employment.

Activity: Researching jobs in radio

Explore the roles in radio that appeal to you by building a portfolio of job descriptions, person specifications and employment contracts for a range of jobs. You can find job ads in the jobs pages of these publications and websites:

- BBC – www.bbc.co.uk/jobs
- BBC – internal weekly newspaper, *Ariel*
- Broadcast magazine – www.broadcastnow.co.uk
- *Guardian* newspaper (Media section, Mondays) – www.guardian.co.uk/jobs
- Media UK – www.mediauk.com
- Media Week Online – www.mediaweekjobs.co.uk

Getting into radio

There is no recognised route into a job in radio. You will need to try any way possible. If you want to work in administration, sales or technical areas, it is likely to be easier to get a job than if you want to work as a presenter, where competition is very high.

You will find it useful to familiarise yourself with the services offered by a number of professional bodies which fulfil specific roles in the radio industry:

- Skillset (the Sector Skills Council for Creative Media)
- NUJ (National Union of Journalists)
- Equity (Actors Union)
- MU (Musicians' Union)
- NAB (National Association of Broadcasters)
- CRCA (RadioCentre)
- CMA (Community Media Association).

Activity: Radio industry bodies

Visit the websites of these professional bodies to find out the function of each in relation to the radio industry. How can they help you in finding a job in radio?

Doing any job effectively requires training. You may be able to get this in the form of voluntary work at one of the hundreds of not-for-profit radio stations while you continue with your BTEC course.

Activity: Finding opportunities for training in radio

Use the *Radio Listeners' Guide*, the *Guardian Media Guide* or *Media 08* to find your nearest local hospital radio and community radio stations. Does your school, college or nearest university have a student radio station? Is there a local special events radio station?

Ask if you can do voluntary work at any of the stations you identify.

Tips

- Do your research: listen to the station you are applying to, and be sure of their style and output.
- Write or email politely, not forgetting to check your spelling – first impressions are vital!
- If you cannot do regular voluntary work, try to arrange at least a visit.
- Get your demo disc made.
- Send it to the station with your CV and a covering letter.

PLTS

Researching job opportunities will help develop your skills as an **independent enquirer**.

Voluntary work at a radio station could eventually lead to the offer of a paid job, or you might make personal contacts who can help you to find work. In any case, it will give you valuable hands-on experience.

When you apply for a job, whether paid or voluntary, you need to prepare your application carefully. You will need **demo material** that demonstrates your skills, and an up-to-date **curriculum vitae (CV)**.

Demo material is a sample of work to demonstrate your practical skills, whether as a presenter, a technician, a journalist or writer, or in some other role; for example including specimens of news reading, introducing and back-crediting music tracks, interviewing, chairing a discussion, reading sports results, continuity linking two programmes, reading weather forecasts, traffic news, scripted speech and so on. If you are **continuity** announcing, it means that you should read 'on air' script that you have written yourself to inform listeners what programme they have just heard and what programme they are about to hear, and to introduce trails for other programmes.

A presenter ensures that speech packages and clips in individual programmes are broadcast in sequence and with no noticeable interruption.

Your CV should summarise your education and qualifications, any paid or voluntary work experience, and the names and contact details of your referees.

Key terms

Demo material – a sample of work to demonstrate your practical skills, whether as a presenter, a technician, a journalist or writer, or in some other role.

Curriculum vitae (CV) – a summary of your education and qualifications, any paid or voluntary work experience, and the names and contact details of referees.

Continuity – ensuring that sequences in individual programmes and programmes in a schedule are broadcast in sequence and with no noticeable interruption.

Activity: Preparing job applications

Prepare the following ready for a job application (use one from your portfolio of job specs):

- demo material (for example, on CD, podcast or via MySpace)
- your CV
- a letter of application giving evidence of how you fit the job description and person specification of a particular job.

PLTS

Producing your career development materials will help develop your skills as an **independent enquirer**, a **creative thinker** and a **self-manager**.

Developing your career in radio

You have secured your first job in radio, but it is not time to relax yet. You need to find ways to advance your career. First jobs in radio tend to be at the lower end of the scale, but you can gain promotion as your skills improve with experience and further training, and through contacts you make through networking.

Case study: Neeta's career development

Although I'm delighted to have my first job in radio – presenting the late-night music programme from 2am to 6am on a small local station – it can be very lonely. I never see my friends, as I am always sleeping or working while they're out having fun, and I'm desperate to get a promotion to a breakfast show or drive-time slot. I've been taking up any on-the-job training going, and I do make an effort to get to know everyone and try to get myself noticed. I've also enrolled for another qualification, studying part-time.

1. What other ways can you think of to develop your career?

Think about it

Collect examples of different radio stations and their styles to build up your own audio library. This will:

- build your awareness of the vast range of radio output
- develop your insight into what constitutes good radio
- help you to decide what type of station you want to work for
- provide a range of reference sources to help with research for new productions.

Radio, ethics and the law

Working successfully in the radio industry is not only a matter of acquiring and using technical knowledge and skills. Whatever your role in the radio industry, you will also need to be familiar with a range of legal and ethical restrictions that apply to all radio broadcasting in the UK.

Radio and the law

Everything broadcast on radio must comply with radio broadcasting standards. The following organisations regulate the radio broadcasting industry in the UK:

- Ofcom – Office of Communications
- CRCA – RadioCentre (formerly Commercial Radio Companies Association)
- ASA – Advertising Standards Authority
- PRS for Music – Performing Rights Society and Mechanical Copyright Protection Society.

Activity: The regulators

Use the websites of these regulators to answer the following questions.

- Which media sectors does each body regulate?
- Which aspects of radio broadcasting does each body regulate?
- How does each body enforce its regulatory powers?
- What are the consequences of not adhering to each regulator's rules and codes of practice?

If you want to work in radio you need to be aware of the wide range of legislation that affects your work.

Defamation is saying or writing something about someone that is not true and that damages their reputation. If you defame someone, they may sue you. The person must still be alive for a statement to be defamatory. Celebrities often have defamatory statements made about them and some famous people have been successful in suing for damages when this has happened.

Libel is writing or recording something false and damaging about someone and is a form of defamation.

Slander is saying something false and damaging about someone and is a form of defamation.

Equality laws prevent anyone from taking advantage of – or discriminating against – someone on grounds of their race, sexual orientation, gender or age. These include the **Race Relations Act** and the **Age Discrimination Act**.

Privacy laws prevent journalists from publicising private facts about individuals, unless it can be proved that knowing the fact is in the public interest.

The Data Protection Act prevents any confidential information or data held on electronic computer files being distributed without the permission of the person concerned.

The Freedom of Information Act allows an individual or a body to request access to information that is held on computer files by a professional organisation or government bodies. See www.direct.gov.uk for more information about the Acts mentioned above.

The Copyright Act and associated laws are very important to media producers. Copyright is held in most assets that are used as part of a media product, including music, words, recordings, archive footage, photographs or newsreel clips. A producer using such material in the making of a media product must seek permission from the copyright owner and pay them royalties. The main organisations that deal with copyright in music are PRS for Music (an alliance between PRS (Performing Rights Society) and MCPS (Mechanical Copyright Protection Society)) and PPL (Phonographic Performances Limited). See www.prsformusic.com and www.ppluk.com for more information.

The BBC Producer Guidelines are a comprehensive set of regulations that apply to any media product produced by the BBC for radio, television, merchandise or their website. They cover everything from programme content to the way in which the titles and credits are written, from programme running times to the technical quality of the media product. They are very complex and occupy hundreds of pages. See www.bbc.co.uk/guidelines for more information.

Activity: Legislation

Choose a few of the issues listed above and discuss how they might affect radio broadcasting.

Ethics

A radio broadcast must not deliberately offend or insult any listener, particularly if it refers to a minority or specific group of people. Jokes in poor taste, such as 'Sachsgate', where a respected actor received an on-air prank telephone call, are not ethical.

Activity: Unethical broadcasting

Find the 'Broadcast bulletin' on Ofcom's website, which provides details of complaints made about radio programmes.

Read five complaints about radio programmes. Summarise the reasons for each complaint and the regulator's findings in each case. Do you agree or disagree with each outcome?

Case study: Legal issues and production techniques

Alex, station manager

When a show is live, there are lots of legal issues to keep in mind. The usual copyright, performing rights and contractual things are taken care of when the programme is planned, but when you're live you just don't know what guests or people phoning in might say. It's really hard to make sure the broadcast doesn't contain anything that could get us prosecuted: defamatory remarks, slander of a living person, profanity, racist or sexist comments. Studio guests are warned about what they can and can't say on air, but sometimes, say in a phone-in, we use a time delay, which gives the presenter up to eight seconds to react and press the 'dump' button to prevent anything unsuitable from being broadcast. To be really safe, we might record part of the programme 'as-live' for later replay, which allows for editing as necessary.

1. How else could a radio station try to avoid broadcasting inappropriate live material?
2. Who is responsible for ensuring that a radio programme complies with the law?

How is a radio programme put together?

This section of the chapter is relevant to Unit 9, LO3, and Unit 17, LO1, LO2, LO3 and LO4.

The production process

All radio programmes are made by following a specific four-stage sequence of events called the production process (see Figure 1).

The third box of the production process flowchart below summarises a complex sequence of technical events. In Unit 17 of the Radio pathway you will focus in some detail on the technical skills that you will need if you intend to work in technical production in radio; that is, recording, editing, mixing and balancing sound for broadcast. The sub-sections that follow provide an overview of some of the main technical skills that you will learn about.

Initiation
The idea for the programme is first thought up, proposed, pitched and commissioned

Planning
The proposal is expanded into a treatment, contributors identified, content researched, scripted and schedules assembled

Production
The material is recorded, edited, mixed and balanced

Completion
The programme is exported to an appropriate format and packaged for distribution

Figure 1: Which stages do you know most and least about?

Recording sound

Did you know?

A sound has three different components. They are the 'attack', 'duration' and 'decay' (see Figure 2).

The attack is the time the sound takes from silence to reach its peak, the duration is the period of time the sound stays at its loudest and the decay is the time the sound takes to die down to silence. There is then a period of silence before the next sound. All sounds have these three components, but the environment in which a sound is generated will affect the attack and the decay to varying degrees. This information may also be useful if you are following the Sound recording pathway.

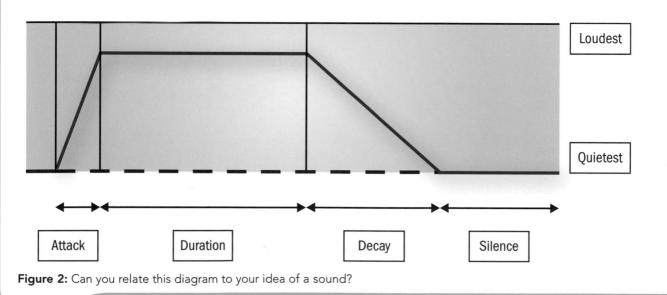

Loudest

Quietest

Attack | Duration | Decay | Silence

Figure 2: Can you relate this diagram to your idea of a sound?

Audio capture

Audio for a radio programme may be from the controlled environment of the studio, either live or pre-recorded, or from a location, most likely to be live. Each situation has its own complications.

- Studio audio includes pre-recorded music, commercials, trails, idents (identification jingles) and fillers (usually stored on a computer hard drive), live interviews, reading news and weather bulletins, continuity announcements, and so on.

- Location audio includes relaying live events and performances, live interviewing of the public, politicians and celebrities, and other situations with a live audience, some of whom may also be contributing.

Pre-recorded sources

The first main pre-recorded audio in a radio studio was on vinyl, tape cartridge and open reel tape. That was followed by CD, the disc cartridge 'Discart'™ and the DAT recorder. For a while the Minidisc™ superseded the DAT recorder. Now usual practice is to play all music, commercials, trails and links from a PC hard drive and record audio on location using a hard disc or flash drive portable recorder. (It is worth emphasising that MP3 and other compressed file formats are meant for domestic use.)

Some radio programmes are pre-recorded 'as live' and simply played out at the appropriate time. They are usually announced as such and in the light of misleading practice it has become unacceptable to offer a pre-recorded programme as being live. Some live material is deliberately recorded for later replay, such as sports highlights commentaries and programmes where content may need to be edited for legal reasons. Radio stations, particularly the BBC, hold large recordings libraries from which they can gather clips to illustrate issues raised in programme items.

Activity: Pre-recorded programme content

Using a radio listings magazine and the BBC radio website, list all the programmes that you think will use pre-recorded material, either speech or music.

Recording equipment

While hard disc and flash drive portable recorders are portable and are used for location recordings, the centre of any sound or radio studio is the mixing desk, which appropriately in the radio industry is known as the radio desk.

There are two important differences between a mixing desk used in a recording studio and the desk used in a radio studio: the master faders, and the choice of meters used to monitor the signal output of the desk. Radio desks do not usually have master faders unless they are production/mixing desks which have been adapted for use in a radio studio. In a recording studio, desks generally use VU (Volume Unit) meters and their optimum output level is between −4 and 0 db, while radio desks are fitted with PPM (Peak Programme Meters) with an optimum output of PPM 6, although this can vary from radio station to radio station.

- PPM – slow response, doesn't register initial peaks which the human ear can tolerate.

- VU meter – averages out short peaks and troughs to register the perceived loudness of a signal.

Case study: Cassie, radio engineer

We don't have master faders on a radio desk because the output of the desk is governed by the audio source that is playing. If you think about what you hear on the radio at any time, it's one music track, one voice, one pre-recorded programme, one commercial or one continuity announcement. The only time you hear more than one signal is during an interview (two microphones) or a discussion, but the protocol then is for the presenter or interviewer to make sure that only one person talks at a time.

1. Why is it desirable to hear only one voice at a time on radio?

2. Why do you think the volume on the radio stays the same regardless of who is speaking or what is playing?

The radio desk can have as many as 20 input signals but they are used individually so once the level of each is set there is no need for a final level to be adjusted. The signal is metered and monitored electronically to keep it the same so the listener does not have to keep adjusting the volume of their radio (or computer or iPod). In many radio stations the presenter, particularly in a music sequence, will 'drive' the desk themselves; that is, act as the technical operator as well.

Did you know?

When you make pre-recorded drama, discussion and other programmes using multiple sound sources, you use either a PC or a MAC workstation.

- It may be linked to a mixing desk.
- You may be using Pro Tools.
- You will be recording in stereo.
- The signals will be digital.

What skills will you need in order to drive a radio desk and present simultaneously?

What would you need to think about when setting up the studio for recording a radio drama?

Microphone types and characteristics

Your choice of microphone will depend on the particular purpose and type of audio to be captured.

The basic types of microphone are grouped according to method of construction, and polar response pattern, as shown in Table 1.

Table 1: Common microphone types by construction.

Polar response	Type	Construction	Purpose
Omni-directional	Dynamic Capacitor or condenser	(Rugged) Lavalier/tie clip Hand-held Pole-mounted Stand-mounted	On-location speech Reporting Speech Ambience
Uni-directional – cardiod Uni-directional – hyper-cardiod	Dynamic Capacitor or condenser	(Sturdy) Hand-held Pole-mounted Stand-mounted	Stage vocal Instrument Distant speech
Bi-directional/Figure of eight	Ribbon – noise-cancelling	(Fragile) Stand-mounted	Commentary Studio speech

Can you identify each of these microphones? For what purpose would each be used, for example, speech instrument, location, studio?

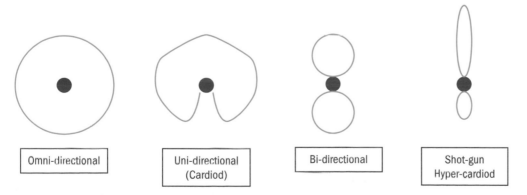

Omni-directional	Uni-directional (Cardiod)	Bi-directional	Shot-gun Hyper-cardiod

Figure 3: Can you see the ways in which different microphone types pick up sound?

Audio formats

Sound can be recorded in a number of formats, as shown in Table 2. It may help to clarify a few of the terms used in the table. **Compression** is a way of reducing the file size to take up less space. **Linear** file formats can only be accessed from the beginning of the file, as opposed to **non-linear** file formats, which may be accessed at any point on the time line.

Table 2: Audio formats.

File format	Player	File type	Linear/Non-linear
MP3	iPod	Compressed	Linear/non-linear
ATRAC (Adaptive Transform Acoustic Coding)	Minidisc™	Compressed	Linear
WAV (Waveform audio format)	Used by IBM and Microsoft on the PC platform	Uncompressed	Non-linear
AIFF (Audio Interleaved File Format)	Used by Amiga and Apple on the MAC platform. Used in Apple's iTunes, Garageband applications and can be played on iPods	Uncompressed	Non-linear
AIFF-C (Audio Interleaved File Format Compressed)	Used by Amiga and Apple on the MAC platform. Used in Apple's iTunes, Garageband applications and can be played on iPods	Compressed	Non-linear
CDDA (Compact Disc Digital Audio)	Playable in PC, Mac, CD and some DVD players	Uncompressed	Non-linear
OMFI (Open Media Framework Interchange)	Universal format for transferring files between multi-track recording systems. Multi-track formats that are supported include Cubase, Pro Tools, SADiE and Digital Performer	Uncompressed	Non-linear

Key terms

Compression – a means of reducing file size to accommodate more material.

Linear – files that can only be accessed from the beginning of the file.

Non-linear – files that may be accessed at any point on the time line.

Acoustics – the study of sound and the way it behaves in different environments.

Acoustics

When choosing a suitable environment in which to record sound, a number of factors must be taken into consideration according to whether it is an interior or an exterior location.

Where are you right now? In a classroom or at home in your own room? How does it sound? In some rooms you may notice an echo when you speak; in others it can be difficult to hear what someone is saying. This is because of the materials from which the walls, floor, ceiling and furniture are made, and the number of windows in the room. Some surfaces reflect sound; others absorb it. Studios, theatres, cinemas and other places where sound is produced professionally have specially prepared surfaces that either absorb or reflect sound according to what is required. The study of sound, the way it behaves in spaces and the way buildings are designed to modify this behaviour is called **acoustic** engineering and is a lucrative industry.

Did you know?

- Hard surfaces reflect sound: tiled bathrooms, bare walls, floorboards, vinyl.
- Soft surfaces absorb sound: carpeted floors, heavy drapes, sofas, upholstered furniture.

The walls, floors and ceilings of radio and sound studios are designed to ensure that the clearest untreated sound is produced. It is easy to add **reverberation** (a characteristic of sound in a reflective environment) and other effects to recorded sounds, but impossible to remove them from a recording. A 'live' room is used for recording vocals and instrumentals and has a fast decay time. A 'talks' studio will be very 'dead' in terms of its reverberation time, as will be the control room of a studio.

Activity: Interior acoustics

Wherever you are, sit quietly and listen for half a minute or so. What can you hear?

You may have thought the room was quiet but by concentrating you will probably hear sounds: a ticking clock, a humming computer fan or fridge motor, a gurgling radiator or the dull low sound of a television or music in another room.

This background noise is noise pollution. When recording, it is important to ensure that it is at an absolute minimum (unless you want to contextualise a sound in a particular location). That is why studios are provided with acoustic insulation.

Did you know?

Soundproofing is a much misused term as it is virtually impossible, except at great expense, to soundproof a space fully.

Sound recorded outdoors is said to have been recorded 'on location'. Location recording is done for a specific purpose, either because a particular effect is required or because the person being recorded is unable or unwilling to travel to a studio. Drama is often recorded on location to give an authentic feel to the dialogue by providing appropriate background noise or 'ambience' to the recording. News interviews at locations of events such as accidents, political rallies or opening ceremonies often contextualise the content of the piece using ambient sounds.

Key terms

Reverberation – characteristic of sound in a reflective environment.

Surround sound – the effect of creating sound around the listener by the use of multiple speakers.

Activity: Outdoor acoustics

- Go to an outdoor location and listen to the sounds around you. Is it windy enough to cause microphone noise? Is there any noise from traffic, aeroplanes, or nearby people or natural sounds such as birdsong?

- What can you do to reduce the ambient or background sound when you make an audio recording?

Sound treatments

It is desirable to record sounds 'dry', without any special effects, and to add 'treatments' in the mixing and balancing stage of the recording process to create the simulated acoustics of your choice. Treatments that can be applied to recorded sound include:

- reverberation
- echo
- dynamic filtering
- compression
- limiting.

Activity: Sound treatments

- Find out what effect can be achieved using each of the treatments listed above.

- Which of these treatments is used in Automatic Gain Control (AGC)?

- Which treatment would you use to achieve a 'telephone voice'?

PLTS

Deciding on the use of appropriate technology will help develop your skills as a **creative thinker**.

Many sounds are recorded using a monophonic or mono (single channel) microphone, whereas we hear sound stereophonically, that is, with two ears. Often mono sounds will be recorded and added layer by layer to a multi-track or multi-channel recorder. They are then balanced across the sound stage of the channels of a play-out system that can be stereo, 3.1, 5.1 or 7.1 **surround sound**, and mastered accordingly. Surround sound is the effect of creating sound around the listener by the use of multiple audio channels feeding multiple speakers. Home cinema and other stereo sound systems have developed along the lines of 3.1, 5.1 and 7.1 (pronounced 'three point one', and so on) and are known generically as 'surround sound'.

3.1 means three speakers: left, centre and right. 5.1 means five speakers: left, centre, right, left rear and right rear. 7.1 means that the speakers are positioned as for 5.1, plus intermediate mid-side-left and mid-side-right rear speakers.

It is important when working in this way for the signals to be 'in phase' or moving in the same direction at the same time. This is achieved using time delay in the recording process.

Mixing and editing for radio

Mixing

The mixing stage takes place both in live broadcasts and in making pre-recorded programmes. Music that could be recorded for radio broadcasting includes sessions recorded by live bands, church events on local radio and the Proms at the Royal Albert Hall.

As you have seen, the requirements for live radio are for hearing one sound source at a time but nevertheless being set up so that multiple sources can function simultaneously. Live radio does not use special effects. The requirement is to mix live voices and pre-recorded sources as appropriate, maintaining individual levels and ensuring no signal exceeds its preset level.

Editing

Recorded speech needs editing to ensure it is the correct length or running time, contains an appropriate balance of comment and to remove errors and incidental noise.

All editing is now non-linear accessed (that is, any part of the recording can be accessed directly; you do not have to start at the beginning and work through to the part that you want). You may need to edit some music clips for inclusion in other programmes, or compile play lists, according to the degree of automation in the station.

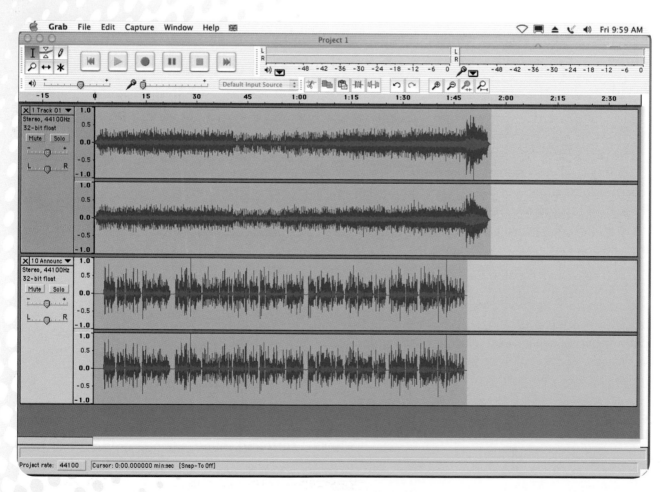

Figure 4: Can you see the different tracks in this multi-track workstation display?

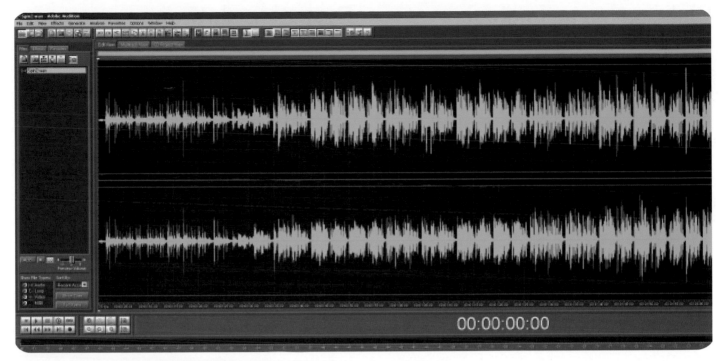

00:00:00:00

Figure 5: Compare this stereo edit workstation display with the multi-track display.

Radio technology: the future

This section of the chapter is relevant to Unit 9, LO4.

Radio has developed in many ways since 1922 when the first test broadcasts were made. We have moved from terrestrial radio to satellite radio which can be received on television; from mono **AM** (Amplitude Modulation) to stereo **FM** (Frequency Modulation) and simultaneous radio and television broadcasts. As new technologies develop they will continue to take radio to new audiences and increase sound quality.

Digital technologies

The two main digital technologies are **DAB** (Digital Audio Broadcasting) and **DRM**. DRM, or Digital Radio Mondiale, is a universal, standard digital broadcasting system covering frequencies up to 174MHz, including AM long-, medium- and short-wave and FM. It can accommodate more channels in less bandwidth and at higher quality than AM. The digital switchover for radio has been delayed.

Activity: Digital radio

Find out about the current situation regarding UK digital radio switchover.

- What is the date for the radio switchover?
- Why has the radio switchover been delayed?
- Which of the two digital platforms is likely to be used in the UK and why?

PLTS

Describing developing technologies will help develop your skills as a **reflective learner**.

Key terms

AM – Amplitude Modulation: one of the ways in which radio waves are propagated.

FM – Frequency Modulation: one of the ways in which radio waves are propagated.

DAB – Digital Audio Broadcasting.

DRM – Digital Radio Mondiale.

Distribution technologies

Distribution technologies are the ways in which radio is distributed to its audience. They include:

- terrestrial – radio waves are sent from a transmitter and received by radios
- cable – programmes are sent down a telephone wire or fibre optic cable
- satellite – the signal is sent to a satellite and received by a dish which feeds through a set top box to a television
- Internet – the radio programme is received on a computer.

Another change in distribution technology has affected the way that independent radio programme producers submit completed programmes to their commissioners for broadcast. Formerly the standard was CD (Compact Disc), but programmes are now sent electronically via broadband Internet (for example, FTP) as BWAV (Broadcast WAV) files. These are WAV files with embedded metadata (such as the programme name).

How many ways of listening to radio can you think of? What are the advantages and disadvantages of each?

Reception platforms

New methods of distribution have had a significant effect on how the audience receives and listens to radio.

- Satellite broadcasting has added to its pay providers the one-off Freesat platform, offering the audience a large number of radio stations.
- The audience can access many BBC programmes as podcasts.
- Some people get radio through their cable telecommunications providers.
- Mobile phone users can access radio via Internet connections.

Activity: Reception platforms

- What might be the effect on advertising of accessing programmes on demand?
- What is the significance of the reception delay between terrestrial reception and online reception?
- What influence might on-demand access have on programme content?

Paul Stirling
Freelance radio producer

My role is very varied and involves me with a wide range of radio stations, carrying programmes through from proposal to broadcast. Since I completed my BTEC National Diploma in Media Production, my career has required me to move to different places. I started as a part-time station assistant while still a student, moving on to be audio controller and producer. I then added music manager to my range of job roles. Then came an opportunity to help develop digital radio, as digital network producer for a national independent radio broadcaster.

Working in the new technology of digital radio has presented all sorts of new challenges and opportunities; digital radio has really revived the industry.

In the radio industry you have to be able to turn your hand to any job that comes up, because the show must go on, whether it's devising a new programme or standing in for someone who is ill. Not all radio studios are the same and there is quite a range of technical equipment to get to know about.

That's partly why I decided to freelance; that and the variety that this work brings. I have to work closely with other members of the production team and get involved with a whole range of different job roles. This has provided me with a valuable overview of the whole production process, enabling me to develop my technical skills and knowledge. I also have to be a good communicator, as I have to deal with lots of different sorts of people including presenters, producers and technical operators, and I have to make sure that the information we get from our clients is accurate.

Having a flexible approach to your work and having a broad knowledge base of the whole industry is very important to working in radio broadcasting. You also have to be highly motivated and be able to work well on your own, as well as being an effective team member.

Being organised is very important as programmes have to be carefully planned out and scheduled and we often have to work to very tight deadlines. I also have to work very accurately and get things right first time.

Think about it!

- Why do you need to be highly organised and work quickly and accurately in the radio industry?
- What skills do you already possess that would help you to work well in a radio production environment?
- How have changes in technology impacted on the radio production industry?

Just checking

1. How can you find out about the radio industry of which you plan to become a part?
2. How many job roles in the radio industry can you list? Can others in your group think of any more? Do you fully understand all these jobs? How can you find out more about them?
3. Where might there be opportunities for bi-media work in radio?
4. What is an ISDN line and what is it used for in a radio studio?
5. What is a delay line as used in a radio phone-in and why might it be used?

edexcel :::

Assignment tips

- Use the technical vocabulary of the industry appropriately and confidently in your assignments.

- Make sure any written work is neat, methodical and check carefully for any errors.

- Use carefully chosen examples to help you explain your points in depth. If you hope to achieve the highest grades, it is not enough simply to mention examples. You need to explain their relevance, use them to illustrate your points and demonstrate that you have fully understood the issues.

- Keep a thorough log of your practical production work, including any changes you make, and why. The highest grades will be awarded for reflective work showing the ability to make well-judged decisions based on excellent theoretical understanding and thorough knowledge. You will need to explain your decisions, demonstrating how your understanding of the relevant technical and professional issues has contributed to your work.

- Make sure you can provide clear evidence of your ability to work independently to near-professional standards, showing your technical ability, creative flair, and ability to work within legal and ethical constraints. Will your assessor be able to see that you have not only worked on technical detail professionally, but have also thought about developing the production as a whole as a marketable product? You cannot assume that they will, unless you provide good evidence in the form of a thorough log and work in progress with well-documented decisions.

Sound recording

Sound recording is part of every discipline in the media, music and entertainment industries. Specialising in sound opens up a wide range of fields and with the development of new technologies the sound industry is global, offering employment options throughout your career and around the world.

This chapter supports your study of the two specialist mandatory sound recording pathway units: Unit 10, Understanding the sound recording industry and Unit 17, Audio production processes and techniques.

The first section of this chapter introduces the sound recording industry. It gives you the opportunity to investigate professional organisations related to the industry, and to explore the range of recording studios and related businesses that comprise the industry.

The next section looks at what it is like to work in the industry, and where and how to look for jobs in sound. You will also develop your own professional image and practice in preparation for entering the industry.

The focus is then on the production process. You will be supported in acquiring the theoretical knowledge and practical skills in recording, editing and mixing sound that you will need to complete any brief and to prepare you to make excellent recordings for any production in your career in the sound industry.

This chapter supplements the information supplied in the Radio pathway chapter (both chapters are relevant to Unit 17). You should read the Radio pathway chapter first, and use this chapter to broaden the focus from radio to other areas of the sound recording industry.

This chapter is designed to give you an overview of the sound recording industry and the types of skills you will need for this pathway. You will find details of the learning outcomes and the assessment and grading criteria for the Sound recording pathway on pages 256–258. Unit 17 is mandatory for both the Sound recording and Radio pathways, so you may also find it useful to look at the Radio pathway.

Rosie, becoming a sound engineer

I studied for a BTEC National Diploma in Sound Recording and I'm now in the second year of my BA in Sound Recording. When I started my BTEC National Diploma, I was mainly interested in music recording but the course made me see all the other areas of the creative media industries that I could work in. I studied the technical and practical aspects of recording and completed projects for radio, music studios, films and games.

Covering all these different recording contexts has really helped me at university and I'm now working with people from several other courses, doing the sound on their projects. Studying all types of sound recording has also helped me to earn money to help with university! Right now I'm doing sound for a club two nights a week and I also get occasional work for a local recording studio and editing interviews for a radio station. It's not just the money that's useful, of course, but the experience as well. I'm getting a chance to use and develop the skills I'm learning in my course, and I'm starting to make contacts with people working in the industry, with an eye to the future. I'm getting to know a lot of people, not just on my course but on other courses as well, through working on their projects with them, and who knows where these things might lead in the future?

When I leave university I want to be a freelance sound engineer and ideally work all over the world.

Over to you!

* What area of the Sound recording pathway interests you most?
* What sort of sound would you like to record?

The sound recording industry

This section of the chapter is relevant to Unit 10, LO1, and Unit 17, LO2.

Set up

Sound recorded products

How many types of sound recorded products can you think of?

Make a list of as many products you can think of that have had sound recorded. (Remember to include virtual and hard forms of media.)

Sort your list into the following categories:

- television
- film
- music
- communications
- media.

This chapter will build on the information in the Radio pathway chapter to explore aspects of audio production relevant to the broader sound recording industry. Read and familiarise yourself with the Radio chapter before studying this one, which supplements it.

The sound recording industry: an overview

Sound recording is a very wide-ranging industry. Depending on what you want to do, you could find yourself working in many different contexts: film, television, radio, commercials, music, speech, talking books, communications and many more.

The sound recording industry also includes a wide variety of disciplines, spanning technical and creative areas. Whatever the product or context, however, some aspect of the recording, editing, synchronisation or mastering will be completed in a recording studio. Until the 1980s, only a few recording studios were equipped to produce professional recordings and these studios were predominantly owned by huge media companies, record labels or television and film studios. With new developments in technology, recording studios are now available to everyone who owns a personal computer in one form or another. This has had a huge impact on the sound recording industry, and change is ongoing.

Permanent, full-time jobs in large organisations, which used to be the norm, have become scarce within the industry. Freelancing has become a common way to work, and the range of possible employers is constantly changing as technological advances bring about new developments across the creative media sector.

The sound recording industry landscape is therefore vast, complex and ever-changing.

How many studios have you been in?
What type of mixing desks did they have?
What types of recordings have you made?

Activity: The structure of the sound recording industry

The sound recording industry cannot easily be summarised as it covers such a wide range of associated businesses and practices.

- Find and explore:
  - the industry structure maps produced by the British Phonographic Institute (BPI) – search in the 'Music business' area of their website: www.bpi.co.uk
  - the 'Music universe' diagram produced by the Performing Rights Society – search on their website: www.prsformusic.com
- How many contexts can you identify where recorded music is used?
- What areas of recorded sound are not included on these diagrams, and which industries do these belong to? Can you find maps of their structure?

Professional organisations

The following are just a few of the many organisations that support the sound recording industry.

Association of Professional Recording Services
www2.aprs.co.uk

Audio Engineering Society
www.aes.org

British Phonographic Institute
www.bpi.co.uk

Music Producers Guild (UK)
www.mpg.org.uk

Performing Rights Society
www.prsformusic.com

PLTS

Researching industry bodies and the information and services they can offer will help develop your skills as an **independent enquirer**.

Activity: Who does what?

How much do you know about the role of each of these professional organisations? Investigate their websites and make notes of your findings.

- Which organisation collects and distributes royalties for performance of recorded music?
- Which organisation(s) offer(s) information about industry events such as trade shows and conferences?
- Where can you find information about new technology and equipment?

Recording studios
Studio design

Traditionally, all recording studios tended to have much the same general design. However, with the development of technology in recent years, the general idea of what a recording studio might look like has changed enormously. You will need to understand and familiarise yourself with the range of recording studios and who owns them as you prepare to gain employment in the industry.

So what are the differences in studios?

Many recording studios specialise in one aspect of recording and this gives a clue about the likely design, features, function and equipment that are used within them. Keep in mind, though, that there will always be variations, since any studio will need to diversify and undertake as many different types of recording as possible in order to stay in business.

Table 1: Some of the features that contribute to the design of a studio.

Type of recording	Design features	Equipment needs
Music recordings	Live room Control room	Range of equipment needed to cater for diverse recording scenarios
Classical recordings	Large live room Control room	Large number of inputs, microphones to accommodate many musicians being recorded at once
Location recordings	No live room needed No control room needed	High quality mobile recording devices and microphones needed to ensure the best possible recordings are made as re-recording is not always possible
Post-production recordings	No live room needed Control room	Audio-visual hybrid equipment needed to satisfy the demands of sound and vision, including dialogue, music and Foley sound High-end monitors for detailed listening environment
Mastering suite	No live room needed Control room	Exceptional high-quality equipment needed, including high-end monitors for detailed listening environment
Sound design	No live room needed No control room needed	Large amount of sound generation equipment and programs Good set of monitors needed
Multimedia authoring	No live room needed No control room needed	High specification computer-based software and hardware Quality monitoring for listening detail

While Table 1 gives only a very general view of the features and factors needed for each kind of studio, it does demonstrate some basic elements that will help you to start defining the disciplines covered by the studio and what you may find there.

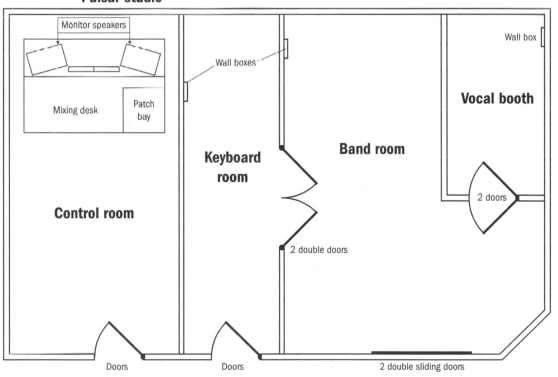

Figure 1: Can you relate this professional studio floor plan to a studio you have used?

Finding out about studios

Many studios have an online presence and sometimes include virtual tours of their facilities. This information can give you a real opportunity to build your knowledge of equipment you may have never used, and to develop your professionalism in terms of understanding the range of establishments, specialisations and types of equipment and services on offer. If you get the chance to visit or do work experience in a studio, do all you can to make sure that you have researched the host company as thoroughly as possible so that you are well informed in advance, and will be able to show that you know what you are talking about.

Activity: Facilities and ownership

The following websites give overviews of many recording studios in the UK, including information about what the studios do, who owns them and their facilities and equipment. There are also virtual tours of studios and interviews with producers who work there.

www.recordproduction.com

www2.aprs.co.uk

Use these websites (or others you may find) to research the ownership, facilities and type of work undertaken by a range of UK recording studios.

- Which kinds of studios and facilities are you most interested in?
- Which areas of work and equipment do you need to know more about?

Remember to use your experience to build up a more detailed picture of the functions and equipment found in studios. Keep a log with as much detail as possible about the facilities you come across in your studio visits, work experience, research activities and practical projects for your course. This log will help you to reflect on the diversity of the industry and build up your own expertise.

Case study: Phil, student

When working in a studio, one thing I realised is that it isn't only keeping up with new technology that's important. Learning as much as you can about older systems can also be really useful. One studio I've worked in had some vintage recording equipment that is scarcely available anywhere now, but some really big artists come to them especially to use that set-up because they can't get that particular sound any other way, or in any other studio. Of course this all depends on the engineers knowing how to maintain and operate what's usually considered out-dated equipment, which is no longer common knowledge. It's a specialist area that would really interest me.

I've noticed that some studios have collections of special vintage instruments, which can also be a unique selling point in the facilities they offer.

1. What is analogue recording?
2. Can you find a studio that does analogue recording? Which artists use it and what does analogue recording do to the sound?
3. Ask your tutor if there are analogue recorders in your school or college, so that you can have a go.

Working in the sound recording industry

This section of the chapter is relevant to Unit 10, LO2 and LO5.

Sound industry jobs

There are many jobs in the sound recording industry. The majority are concerned with the capture (recording), manipulation (editing) and preparation for mass distribution (mastering) of sound. There are also many jobs that relate directly to the recorded product, based in the studio and outside. These jobs include producer, sound engineer, assistant engineer, sound technician, audio engineer for video, re-recording mixer, set-up engineer, sound designer, boom operator and multimedia developer. If you are planning to work in the industry, it is crucial for you to understand how to find these jobs and identify the skills and knowledge you will need to operate successfully in one of these roles. The 'Finding a job' activity may help you with this.

Remember

Remember also to refer to the related sections of the Radio pathway chapter that contain information and advice specific to jobs within the radio industry.

Did you know?

Many of the sound industry professional bodies offer student memberships. Benefits may include opportunities for training, employment and keeping up with the latest technology. You may be able to attend their conferences where you can hear about new developments, meet professionals who work in the industry, and do some networking with potential employers.

Getting into the industry

There is no set route for entry into the sound recording industry and every person who works in sound recording will tell you their own unique story of how they got there. In recent years, full-time permanent jobs in the recording industry have become few and far between. Freelancing and short-term contract work has become the norm.

Freelancing means you are not tied to one employer and you may get to work in many different areas for a range of organisations, from large studios to smaller studios with relatively little equipment and lower overheads and costs. Working freelance means you can develop a wide range of experience and develop your skills with every production, but it also means that you constantly have to secure your next job.

Activity: Finding a job

1. Use the websites below to find out about a range of jobs in the sound recording industry. List the different jobs you find, and note down the skills, qualities and knowledge that are needed to begin work in these roles.

   Association of Motion Picture Sound (AMPS) www.amps.net (search for 'Sound job descriptions')

   Association of Professional Recording Services (APRS) www2.aprs.co.uk

   Audio Engineering Society (AES) www.aes.org

   RecordProduction.com www.recordproduction.com

   Sector Skills Council for Creative Media www.skillset.org (search for 'sound')

2. Search for job advertisements for the sound industry roles that interest you. The following may help you.

   BBC www.bbc.co.uk/jobs (includes radio, television and BBC Worldwide)

   Broadcast www.broadcastnow.co.uk (careers in broadcasting)

   The Grapevine www.grapevinejobs.com (jobs in broadcast and media)

   The Guardian www.guardian.co.uk/jobs (the media supplement is published on Mondays)

   Mandy's www.mandy.com (film and television production resources)

   Production Base www.productionbase.co.uk (film, television and commercials network)

   UK Music Jobs http://uk.music-jobs.com

No matter which part of the sound recording industry you want to work in, what any prospective employer will want to hear is how good you are at recording. In order to present the best possible portfolio you should be recording as much as possible.

An audio portfolio should be as diverse as possible in terms of content. This will demonstrate your suitability for the widest possible range of jobs and help you to keep your options open.

Activity: Audio portfolio

Build up your audio portfolio. Include a wide selection of projects to demonstrate a wide range of skills, such as:

- music (acoustic and electronic)
- spoken work
- audio books
- interviews (location and studio)
- sound design
- soundtrack
- dialogue
- sound effects
- games music.

A CD, digital audio tape (DAT) and digital recorder. Have you used appropriate set-ups and equipment for the recordings you have made? What types of recording media have you used?

PLTS

Developing your personal audio portfolio will help develop your skills as a **self-manager**.

Case study: Debbie, sound industry freelance

How do you get a job in the modern recording industry? Well, many people first get a foot in the door by volunteering their time for nothing. This gives you some experience and some contacts, and might give you a chance to apply for a paid job as a general dogsbody. Then over the years you can work your way up through a mixture of having the right skills in the right place at the right time, and making contacts who may be able to put work your way. Some permanent jobs are advertised but others can come up through word of mouth.

The sound recording industry is fiercely competitive and the bottom line is always going to be your ability to record audio. You need to get as much experience as you can, practise and keep practising, keep your technical know-how right up to date and constantly look out for any opportunities to take the next step.

1. Have you researched local studios or other settings where you may be able to gain experience in sound recording?

2. Which kinds of recording do you still need to practise and add to your portfolio?

The quantity and quality of work you will be offered and money you will earn in the UK sound recording industry will be directly related to your ability to capture, edit, mix and master recordings to the highest possible quality. Simply put, the greater your skills and knowledge in all aspects of sound and its recording, the more highly regarded you will be in the industry.

Activity: Work experience

- Try to get voluntary work experience in a recording studio. See how they work and what tasks they undertake day to day. Always ask questions.

- Start a sound library of recordings you have done. Try and make them as varied as possible so you can compile targeted demos of your work.

- Make a point of networking and developing contacts in the industry, as word of mouth is still the main way to find work in sound recording. Use your student credentials to ask for a tour of the studio for your college project. Do this in as many studios as you can get to.

- Check your written work, CV and any letters or emails you write for accuracy.

- Always present a professional image when working. Reputations are won and lost on time keeping, courtesy, efficiency and technical expertise.

Developing your career in the sound recording industry

Getting a job is just the first step. Once you are employed, keeping up to date with the technology and current practices can feel like a full-time job in itself. Every recording scenario is different and you must be ready to tackle anything. If you work for a large studio, you may be sent on training courses to keep up to date. Such courses can cost hundreds of pounds and as a freelancer you may not be able to afford to take such training. You will need to find other ways to develop your skills and knowledge through your own efforts.

- Keep a log of all your sound recording endeavours; this should include all the equipment you use and the nature of the projects undertaken.

- Take an active interest in other people's projects and experience, and be ready to learn from them.

- Take out membership of professional bodies which may offer free seminars and technical tips to update your knowledge.

- Trade magazines are also a great source of information. These include: *Sound on Sound*, *Audio Media*, *Light and Sound International*, *Pro Sound News* and *Resolution*.

Trade shows

Trade shows are run by the industry and take place around the UK. These are great opportunities to network, get in among the industry professionals, have a good look at the latest equipment and attend seminars and talks on new developments.

Trade shows may also potentially offer the opportunity to work as a demonstrator for equipment and sound industry businesses.

Activity: Trade secrets

Research upcoming music and sound recording industry trade shows and conferences in the UK and around the world by finding the trade show listings on this website: http://pro-music-news.com

- Explore the associated websites for a range of events that interest you.

- What range of businesses and organisations are exhibiting at these events?

- What professional development opportunities do these trade shows offer?

- Can you organise a trip to a trade show through your school or college?

If you visited a trade show, what would most interest you and what would be of most use to you?

Working in the sound recording industry for your whole career is difficult to do. You need to have excellent, diverse skills, be flexible, and keep up to date with all aspects of the industry. Although it involves a lot of hard work, being able to spend your entire career in the recording industry can also be very rewarding and interesting and can allow you to travel all round the world.

Adam Blunt
Post-production engineer

I'm an assistant engineer in a post-production house in London, working mainly on television programmes and films, making sure the speech is synced to the pictures and the music is put in at the right places. I sometimes also have to find and place the right sound effects.

Films can cost millions of pounds to make so the sound has to be right. I use very specialist equipment which is constantly being updated so I go on a lot of training courses. I have to work quickly and accurately, for long and weird hours. Time is money in this industry and you just have to get on with it.

The most important part of my job is using my ears. All those lessons in acoustics that were so hard, and I never thought I'd use, have been crucial in helping me to match the right sound to the acoustic environment of films and television programmes.

Working in the sound industry is better than I ever thought it would be. I love it. It's always interesting and it's great going to the cinema and seeing a film I've worked on. That's really intense!

Think about it!

- What pressures does Adam work under?
- Which aspects of working in the sound industry do you think you will find most enjoyable? What will you find the most challenging?

Creating sound recordings

This section of the chapter is relevant to Unit 17, LO1, LO2, LO3 and LO4.

The production process

At the heart of the sound recording industry is sound itself. Before recording technology had developed, the only way to experience a sound-related performance was to see it live or read a transcript of what had occurred. Now with the ability to capture, edit and reproduce sound, easy access to performances and events is not only possible but has become expected as a normal part of everyday life.

The main elements of the recording process are the capture, editing and mixing of sound. Either side of these are the pre-production and post-production, or mastering, stages.

Figure 2 summarises some of the main activities and elements that might need to be undertaken or considered at each stage of the process.

There are no strict rules about what might belong in each of these boxes: every engineer and producer has their own unique style of sound production which has developed from their own experience as well as influences from other people.

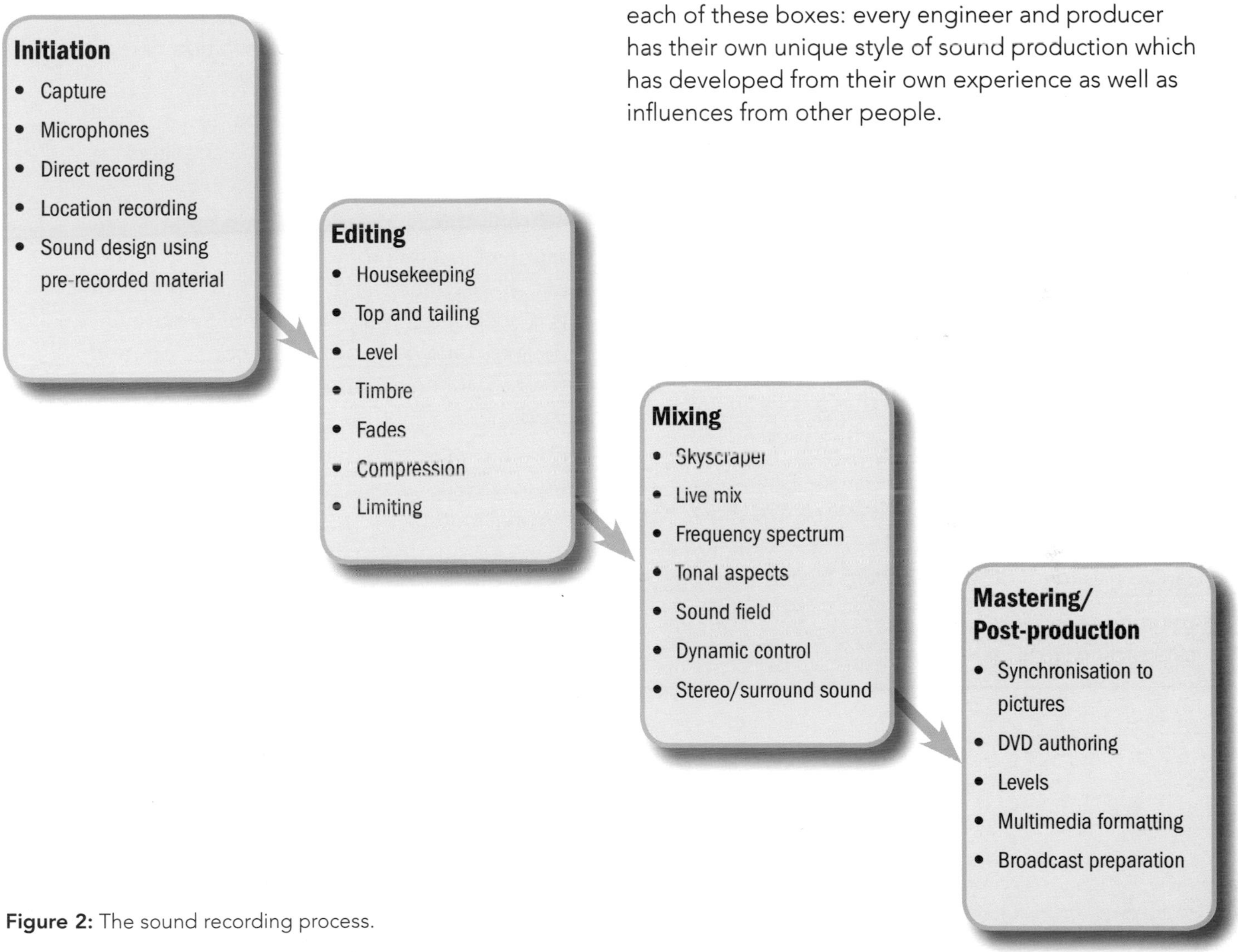

Initiation
- Capture
- Microphones
- Direct recording
- Location recording
- Sound design using pre-recorded material

Editing
- Housekeeping
- Top and tailing
- Level
- Timbre
- Fades
- Compression
- Limiting

Mixing
- Skyscraper
- Live mix
- Frequency spectrum
- Tonal aspects
- Sound field
- Dynamic control
- Stereo/surround sound

Mastering/ Post-production
- Synchronisation to pictures
- DVD authoring
- Levels
- Multimedia formatting
- Broadcast preparation

Figure 2: The sound recording process.

Remember

Read the production process sections of the Radio pathway chapter in conjunction with this section. This section supplements the information you will read in the Radio chapter.

Here is some of the terminology used in the sound recording industry. Do you understand all of these terms and processes?

Broadcast preparation – ensuring the audio is in the correct format for media type – radio, film or music production.

Compression – a tool used within a studio to control and manipulate the dynamic range of recorded audio in order to achieve more control.

DVD authoring – ensuring all the audio and visual files are correct in the right order and the menus are designed and linked properly.

Dynamic range – the difference in loudness between the softest and loudest passages that an audio system can reproduce.

Fades – used to fade audio tracks in (getting louder) or fade out (getting quieter) in sound production.

Frequency spectrum – measured in Hertz and contains bass middle and treble.

Limiting – the use of a device that strictly limits the maximum volume output; often used in live sound.

Live mix – working on the sound for a live show, generally done on the fly and must be corrected as you go along; notoriously hard to do.

Location recording – recording not carried out in a recording studio.

Multimedia formatting – ensuring sound is correctly formatted for use in for example, DVDs and websites.

Skyscraper – a mixing technique that entails building up a mix one layer at a time, like constructing a building.

Sound design – the creation of sound by either manipulating existing audio or creating audio from its most basic components; can be used for sound effects or in music the emulation of real sounds or creation of new sounds.

Sound field – the space that is created in which sound can be placed between the speakers on a system.

Synchronisation – includes ensuring that equipment in a recording and post-production studio all keep the same timing and run together. This is achieved through the use of Samtpe code, Midi time code or Digital word clock and is essential for any context where automation is used.

Timbre – comes from the French word meaning tone; in common use in all areas of acoustic and electronic music.

Tonal aspects – in mixing, tonal aspects are concerned with the frequency content of sound and the balance of bass, middle and treble content.

Traditionally mastering and post-production engineering were carried out in highly specialised studios with esoteric equipment by sound engineers at the very top of their field. These processes are now much more accessible across the industry because of the advent of affordable technology (hardware and software), processing power (microchips) and the explosion of sound formats (CD, Blu-ray, DVD multimedia and online content) and output formats (surround sound, iTunes, Dolby output formats).

A post-production facility. How does this studio differ from the ones you have used and what would you find difficult to record in there? Think about the advantages and disadvantages.

Case study: Kevin Bacon of Bacon & Quarmby and Artists Without A Label

Technology has, not surprisingly, played a major role in the production process over the last 15 years, changing the entire decision-making process and allowing for much more client involvement in the latter stages.

In the old 'analogue' model, what was recorded at the time was committed to the finished product except where huge budgets were available to re-record and re-trace.

Digital changed the landscape totally. Every stage of the process from the very beginning can be reverted to or combinations created almost instantly, offering the client the ability to make 'A to B' comparisons at the click of a mouse.

In spite of the fact that this offering can sometimes slow down the final approval process it is insignificant compared with the amount of time and budget saved in production.

1. How has modern technology changed the production process?

2. What advantages does technology offer for the client?

Activity: The recording process

Think about one of your own recording productions.

Draw a graphic representation of the recording process, using the following headings:

- pre-production
- capture
- editing
- mixing
- mastering/post-production.

Can you research and identify the equipment in this studio?

Editing, mixing and post-production

Post-production consists of a number of activities such as editing, mixing and 'mastering'.

Mixing and editing may be some of the most challenging technical skills to master but they can also be among the most creative, exciting and rewarding tasks.

'Mastering' consists of ensuring the dialogue, music and Foley sound are synchronised with the moving images. For the production of music it includes ensuring the final file has the best signal-to-noise ratio, balance and tone throughout. Both contexts require very high-quality equipment and experienced engineers with excellent attention to detail.

Activity: Art or science?

You may hear sound mixing described as 'the science of mixing' as well as 'the art of mixing'.

In pairs or threes, discuss why you think this is.

Do you see mixing more as a creative task or as a technical one?

Developing your skills in using sound recording technology to make quality recordings is essential to success, but that is not all. You will need basic computer hardware and software knowledge and basic electrical engineering knowledge, but it is not always necessary to study these subjects individually: you will develop skills and acquire knowledge of them through your experience of recording equipment and processes.

You will also need to 'speak the language' of the recording process and understand the conventions and terminology used in the production of sound. Learning the language will mean you can understand exactly what people in the industry are asking of you, and your ability to use the right words properly yourself will give others confidence that you know what you are talking about, too. And when you come to do your own productions, you will be able to put across your creative and technical ideas and requirements effectively so that people know exactly what you want.

Finally, and perhaps most importantly, you will need to develop your own professional judgement. You may be competent at using the equipment to capture the best sound possible but then you need to use your creativity to judge how best to mix, edit and present the results. Your professional reputation and future work requests will depend on your listening skills and your judgement just as much as on your technical abilities.

Technical considerations

File formats

Computer-based technology is now involved in all areas of sound recording, offering a wide range of options for capture, manipulation, reproduction and distribution.

Perhaps the single most important innovation in sound recording is the move from analogue to digital. With the advent of digital technology, the compact disc and digital audio tape (DAT) became the norm for the recording industry, taking over from the vinyl records and tapes of earlier days. File types such as WAV and AIFF have become the standard file types, with the quality of recordings increasing as the computers used to capture and manipulate them have become faster and faster.

As communication technology such as broadband and digital streaming become commonplace, so podcasts are becoming widespread, where the consumer does not need to own the physical media product, but instead can obtain a virtual product. Digital technology has also had a significant effect on how music is presented for playback in the listening environment. This information may also be useful if you are following the Radio pathway.

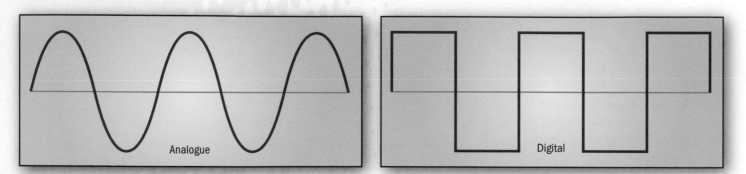

Figure 3: Analogue and digital waveforms. How is sound quality measured? When using audio editors, try zooming in to sample point resolution in order to see the detail of a waveform.

Acoustics

Acoustics refers to the study of sound and the way it behaves in different environments. You could spend a lifetime becoming an expert in this field alone. Acoustic environment is crucial in determining the 'feel' and atmosphere of recording and will significantly affect the quality of your recording. In modern recording scenarios decisions must be made regarding the use of natural acoustics or simulated acoustics and must be considered throughout the production process.

Whether the sound is captured as 'dry' or 'wet' has a profound effect on what you can do with it. A **dry sound** allows you to add a simulated acoustic environment in the studio with the aid of effects units which allow you to choose and control the acoustic environment. This is crucial in areas of film soundtracks, for example, where the environment in the pictures needs to be supported by the sound. If sound is recorded 'wet', with the acoustic environment included, it is almost impossible to treat the sound with further simulation without affecting clarity. **Wet sound** recordings are, however, useful in classical music recordings, where the effect of the environment in which the music is performed (for example, the Royal Albert Hall or the Sydney Opera House) is a crucial aspect of the overall sound.

Did you know?

When you hear a sound indoors, approximately 40 per cent of the sound goes directly from the sound source to your ears and the other 60 per cent reaches your ears after first reflecting off the surfaces in the environment. When recording, the balance of direct versus reflected sound can be controlled either through technical means or by the choice of setting, for example, by selecting either a 'dead' space or a reflective space in the studio.

Key terms

Dry sound – capturing audio with no acoustic environment properties at all; often referred to as a skill in recording, editing and mixing 'dead' sound.

Wet sound – capturing audio with elements of the acoustic environment present.

Activity: Wet or dry?

Next time you are recording in the studio, try to experiment with recording sounds that are wet and dry, and listen to the difference.

Experiment creatively with record sounds as dry as possible. Use the processors in the studio to add various simulated acoustic environments and analyse the results.

Listening formats

The first listening format was mono. This means that however many tracks were recorded, and wherever the sound origins were positioned, all of the recorded sound came out of one speaker. This is not how sound is heard in real life. When stereo became the standard, this allowed sound to be placed in a sound field of left and right speakers. Sounds and music could then be spread out to simulate a more realistic 'three-dimensional' presentation of how sound is in real life.

Activity: Sound formats

Investigate the formats below and describe how the speakers are arranged and how the sound can be outputted to make the listening experience nearer to real life:

- quadraphonic
- surround sound
- 5.1 surround
- 7.1 surround
- Sonic Whole Overhead Sound.

A modern surround sound facility using computer-based DAW and a control surface. Have you ever seen or used this type of studio before?

The sound recording industry and the law

This section of the chapter is relevant to Unit 10, LO3 and LO4.

Copyright

The sound recording industry, like all others, is subject to laws and legal requirements that govern the way in which it operates. The main areas of law that govern the sound recording industry relate to issues of copyright (who owns the rights to the recorded material), the reproduction of material (how many copies and in what format) and the distribution and broadcast (where and when it is played). These areas are crucial in determining that all the right people get paid for their work.

The creators of creative and artistic works of all kinds have the right to control how their material is used, including broadcast and public performance, copying, adapting, issuing, renting and lending copies to the public. This protection extends to most countries worldwide, under international conventions.

PRS for Music

Within the sound recording industry it is usual for everyone involved in a recording to get paid, including the writer or composer, any presenters, performers or musicians, and all the technical staff.

Depending on the contributor's role and the agreement they make at the outset, this may not be the only time they get paid for their work on the recording.

The Performing Rights Society (PRS for Music) is responsible for collecting and distributing royalties to all the parties who are entitled to a share (usually the composer, the performer, the publisher of the song and the rights owner). These royalties come from sales and from fees paid by other parties for the use of a recorded piece of music in any public place, such as for broadcast, advertising, in shops and restaurants and many other contexts.

Activity: Royalties

Visit www.prsformusic.com to find out more about royalties associated with the use of sound recordings.

File sharing

New technologies have had a significant effect on the distribution of media products. With the development of the Internet and file sharing technology, issues around sharing music and films without paying have been highly debated in the creative industries and the media.

Did you know?

In a recent report following research across 16 countries over three years, the IFPI (International Federation of the Phonographic Industry) estimated that:

- more than 40 billion files were illegally shared in 2008
- in the UK alone the loss of revenue due to online piracy stood at £180 million a year.

(Source: IFPI Digital Music Report 2009: Key statistics.)

Technology is constantly being developed in the area of virtual security to prevent online piracy. Technologies such as Digital Rights Management and Digital Watermarking are currently at the forefront of technological protection. This will become a very important area for anyone working within the sound recording industry to become familiar with.

Activity: Sharing recordings

Discuss the following questions in your group.

- What kinds of recordings are protected under copyright law?
- Is it fair to share recordings that you have not paid for?
- How would you feel if people shared your work so you never got paid properly for the work you did?

Stephen Buckley
Assistant producer

I work as assistant producer at Voiceovers-UK (www.voiceovers-uk.com), a company that specialises in the production of voiceovers for a wide variety of productions and clients, including television, radio, educational products, phone prompts, DVDs, podcasts, games and talking books.

Like a lot of people my age, I got into sound recording using an old Tascam 4-track cassette recorder. After a couple of years I got myself a computer, and made a lot of music using simple programs like Fruity Loops. I pretty much taught myself and picked up bits and pieces as I went along. I eventually got hold of Cubase and a decent microphone (Shure SM58), and got more used to recording my own sounds as opposed to using samples and software synths. I managed to get on a degree course which wasn't strictly sound engineering, but included a lot of audio work, and gave me access to lots of equipment and software that would otherwise have been unavailable.

After that I took up any dead-end job I could, with the intention of getting enough money to move away and find a job in the music or recording industry. After two years with no success, I was lucky enough to get an opportunity to go along to a local studio and help out with their business, which included a voiceover agency.

After working for free for a while, I eventually started becoming more useful. I picked up skills and knowledge far faster than I did while at home and trying to work it out by myself! I had access to industry standard facilities like Pro Tools software, and eventually started getting paid. I used the money to move to a new place and get some equipment of my own, which also sped up my learning curve, as it meant I could spend a lot of my free time recording bands and suchlike, which also improved my understanding and abilities.

I now work full-time at the studio, and am involved in all aspects of the business, from recording and producing voiceovers for radio and television, through to admin and marketing. I continue to develop my understanding of both the business and the technical side of the job.

Think about it!

- What kinds of recordings do you most enjoy making for your own pleasure?
- How can you use your areas of interest in your career in sound recording? Which areas of the sound recording industry are they most relevant to?

Just checking

1. How many types of recording studio can you name?
2. What does the APRS do in the recording industry?
3. How many jobs in the sound industry can you name and what do they specialise in?
4. What are the main types of employment in the sound recording industry?
5. How does the PRS for Music help people to get paid?
6. What is the single most important legal issue facing the recording industry today?
7. Write down what you know about:
   - decibels
   - recording formats and playback systems
   - patch bays and operating levels
   - computer-based systems and performance indicators
   - roles in a recording studio
   - the professional industry bodies (BPI, APRS, MPG, PRS for Music, ABU, EBU, BBC)
   - studio design, layout, equipment and configuration.
8. How will knowledge of each of these subjects be of use in your own professional practice?

edexcel

Assignment tips

- Merit and distinction grades are awarded in this pathway when research and development work are thorough and well documented, showing good understanding and use of industry terminology, and practical work is independently produced with creativity and flair to professional standards, in an appropriate response to the brief.

- Keep a careful log of your work so you can demonstrate how you have followed the production process and explain the decisions you have made and any rethinking you have done in the light of your experience.

- Develop your own sound recordings library for reference and draw on this to demonstrate your ideas.

Print-based media

Print is the oldest form of mass media. Like all creative media industries, the print-based media industries have gone through a period of rapid change and development in recent years, embracing new digital technology and more integrated production processes. Many of the traditional print techniques and practices have been replaced by new methods of production and distribution centred on computer-based technology, and this has led to a need for a highly skilled and flexible workforce with an understanding and awareness of different printed media forms and digital technology.

Multi-skilling is an increasingly important factor for employment in these industries as publishers develop and expand online versions of their paper-based products, and use ever more sophisticated hardware and software packages to originate, design and construct their print-based products.

As with all commercial media products, print-based media products such as newspapers, magazines, comics, books and promotional material including posters, fliers and leaflets need to be produced within a viable financial context. If you want to work within the sector you need to have an understanding of the economics of print production. Print-based products are targeted at specific audiences and those working within the industry require a good understanding of the legal, ethical and professional constraints and practices that help to ensure that these audiences are properly served and that the industry remains a viable and successful one.

Undertaking the Print-based media pathway will allow you to develop your knowledge and understanding of the industry and its production techniques and technologies. The pathway includes two mandatory units: Unit 11, Understanding the print-based media industries and Unit 18, Producing print-based media.

This chapter is designed to give you an overview of the print-based media industries and the types of skills you will need for this pathway. You will find details of the learning outcomes and the assessment and grading criteria for the Print-based media pathway on pages 259–261.

Frank, Print-based media student

I have always been interested in writing and would like to be a journalist after I have been to university. My college has its own small printing department so choosing the print-based media pathway was a good idea as it meant I could get some practical, hands-on experience of using different forms of print technology as well as further developing my writing skills.

I enjoyed researching the print industry and finding out about the different roles people undertake and the different types of products the print sector produces. I also had to research the production processes and techniques that are used to create these products and I learned about the different printing methods and digital printing techniques that are used today.

I also enjoyed investigating the print-based media products themselves and finding out about the different elements that go into their construction. This helped me in my practical production work as it made me think about the production process more carefully and saved me making a lot of costly mistakes.

I made links with the college's marketing department and was able to help them in the production of a student magazine. This was really good as I was able to use the latest desktop publishing software (DTP) that the college's marketing department use.

Over to you!

- Why did you choose the Print-based media pathway?
- What links can you make to help you get hands-on experience of print technology?
- What skills do you think you will need to develop to succeed on this pathway?

Working in the print-based media industries

This section of the chapter is relevant to Unit 11, LO1, LO2 and LO5.

Set up

Range of print-media products

There are print-based media products all around us. Discuss and list all the print-based media products that you and your group can think of.

Do some research to find out how a range of these products were produced, who produced them and how many copies were printed. Write up the information in a short report.

Try to find some examples of the products that you have listed and include them in a supplementary folder to support your report.

The print-based media industries are dynamic and exciting places to work and, like all creative industries, are going through a sustained period of change and development. This is having an impact on the skills needed by those working within the industries.

Flexibility and the ability to work in a number of different areas, at different levels and within different media (referred to as multiskilling), are increasingly important for employment in these industries as they develop and respond to the potential that new technologies bring and the associated demands and expectations of audiences.

Who works in publishing?

A recent report by Skillset, the Sector Skills Council for Creative Media, showed that the publishing industry represents over 38 per cent of the creative media workforce, employing over 180,000 people. Of these:

- 51,000 people are employed in the newspaper sector
- 41,000 work in journals and magazines
- 34,000 work in the book industry
- 8,000 work in news agencies.

The report also showed that around 13 per cent of the workforce operates on a self-employed freelance basis.

(Source: Labour Force Survey, Apr 2009–Mar 2010)

As with other industries in the creative media sector, many local and regional print-media organisations have been subsumed by expanding national and multi-national conglomerates that now dominate the mass publishing markets.

Independent and local publishers and production companies still exist but they often have to find niche markets for their products rather than trying to compete with the mass market multinationals.

Activity: The print-based media industry

Visit the Skillset website (www.skillset.org) for more information about working in the print-based media industry and to help you to prepare your personal career development material for LO5 of Unit 11, Understanding the print-based media industries.

1. What are the advantages and disadvantages of working as a freelancer?
2. Which sector of the print-based media industry would you like to work in?
3. Which skills do you need to develop to succeed?

Case study: Periodical Publishers Association (PPA)

The magazine and business-to-business publishing industry is one area that still has a large number of independent organisations producing print-media products.

The Periodical Publishers Association (PPA) is a trade organisation that promotes the interests of the UK magazine and business media industry. Its website contains links to almost 300 companies that publish over 3,000 consumer, business and customer magazines.

Visit the PPA website (www.ppa.co.uk) and find out the answers to the following questions from its key facts page.

1. How many business magazines are published in the UK?
2. How many magazines does the average UK adult buy each year?
3. How much money is spent on advertising in business magazines every year?

Job roles

Most printed material consists of a combination of words (copy) and images. The print-based media industry employs a range of people to generate and manipulate this raw material, which forms the building blocks of their commercial products.

Working on words

Producing original copy can be a demanding job, and is often done to very tight deadlines. Journalists and copywriters need a very clear understanding of the audience that they are writing for, the context in which their words will be placed and what the purpose of the writing is.

Activity: National Council for the Training of Journalists

The National Council for the Training of Journalists (NCTJ) is an independent registered charity which offers professional training for journalists and sets standards that influence the industry, its practices and employment conditions.

It was established in 1951 and now plays an influential role in all aspects of journalism education and training. Education providers across the UK have been accredited by the NCTJ to offer approved journalism training courses, and the NCTJ also offers distance learning courses and publishes its own training CDs and manuals.

Visit the NCTJ website (www.nctj.com) for more information and to find the answers to the following questions.

1. Where is your nearest NCTJ-accredited centre?
2. Which centre offers an NCTJ-accredited press photography and photojournalism course?
3. What other types of course are available through the NCTJ?

Activity: Newspaper analysis

Look through a selection of newspapers from the same day and select examples of the same story that appears in more than one paper.

Try to identify the different styles and writing techniques used in each paper. Look at the types of words that are used. Are they emotive words or has the writer chosen words that are more neutral? Are they negative or positive words? Are the sentences long or short?

Explain why these different techniques have been used and what their impact on the reader might be.

Different newspapers target different audiences. What newspapers and magazines do you read? Why?

Working on images

Images are just as important as the printed word, if not more important, and can communicate powerful messages. Digitally produced images are widely used within print-based media. Modern digital photographic equipment produces high quality images that can easily be enhanced, manipulated and transferred quickly all over the world.

> ### Think about it
>
> There is a saying that 'the camera never lies'. To what extent is this true?

Photographs are not the only images used in printed products. Cartoons, line drawings, logos, charts and diagrams can all be used to illustrate a piece of copy and attract the attention of potential readers. The industry uses the skills of photographers and graphic designers to produce images for their products. Many of them are commissioned to produce specific images for a specific publication on a freelance basis.

Many photographers also sell images to picture libraries and photo agencies which charge a fee to print-based media producers to allow them to reproduce the images in their products.

> ### Activity: Images
>
> Collect at least five images from printed media products. Write down what these images communicate and what the relationship is between the image and the words that accompany it.

Putting copy, images and graphics together in a way that is pleasing to the eye and satisfies the demands of the brief is a skilled job. Pre-press designers and layout artists use desktop publishing and design software packages to help them work quickly and efficiently.

Combining words and images: the editing process

Once the copy and images have been produced and combined, editing takes place to check that the material fits the brief and the finished product makes sense and doesn't have any mistakes.

The publishers of newspapers and magazines employ an editor to oversee the whole product, who will in turn use sub-editors to edit specific parts of the publication.

For the written material, a sub-editor might be responsible for restructuring the material, checking the copy for accuracy, adding or deleting text to make it fit the required word count, adding headlines and sub-headings or making other necessary adjustments to the copy.

A sub-editor who is responsible for images might select or commission the image or graphic, scale it (increase or decrease the size) to make it fit the available space, crop the image to get rid of unwanted parts of the picture, or add a caption to make its meaning clearer.

Once the content has been finalised and signed off by the editor it is ready to be printed. The stages of the print production process are explained in more detail in Unit 18, Producing print-based media. Here we can note that large-scale print houses will employ printers, print-coordinators and print finishers to produce a broad range of print-media products, often from many different sources and organisations.

Digital technology has had a very large impact on the print industry which, until relatively recently, relied on more traditional mechanical methods of print production. New methods of production and distribution have led to a greater emphasis on computer-based technology, and a need for a highly skilled workforce.

Pages are now usually produced by publishers as PDFs (a file format called Portable Document Format, a stable and secure way for document exchange), which are then digitally transferred into printing online scheduling tools. Printing plates are created directly from these digital files which are then loaded into printing presses.

Working in the print-based industries

The industry requires recruits with strong project management skills across digital and print formats, and good skills in new technologies in this fast-changing environment, as well as skilled producers of the actual content in terms of words, images, design and print.

Many of these roles are carried out on a freelance basis (for example, see the case study below).

Skillset reports that 13 per cent of the publishing workforce is freelance, though there are variations within this overall figure. In the book publishing sector, the figure is 19 per cent but in newspapers it falls to just 5 per cent.

(Source: Labour Force Survey, Apr 2009–Mar 2010).

Case study: Carl, freelance page layout artist

Carl studied graphic design at university and after working for an advertising agency on a part-time contract decided to go freelance. He now works for a number of different advertising agencies and production houses on short-term commissions.

He mainly works from home and enjoys the flexibility that freelance work brings, though he has to manage his finances very carefully, as working in this way means that he does not have a guaranteed wage coming in each month.

He has a fast broadband connection and receives most of his work via email attachments. He works on these using page layout design software applications, according to the specific brief that has been supplied with the copy and images.

These are then converted into PDFs and emailed to the client.

For some of the larger projects he is commissioned for he will work in the offices of an agency or production house on their own computers with a team of other designers all working together on a specific publication.

1. What are the advantages and the disadvantages of working on short-term commissions?

2. Why will Carl need to read the brief he receives from the client very carefully?

3. What are the differences between working from home and working in an office as part of a team of people?

Activity: Researching jobs in print-based media industries

The final learning outcome of Unit 11 requires you to produce personal development material, which includes plans for your future career achievements. To achieve a higher grade for this you will need to relate your understanding of relevant job roles to your personal career path, identifying any skills gaps that you have and suggesting realistic personal development plans for filling those gaps. You will also need to show how your personal skills can best be used in the industry.

1. Explore the roles in print-based media that appeal to you by building a portfolio of job descriptions, person specifications and employment contracts for a range of jobs. The following publications and websites may help:

- *The Bookseller*: www.thebookseller.com
- British Printing Industries Federation (BPIF): www.britishprint.com
- *The Guardian* newspaper (Media section, Mondays): www.guardian.co.uk
- www.journalism.co.uk
- Periodical Publishers Association: www.ppa.co.uk
- PrintWeek jobs: www.printweek.com

2. What skills and qualifications are needed for the roles that interest you?

3. Write an application letter for one of them.

The print-based media industry as a business

This section of the chapter is relevant to Unit 11, LO3 and LO4.

Finance and expenditure

As with all commercial media businesses, assessing the financial viability of a proposed print-based media production is an important aspect of working in the industry. This involves two factors: understanding the potential sources of finance for a specific product (such as selling advertising space, sponsorship, subscription fees, cover price); and the expenditure involved in its production (such elements as staffing and personnel, equipment hire or purchase or maintenance costs, materials, research and development, marketing and promotion, distribution, copyright and legal costs).

The productions you undertake for your practical units will probably be subsidised by your college, as you will be using their equipment and materials and will not have to pay for your own crew. This means that your financial needs will be minimal and you will not necessarily need to secure funding for your projects.

However, you need to demonstrate that you are able to work in a realistic vocational context and that you understand the financial and market influences on your print-production work. You should therefore explore the potential funding for your project work as well as the potential costs, as both of these factors are critical to all creative media productions if they are to be viable.

The print-media marketplace is highly competitive, with many titles jostling for readers. To try to get ahead, print-media producers often undertake or commission detailed market research to get a better understanding of their target market. They are interested in what the market looks like, who the competitors are and what their products are like. They are particularly interested in the economic factors and the potential revenue available within the market.

Activity: UK newspaper market

News International Ltd is owned by Rupert Murdoch's News Corporation and publishes the *Sun*, *The Times*, the *Sunday Times* and the *News of the World*. Find out more about the UK national newspaper market and the position of these four newspapers in this market.

The print-based industries and the law

When you work within the print-based media industry producing material for published products, you must be aware of the legal, ethical and professional constraints that apply and ensure that you abide by these and do not get yourself, or your publication, into trouble.

Laws on data protection, libel and the publication of obscene or offensive material are relatively clear, but the UK, unlike many other countries, has no clear law on privacy. Therefore newspapers and magazines have to be very careful when planning stories and articles.

When planning the content of your print-based product you may want to use some existing material, such as graphics or photographs from a picture library or sourced from the Internet, or to reproduce text from an existing source. In such cases you will need to be aware of copyright.

When investigating the print-based media industry and undertaking your own print-production work, you also

Activity: Sources of finance

Research the potential sources of finance available for a range of different print-based media products.

- How much income can be generated from these sources?
- What processes and practices do organisations use to try to secure this income?
- What specific items of expenditure are needed to produce these products?

Write up your findings in the form of a short report.

need to be aware of the relevant regulatory bodies that help to control the industry.

The **Advertising Standards Authority (ASA)** is the independent regulator of the advertising industry (www.asa.org.uk).

The **Press Complaints Commission (PCC)** is an independent self-regulatory body that deals with complaints about the content of newspapers and magazines. It produces a Code of Practice for the industry to help regulate what can and cannot be printed (www.pcc.org.uk).

The **Editors' Code of Practice Committee** is a group which publishes *The Editors' Codebook*, a practical guide to how the PCC interprets the self-regulating press Code of Practice (www.editorscode.org.uk).

Activity: Regulatory bodies

- Visit the website of the ASA to find more information about the organisation. Write up your findings in a short report.
- Use the PCC website or *The Editors' Codebook* (available online from the website above) to find out how complaints can be resolved by the PCC.

- How are complaints against a newspaper's website usually resolved?
- What are the advantages and disadvantages of the publishing industry using its own Code of Practice to regulate and control newspapers and magazines through the PCC?
- Does the PCC only deal with complaints?

Case study: Intrusive reporting

In 2009 a couple complained to the PCC that an article published in their local newspaper was intrusive and in breach of the Code of Practice.

The article reported the couple's concern that their home had been damaged by a builder and its last paragraph contained the mobile phone number of the husband.

The couple argued that the story was intrusive, that they had not given consent for the story to be published, and they strongly objected to the publication of a private telephone number. They had subsequently received numerous crank calls, and were concerned about their personal security.

The newspaper accepted that it had made a serious error regarding the phone number and explained that the reporter had left it in by mistake and that the sub-editor should have removed it during the editing process. The newspaper's editor apologised unreservedly for this mistake and offered to publish an apology in the paper.

1. Why were the couple particularly unhappy about the inclusion of a personal phone number in the article?
2. Who was responsible for the error?
3. Do you think that the couple would have been happy with the published apology?

Print-based techniques

This section of the chapter is relevant to Unit 18, LO1.

Most of the print products that you thought of in the Set up exercise at the start of this chapter will have been printed by some form of machine, but this has not always been the case. Many traditional hand-operated processes are still in use today, though usually for producing pieces of art and design work, and as a hobby craft, rather than for producing commercial media products.

Methods of printing

There are three main types of printing that you need to understand. These are traditional **hand-operated processes** (including etching, linocut, woodcut and screen printing), **mechanical processes** that use some form of machinery (for example, flexography and gravure), and new **digital processes** that are now widely used within the commercial printing industry (for instance, laser printing, inkjet printing and the use of desktop publishing software).

Key terms

Hand-operated processes – usually used today for producing pieces of art and design rather than for commercial media production; include etching and screen printing.

Mechanical processes – involve the use of some form of machinery and include offset-litho and gravure.

Digital processes – widely used within the commercial printing industry; include photocopying and the use of desktop publishing (DTP) software.

Hand-operated processes

One hand-operated method of printing still popular today is screen printing, a way of making multiple copies of a two-dimensional design on a range of different materials including fabric, paper and card. The screen is made from material such as silk which has a fine mesh and is stretched on to a wooden frame. A stencil of the image to be reproduced is laid on the mesh and ink is forced through the mesh and on to the paper or fabric underneath.

Screen printing can be a very creative process but can also be time-consuming and is only suitable for small print runs. Mechanised and digital versions of traditional hand-operated screen printing equipment are now available and are often used for printing posters, T-shirts, fabric and wallpaper.

Other methods of printing by hand include etching, where etches (or scratches) are made on a copper plate which is then coated with ink and pressed on to paper to reproduce the image. Many famous artists, including Picasso and Rembrandt, used etching to reproduce their pictures.

Woodcut and linocut are similar methods that use different materials for the printing surface. In a woodcut, an image is carved into the surface of a piece of wood, removing the pieces of wood which are not required to print and leaving the remaining parts of the original surface to form the printing image. This is called relief printing. The surface of the wooden block is covered with ink by roller, and the block is pressed on to paper to transfer the ink and reproduce the image.

Linocuts are broadly similar but the image is cut into a sheet of linoleum instead of a block of wood. Linoleum is made from solidified linseed oil and is easier to cut than wood, though it is quite fragile and the linoleum printing plate can deteriorate with continued use.

Did you know?

The pop artist Andy Warhol is famous for his screen prints of celebrities such as Marilyn Monroe and Elvis Presley. He transferred photographic images to a silk screen and then used a rubber squeegee to press different coloured paints through the screen on to paper underneath. By repeating the process the same image is reproduced, but each copy is different.

Mechanised processes

The invention of the mechanical printing press by Johannes Gutenberg in Germany in around 1450 led to the decline in traditional hand methods of printing and the growth in ever more sophisticated mechanical processes as the demand for mass-produced printed material grew.

Before printing was invented, books and manuscripts had to be copied by hand and it could take up to two

Letterpress machines were used in the publishing industry to mass produce newspapers. What were the advantages and disadvantages of this system for producing newspapers?

years to copy a book. The invention of **letterpress printing** using moveable type made from metal characters meant that whole pages of text could be put on to a press and used to produce hundreds of copies of books and manuscripts. At first, print runs were limited to around 200 or 300 copies, but soon much larger print runs were being produced.

Flexography uses much thinner plates made of a flexible material such as rubber or a special type of plastic. The words and images to be printed are transferred to the plates by a photographic process, and the inks used are quick-drying. Flexography can be used to print on materials such as polythene and metallic films, for plastic shopping bags and food packaging.

Recent developments in flexographic inks have made them even faster drying, resulting in faster, more cost-efficient production. As a result many newspaper publishers are moving over to flexo printing.

Lithography also uses flexible plates produced by a photographic process. The plates are attached to a cylinder and the process relies on the fact that oil and water do not mix. Some parts of the printing plate are kept wet so that the oily ink is rejected by the wet areas of the plate and only sticks to the dry areas,

which are the words and images to be printed. These are transferred on to the paper that comes into contact with the inky cylinder.

Offset-litho printing uses the same principle, but the paper does not come into direct contact with the printing plate, as the image is first transferred to a rubber roller, called an offset blanket or offset cylinder. Lithography is used for medium and large print runs of products such as magazines, posters and books.

Offset-litho presses that take one sheet of paper at a time are called sheet-fed presses and are often used for high quality work. Paper can also be fed from a large roll, called a web, and such presses are called **web-litho presses**. They are used for large print runs such as magazines and catalogues.

Case study: Northcliffe Media

Northcliffe Media is part of the Daily Mail and General Trust (DMGT) group which has a wide range of media interests including national and regional newspapers, news and classified websites, radio, exhibitions and information publishing.

Northcliffe Media publishes 110 newspapers, including dailies, weeklies and free sheets, which are read by a total of over 5.8 million readers. Titles include the *Leicester Mercury*, *Bristol Evening Post*, *Essex Chronicle* and *Derby Telegraph*.

Its papers are printed by another company in the DMGT group, Harmsworth Printing, who operate from four sites across the UK. These sites include both web offset and flexographic printing. At their newest print plant in Didcot they have installed state-of-the-art flexo presses which produce every page of the *Daily Mail* and the *Mail on Sunday* in colour.

In total the four sites produce over four million copies of national and regional titles including all the Northcliffe Media titles and over 200 contract print titles.

1. Why does the company use web offset printing presses for printing newspapers?

2. What are the advantages of the flexo press?

3. What are the advantages and disadvantages of being such a large media organisation?

When printing with more than one colour, a different plate is used for each of the main colours, with overprinting using translucent ink allowing different colours to be reproduced. Four-colour printing derives its name from the four colours of ink that are used (see Figure 1). With these, the full range of colours on the spectrum can be printed.

RGB is the other important term used for colours, and stands for red, green and blue. Scanners and digital cameras produce images using a combination of these three colours. Commercial printers have to convert RGB-produced colours into CMYK colours to ensure that their printed products look correct.

Gravure is a web-fed printing process that uses a copper-coated cylinder on to which a reverse image of the print product is engraved. This cylinder prints directly on to the substrate (the material, such as paper, on to which the printing takes place), with a softer roller applying pressure with the substrate. Gravure printing is used for long, high-quality print runs such as magazines, mail-order catalogues, packaging, and printing on to fabric and wallpaper.

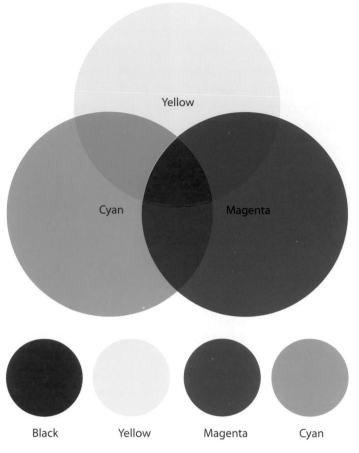

Black   Yellow   Magenta   Cyan

Figure 1: Did you know that the term 'CMYK' derives from the colours used in four-colour printing: cyan (C), magenta (M), yellow (Y) and the 'key plate' black (K)?

A modern-day printing press in action. What printing technology is available to you to help you produce your own print-based media products?

Digital printing

Digital printing is now commonplace in domestic and office environments and becoming increasingly popular for commercial printing. This is because digital printers, such as inkjet and laser printers, are now capable of high-quality colour printing using variable data, and are also cost effective for shorter print runs. 'Variable data' refers to the different information that can be sent to a printer when printing the same product, for example, individually addressed letters printed from a standard template, or personalised promotional material with specific elements targeted at individual people.

Activity: Digital printing

Digital printing allows the use of variable data so that personalised promotional material can be produced relatively cheaply and quickly.

Can you find any examples of material that has been produced using variable printing techniques for your portfolio?

The commercial printing process

The three main stages of the commercial printing process are called pre-press, press and post-press, also known as print finishing.

Pre-press is the generic term for all the design and preparatory work that is needed to get a product ready for print. The **press** stage describes the actual printing process. The **post-press** or **print finishing** stage is when the processes such as cutting, trimming, folding and binding take place on the printed material before a product such as a newspaper or magazine can be distributed.

One of the biggest changes in the print industry has perhaps been on the pre-press side, with the introduction of ever more sophisticated computer-based programs for the design and layout of pages, replacing the traditional labour-intensive physical cut-and-paste methods.

Activity: Software programs

A pre-press designer needs to be familiar with a range of software programs used within the industry to manipulate, control and combine text, images and graphics.

Which software applications are available for your own pre-press work?

Once the design is finalised, the copy written, the images added and the whole product edited and signed off by the client, it needs to be printed, with the choice of printing method dependent on the type of product, the reproduction quality needed, the amount of money available and the size of print run. The printing process needs to be monitored and controlled carefully so that the quality can be maintained throughout the whole run.

As we have noted, print finishing is the range of procedures that follow after a product is printed and before it can be distributed and used. The finishing process usually includes cutting and trimming the product to the appropriate size. If the product is a book, leaflet, newspaper or magazine then the pages need to be collated in the right order, folded, and a form of binding applied. This might be staples, glue or some form of stitching.

Key terms

Pre-press – the generic term for all the work needed to get a product ready for print.

Press – the term for the actual printing process.

Post-press or **print finishing** – the processes that take place on the printed material before a product can be distributed.

Creating print-based products

This section of the chapter is relevant to Unit 18, LO2, LO3 and LO4.

Generating ideas

Much of your time on Unit 18, Producing print-based media, will be focused on the development of ideas for print-based media products which you will take through the pre-production, production and print-finishing processes before finally reflecting upon your own production work.

This creative production process, followed by a period of reflection and self-evaluation, is common to the practical production units in all the pathways. The range of work that you develop and produce for Unit 18 needs to include the use of both traditional and digital production methods, and your centre should write assignments for the practical work that involve real or simulated client briefs that provide a realistic vocational context for the work to be undertaken.

Creative production starts with creative thinking, so it is important to get the ideas flowing as early in the process as you can. If you are working in a group, a good way of starting to generate ideas for your print-based media products is to sit round a table and generate ideas.

It is important that everybody in your group makes a contribution to the session and that all the ideas are recorded in some way so that they are not lost or forgotten. A flip chart or whiteboard can be used to write down the ideas as they emerge, or you might want to record the session so that you have a permanent record of the process.

This session is about getting all the ideas out, no matter how strange they may at first appear. It is important to consider all of the options because you cannot always tell initially which ideas will work, or what else they may inspire.

You should consider a range of different print products, such as newspapers, magazines and newsletters, publicity and promotional material. As the ideas are discussed you should begin to explore some of the more viable ones a little further to assess their potential, considering factors such as:

- the cost of production
- the availability of resources
- the size and quality of the print run
- the profile of the potential audience and market
- any legal regulations that you will need to abide by
- any ethical issues that your proposals might generate.

A **SWOT** analysis might help you to identify the most viable ideas to take forward to production. This involves discussing each idea in terms of its **S**trengths and **W**eaknesses, and any **O**pportunities and **T**hreats (or barriers) that it presents.

Activity: SWOT analysis

Choose a selection of your preferred ideas.

Write the name of each idea on a separate piece of paper and then divide each piece of paper into four areas with a large cross. In the top left section write the word 'Strengths', in the top right write 'Weaknesses', in the bottom left write 'Opportunities' and in the bottom right put 'Threats'.

For each idea, undertake a SWOT analysis by discussing the strengths and weaknesses of each idea, the opportunities that it will bring and the potential barriers that might get in your way of doing it. Summarise your findings in the relevant section of the paper.

At the end of the process, use your analyses to help you decide on the best ideas to take forward to production.

Activity: Generating ideas

What do you think is the best way to make sure that all of your ideas are recorded and captured?

Going into production

Having decided on the best idea to take forward you now have to work it up into a firm proposal that you can take through the pre-press, press and print-finishing processes to complete the finished product (see the Development portfolio activity below).

Activity: Development portfolio

As you develop your ideas and work through the pre-production stages, start to build a development portfolio of evidence in which you log the work undertaken, including supporting information such as developmental images, sketches, thumbnails, ideas sheets, concept drawings and trial prints. These should be clearly annotated to show the progress you have made and the processes you have gone through.

You could work alone to develop your printed material but it is a good idea to work on at least one large project as part of a production team as this more closely reflects the vocational working environment, and you will be able to share ideas and work together to produce a well-designed and professional-looking product.

For example, you and your production team could produce a student newspaper or magazine for your school or college. This is a good idea for this unit as it allows each member of the group to take responsibility for the development, design and production of a specific section of the newspaper or magazine, while you work together on other aspects such as the front cover, marketing and advertising.

Activity: Producing a magazine

Form a production team with other members of your class. Hold a planning meeting to discuss ideas for a new student magazine for your school or college and decide which pages each team member will be responsible for producing.

Discuss the front cover with the group. How you are going to market your product? What potential is there for generating revenue from selling advertising space in the magazine?

Print the magazine using appropriate available printing resources, take it through the print-finishing processes and then distribute it to your audience.

Think about it

- Try to get hands-on experience of as many different types of print production technology and techniques as you can.

- Try to make links with a company or organisation operating in the print-media industry and ask if you can visit to increase your knowledge and understanding.

- Spend time carefully planning your own print-based media products so that you can apply your knowledge and take your ideas through the pre-press, press and print-finishing processes successfully.

Peter Bedford
Printer

My role as a printer within a large FE college is very varied and I'm involved in all stages of the production processes: pre-press, press and print finishing.

We have some large offset-litho and flexography printed presses that we use to produce marketing and promotional material for the college and now also have a digital press that we use for variable data printing so that we can produce material that is targeted at individual clients.

I have to work closely with other members of the print team and get involved with lots of different types of job. So I have to have a good overview of the whole production process and have good technical skills and knowledge. I also have to be a good communicator as I have to deal with lots of different sorts of people and make sure that the information we get from our clients is accurate.

I have learned that having a flexible approach to your work and having a broad knowledge base are very important to working in the print industry and that you have to be able to work well on your own as well as being an effective team member.

Being organised is very important as the production run has to be carefully planned and scheduled and we often have to work to very tight deadlines. I also have to work very accurately and get things right first time. When I press the button to print hundreds of copies of a poster I have to be sure that everything is right or else I will waste a lot of time and money.

Think about it!

- Why do you need to be very organised and work quickly and accurately in the print industry?
- What skills do you have already that would help you to work well in a print production environment?
- What impact do changes in technology have on print-media production?

Just checking

1. Identify the main types of hand printing.
2. Explain the main forms of mechanical printing and what each type is best used for.
3. What does CMYK stand for?
4. What is variable printing?
5. What are the names of the main stages of the commercial printing process?
6. What is text called that is going to be printed?
7. What processes can print finishing include?
8. Explain what the editing process involves.
9. What is copyright and why is it important in the print industry?
10. Identify the main regulatory bodies for the print-based media industries.

edexcel

Assignment tips

- You need to provide clear evidence of how you developed ideas and designs for your print-based media products, for example, pre-press mock-ups and experimental print runs, together with the final products themselves.

- The products on their own will not be enough to secure the highest grades. You need to supplement them with a detailed commentary explaining the developmental and production processes you have undertaken, the technology and techniques you have used and the skills you have developed.

- Keep a thorough log of your practical production work, including any changes you make, and why. The highest grades will be awarded for reflective work showing the ability to make well-judged decisions. You will need to explain your decisions, demonstrating an excellent understanding of the relevant technical and professional issues.

- It is important to show clearly what your individual contribution has been to the group project. Your commentary should be supported by relevant tutor observation records and feedback from your client and target audience.

- To achieve at least a merit grade, your evidence will need to show a clear and considered progression from your original ideas and designs through to the completed production work, which will need to be of a good quality and reflect high standards of design and preparation work.

- You will also need to show that you can work effectively on your own initiative, display good self-management skills and work positively with other team members to meet the required deadlines.

- Allow time at the end of the chapter to ensure your final portfolio of evidence is well organised and presents your work in the best possible way.

Interactive media

Though the interactive media industry is relatively new in comparison with other media industries, its rapid growth means it is now the largest industry in the creative media sector, creating a wide variety of multimedia content for the Internet, computers, kiosks, mobile phones, DVDs, digital television, media players and other emerging technologies. This also means that it overlaps with many other industries.

The industry uses a combination of employed and freelance staff and multi-skilling is an increasingly important factor for employment in this sector. Many roles within the interactive media industry require a combination of both creative and technical computing skills. While some employees within the industry will specialise in one or two complex programs for creating interactive media content, many others will need to be able to use a wide range of software, as well as have traditional visualisation skills.

Interactive media often need to be produced within short deadlines and tight budgets, and you will need to have an understanding of the constraints of interactive media production. Interactive products are targeted at specific audiences and those working within the industry also require a good understanding of the legal, ethical and professional constraints and practices that help to ensure that these audiences are properly served.

Undertaking the Interactive media pathway will allow you to develop your knowledge and understanding of the industry and the production techniques and technologies that it uses. The pathway includes two specific mandatory units: Unit 12, Understanding the interactive media industry and Unit 19, Digital graphics for interactive media.

This chapter is designed to give you an overview of the interactive media industry and the types of skills you will need for this pathway. You will find details of the learning outcomes and the assessment and grading criteria for the Interactive media pathway on pages 262–264.

Nicola, Interactive media pathway student

I have always enjoyed drawing, but I also like to use computers so wanted a course that would allow me to continue to develop my skills in both areas. As part of my IT qualification at school I designed a website and am considering a career in web design, but also enjoy a lot of the other skills I have learned on the Interactive media pathway.

I enjoyed researching the interactive media industry and finding out about the different roles available and the different types of products that the interactive media industry produces.

I also enjoyed finding out about the different types of digital graphics which are used in interactive media products, the different computer programmes used to produce them and which are most appropriate for which jobs. This helped me in my practical production work as it made me think about the production process more carefully so that the finished work looked better and graphics for websites downloaded faster.

I made links with the college's marketing department and was able to help them in the production of a page showcasing student work on the college intranet. This was really good as the college's marketing department used the same software that we had been studying.

Over to you!

- Why did you choose the Interactive media pathway?
- What links can you make to help you get hands-on experience of interactive media technology?
- What skills do you think you will need to develop to succeed on this pathway?

The interactive media industry

This section of the chapter is relevant to Unit 12, LO1, LO4 and LO5.

Set up

What is interactive media?

What do you understand by the term interactive media?

Make a list of the different types of interactive media content you use regularly, for example, social networking sites.

For each one, list the platforms you can use to access them, for example, PC, DVD player, mobile phone.

Finding out about the industry

The interactive media industry is dynamic and an exciting place to work. Interactive media have developed quickly and continue to do so. The industry includes both very large and very small companies, while many more people work in other industry contexts within an interactive media role, for example many companies produce their own websites in house. As well as this, the interactive media industry itself overlaps with a great number of other media fields. All in all, the interactive media industry is hard to define; Skillset describes it as 'not so much a sector as a discipline'.

Skillset's Employment Census 2009 reports that the interactive media sector employs around 35,000 people. Almost 70 per cent of them work for companies with fewer than 10 employees; only 3 per cent work for companies with more than 50 employees. (This number excludes interactive media specialists working in associated industries such as animation and those employed outside the sector, for example, in banks or government departments.)

The majority of those working in the industry are involved in the production of online content for the web or Internet, with the remainder working in offline multimedia, interactive television and mobile content. An increasing number (around 21 per cent) of the workforce operates on a self-employed freelance basis.

As is the case within other industries in the creative media sector, many local and regional interactive media organisations have been subsumed by expanding national and multinational organisations. However, there is still a large number of small local businesses flourishing within the industry.

Employees and freelancers within the industry constantly need to update their skills in response to the challenges that new technologies bring and the associated demands and expectations of audiences. Flexibility and multi-skilling (the ability to work in a number of different areas and within different media) is an increasingly important factor for employment in these industries.

The organisations listed below, among others, are associated with the interactive media industry.

- The Chartered Institute for IT (BCS) – www.bcs.org
- British Interactive Media Association (BIMA) – www.bima.co.uk
- Entertainment and Leisure Software Publishers Association (ELSPA) – www.elspa.com
- The Independent Game Developers' Association (TIGA) – www.tiga.org
- International Game Developers Association (IGDA) – www.igda.org
- Producers Alliance for Cinema and Television (Pact) – www.pact.co.uk

Activity: Organisations

Investigate the role of each of the organisations on page 213. Then answer the questions below.

1. Where can you find news about industry events and new technology?

2. Where can you find out about conferences, trade shows and other events for the interactive media industry?

3. Where can you find out about anti-piracy law and technologies?

4. Which organisations offer student membership or other forms of support and information for students?

5. Which organisations offer career development opportunities?

PLTS

Researching information independently will help develop your skills as an **independent enquirer**.

Job roles and skills

Interactive media material may comprise a combination of words (copy), images, animation, video, audio and interactive content. People working in the industry are often multi-skilled and are able to work in more than one of these areas, for example creating and manipulating digital images and then incorporating them into an interactive product.

Creative and technical roles include:

- multimedia design
- multimedia production
- web developing
- photo imaging
- graphic design
- applications developing
- analysis
- content strategy
- information architecture
- animation
- scriptwriting
- Search Engine Optimisation (SEO)
- usability

- 3D modelling
- programming
- quality assurance testing.

As well as creative and technical production staff the industry also offers employment in such areas as project management and production coordination, editorial, marketing, management, administration, law and finance.

Throughout the industry, key activities include a range of organisational, planning and research skills as well as the ability to communicate clearly, respond to a brief creatively and manage and review a production process efficiently, accurately, within budget and on schedule.

Activity: Skillset

Skillset is the Sector Skills Council for Creative Media, including interactive media. The Skillset website contains a wealth of information about careers and job roles in the industry.

1. Visit www.skillset.org and find out about a range of interactive media job roles. For each job, note down the main activities and responsibilities, and the technical skills, personal qualities and knowledge that are needed to begin work in these roles.

2. Which area of the interactive media industry do you feel you might enjoy working in or might be suited to? Which of the necessary skills and qualities do you already possess? Which skills and qualities do you feel you need to develop?

PLTS

Researching roles and contractual details will help develop your skills as an **independent enquirer**.

Entering the industry

Since the industry is so wide-ranging, ways into the industry can also be many and varied. In common with other creative media industries, the interactive media industry sometimes has openings for new entrants as production assistants or other starter-level posts. While the trade press for the interactive media industry will include advertisements for a range of current vacancies, you may also need to think laterally and explore the press for related industries where interactive media work may also be available.

Activity: Finding a way in

Try to make some links with a local company or organisation operating within the interactive media industry. Ask them if you can go on a visit to increase your knowledge and understanding – and of course to build up personal contacts for the future.

The trade press

The following organisations, publications and websites are worth exploring for industry news, developments, training events, trade fairs and current vacancies.

- *Creative Review* – www.creativereview.co.uk
- *Develop* – www.develop-online.net
- *Edge* – www.edge-online.com
- *The Guardian* – www.guardian.co.uk/jobs
- MCV – www.mcvuk.com
- Mobile Entertainment Forum (MEF) – www.m-e-f.org
- *New Media Age* – www.nma.co.uk

Trade shows may provide an opportunity to meet employers in your chosen industry, as well as giving you an insight into recent developments in the trade and what is on the market, both in terms of the products themselves, and in terms of new technologies for producing interactive media products.

Activity: Trade shows

Research past and future industry exhibitions, trade fairs and conferences in the events diary listings and news coverage of the trade press. Explore the associated websites for a range of events that interest you.

- What range of businesses and organisations exhibit at these events?
- What professional development opportunities do these trade shows offer?
- Can you organise a trip to a trade show through your school or college?

No matter which part of the interactive media industry you want to work in, any prospective employer will want to see evidence of your skills. You will need to be able to demonstrate creative and original thinking as well as technical skills, and the ability to turn your ideas into successful interactive media products.

The best way to provide evidence of your abilities is to build up a digital portfolio of your work. Your digital portfolio could take the form of a showreel, a DVD of work or a personal website. It should be as diverse as possible in terms of content to help you demonstrate a wide range of skills. It also needs to be as professionally produced as possible, with menus, navigation and titles all in place and fully functioning, so that it looks professional and does the job of demonstrating your abilities, skills and strengths.

You will also need a carefully written CV, which should sum up your skills, experience and personal qualities succinctly and effectively. While it is good to create a version that includes all of your skills and experience, remember that the employer will be looking for evidence that you will fit the particular job on offer, so for each job application tailor your basic CV to highlight the relevant experience, and leave out details that are irrelevant for the job you are applying for. You need to persuade the employer that you can do this particular job and are worth interviewing, and they need to be able to find clear, relevant information that will convince them of this, quickly and easily.

Activity: Tailoring your CV

1. Collect a selection of job advertisements for a range of interactive media roles. Create a tailored CV and write a letter of application for one or two jobs that interest you. Think about how to adjust them according to the different requirements of the jobs.

2. Build up your digital portfolio. Include a wide selection of projects (for example, websites, interactive CD or DVD) to demonstrate a wide range of skills.

PLTS

Preparing your own career development materials will help develop your skills as a **reflective learner**.

Developing your digital portfolio will help develop your skills as a **creative thinker** and a **self-manager**.

Luke Campbell
Freelance web designer

I studied web design at university and after working on the web team of a large design agency for two years, I decided to go freelance.

It was hard to find clients at first, but I now have a number of regular clients as well as working on short-term commissions for different agencies and production houses during their busy periods or to provide holiday cover.

When producing websites for clients I work from home but have to travel to meet with them. When I'm working for agencies or production houses I sometimes produce content from home but sometimes work for them in-house in their offices on their own computers.

I enjoy the flexibility that freelance work brings, but it can be hard to balance the demands of the agencies with those of my own clients. I have to manage finances very carefully as freelancing means that I don't have a guaranteed wage coming in each month.

I use a variety of programs. As well as designing web pages I sometimes design digital animations for banners and edit photographs or even video clips and optimise them for the web. I have to make sure the sites I design work using all the major Internet browsers. Clients may also want sites that can be used on a variety of platforms such as mobile phones as well as PCs. It's also my job to make sure that the sites I design get high rankings on search engines. I have a fast broadband connection and communicate with clients mainly by phone or email. I upload proposed web designs to private areas on the Internet for clients to view them.

For some of the larger projects, I'm commissioned to work as part of a team alongside programmers or specialist content developers, such as animators or designers working on 3D digital content.

Think about it!

- What do you think are the main advantages and disadvantages of working freelance? Make a list and discuss these with your group.
- Do you think you would prefer the flexibility of freelancing or the security of a permanent position?

Developing an interactive media production

This section of the chapter is relevant to Unit 12, LO2 and LO3, and Unit 19, LO2.

Developing ideas and originating designs

The range of services and products offered within the interactive media industry is considerable. You will need to understand the breadth of activities in the industry, and can begin by looking at some current trends.

Creative production starts with a creative approach to the brief. First you need a clear understanding of what the client, or whoever sets the brief, requires. When you are sure you understand what is required, it is important to get the ideas flowing as early in the process as you can. If you are working in a group then a good way of starting to generate ideas for your interactive media products is to sit round a table and share ideas.

It is important that everybody in your group makes a contribution to this session and that all of the ideas are recorded in some way so that they do not become lost or forgotten. A flip chart or whiteboard can be used to write down the ideas as they are discussed or you might want to record the session so that you have a permanent record of the process.

The key point is to get all of the ideas out, no matter how strange they may at first appear. It is important that all of the options are considered because you cannot always tell which ideas will work, or what further ideas they may inspire during discussion.

As you refine your ideas, you will begin to think about your approach in more detail.

When generating and deciding on ideas you need to give some consideration to factors such as:

- the profile of the potential audience and market
- any legal regulations that you will need to abide by, for example, copyright
- any ethical issues that your proposals might generate, for example, confidentiality, representation (race, gender, religion, sexuality), decency, libel
- any specific requirements of the client, for example, colour schemes, fonts or logo use
- the file types used and the best file formats to optimise these for the intended output.

Activity: Graphics

1. Imagine that you have been asked to design graphics for use on a college website. What range of digital graphics will you need to consider?

2. In a group, make a list of ideas for navigation interfaces such as rollover buttons, navigation bars and navigation menus, as well as logos, backgrounds and motion graphics such as animated gifs and web banners.

3. Discuss what other factors you will need to take into consideration as you refine your ideas.

4. Imagine a range of different scenarios for your website production (for example, an advertising campaign encouraging older people to keep fit; a promotional website for a band). How would the different contexts affect the factors you consider, such as the navigational style and imagery?

PLTS

Describing the use of digital graphics technology will help develop your skills as an **independent enquirer**.

Generating ideas for digital graphics will help develop your skills as a **creative thinker** and a **reflective learner**.

Market trends

The range of services and products offered within the interactive media industry is considerable. You will need to understand the breadth of activities in the industry, and can begin by looking at some current trends.

Activity: Products and services

Research three similar companies in the interactive media industry and see what different types of products they offer.

For example, they all may design websites, but do any of them offer search engine optimisation services, web hosting or other services that might set them apart from the competition?

Defining the profile of the potential audience and market for any production is key, whether in your studies or 'out there' in industry. Part of your work for Unit 19, Digital graphics for interactive media, will focus on the development of ideas for interactive media products which you will then take through the production stages following industry practice and reflecting upon your own production work. The range of work that you develop and produce for Unit 19 will be created in response to real or simulated client briefs that provide a realistic vocational context for the work. To do this effectively in your studies or in the real world of work, you will need to understand what clients want and why, and what they expect of you as the commissioned interactive media professional.

Companies may see a website as a necessary expense, or may want a website or other interactive media product to generate profit directly. Either way, they are likely to want to monitor the expenditure involved with its production, covering such elements as staffing and personnel, hardware and software costs, research and development, marketing and promotion, distribution, copyright and legal costs.

Setting objectives is an important aspect of developing a proposed interactive media production. This may include undertaking research into competitor products and the target market, and assessing the financial viability of the product.

Understanding target markets

Any interactive media product needs to be designed with its target audience firmly in mind. A wide variety of interactive media products are often used to popularise and market products towards young adults, since this target audience is generally receptive to – and enthusiastic about – interactive media. For example, teen television programmes such as *Hollyoaks* and *Skins* can build their brands by using their websites to encourage viewers to enter competitions, watch unseen footage, read biographies of the cast, as well as become involved in blogs or sign up for text messages. However, other interactive media products may need to target older audiences, and their design and approach will reflect the interests of the relevant market.

Activity: Marketing using interactive media

Choose a product that is popular with young people, such as a television programme, a media player, mobile phone or soft drink. Research the different ways in which the product is promoted using interactive media.

1. How does the marketing encourage the target market to 'buy into' the brand?

2. Is the product marketed using:
    *   online competitions or interactive games to involve the potential customer?
    *   special offers or discounts for registering online?
    *   viral advertising by email or text message?
    *   spoof sites?
    *   'red button' advertising on digital television?
    *   web 2.0 (such as blogs or social networking) or marketing inside games or virtual worlds?
    *   association with other products, for example, spin-offs, sequels, microsites, charities?

3. Think of a product, service or industry which targets older audiences. Explore how interactive media is used to market the product, and compare it with your findings for the products aimed at a younger market. What are the differences and similarities? How do you explain these differences?

Legal, professional, ethical and contractual considerations

The regulators

The World Wide Web is, for the most part, self-regulated. However, all of those involved in producing material for interactive media products have to be careful not to breach the legal, ethical and professional rules and regulations relating to copyright, data protection, libel, the publication of obscene or offensive material and a host of other issues. Not only the client and the company responsible for designing the website, but also the Internet service provider hosting the website could be in trouble if these rules and regulations are breached, so Internet service providers can be quick to 'take down' websites if complaints are made against them.

When investigating the interactive media industry and when undertaking your own interactive production work you need to be aware of the relevant regulatory and standards bodies that help to control the industry.

Remember

Research the content of your productions carefully to ensure that you do not break any laws or industry guidelines.

What kinds of interactive media advertising campaigns have you experienced? How did these campaigns appeal to you?

Table 1: Regulatory bodies for the interactive media industry.

Advertising Standards Authority (ASA) www.asa.org.uk	The ASA in the independent regulator for the advertising industry. They regulate advertisements in all media, including the following which are relevant to the interactive media industry: • advertisements on the Internet, including banner and display ads and paid-for (sponsored) search results (not claims on companies' own websites) • commercial email and SMS text message advertisements • advertisements on CD-ROMs, DVD and video.
bbfc www.bbfc.co.uk	The British Board of Film Classification is an independent body which classifies films and videos in terms of age suitability.
ISPA UK (Internet Services Providers' Association) www.ispa.org.uk	ISPA UK represents UK providers of Internet services, including making representations on behalf of the industry to government bodies. Membership is voluntary but companies who choose to become members of ISPA UK agree to abide by the ISPA UK Code.
Office of Communications (Ofcom) www.ofcom.org.uk	Ofcom regulates the communications industries, including telecoms, Internet and independent television and radio. The guidelines they produce include: • guidance to broadcasters on interactive television services • guidance on how users can protect themselves against web fraud • a Code of Practice which requires Internet service providers to provide consumers with more information and advice on the maximum broadband speed they can expect to achieve. Where guidance and Codes of Practice fail, Ofcom can consider formal regulation.
Pan European Game Information (PEGI) www.pegi.info	PEGI provides age ratings for computer games using a system recognised across Europe.
World Wide Web Consortium (W3C) www.w3.org	This is an international community that develops standards to ensure the long-term growth of the Web, including accessibility standards – guidelines to make web content accessible to a wider range of people with disabilities, as well as to make web content more accessible to users in general.

Should viral and mobile advertising be regulated?

Copyright

When planning an interactive media product you may want to use some existing archive material, such as photographs or stills from film footage, or material from a sound or photographic library or sourced from the Internet. You might also want to use some existing music or graphics. In all of these cases you will need to be aware of copyright.

Copyright is an automatic right that protects a piece of work (intellectual property) from being copied or used by anyone else without the copyright owner's permission. Copyright owners can choose to grant permission or license others to use the work, usually for a fee, while retaining ownership over the rights themselves. Like other forms of intellectual property, copyright can be bought and sold.

The Internet has made intellectual property a huge issue, for example, the unauthorised use of copyright material on YouTube and illegal video downloads.

Activity: Playing by the rules

Find and look at Ofcom's Broadcasting Code. What are the main areas it covers?

Investigate and discuss in your group the ASA's current position on viral, mobile and online advertising. What are the reasons for and against trying to regulate these areas? What are the practical implications of trying to do so?

What is the current situation with YouTube and/or video downloads and the protection of the intellectual property of television and film makers?

PLTS

Describing contractual, ethical and legal obligations using appropriate subject terminology will help develop your skills as an **independent enquirer**.

Did you know?

It is a common mistake to think that graphics on the Web that do not show the copyright symbol can be freely used… they cannot! All graphics are covered by copyright unless the owners specifically give permission for use or state that the image is 'copyright free'. Sometimes, even in these instances, limitations may still apply, for example, the image may only be copyright free for personal use.

It is also a common error to think that if images are modified using photo editing programmes that copyright no longer applies. In most cases modifying or altering an image infringes the copyright owner's rights unless express permission has been granted.

For more information, visit www.rightsforartists.com/copyright.html

Contracts

When designing work for clients, multimedia design companies enter into a contract with the client company. This normally specifies what the job entails, how much it will cost and how and when payment will be made. In some cases payment will not be due until the project is completed; in other cases the multimedia company may ask for a percentage of the fee in advance. The contract may also include other clauses agreed by the company and the client.

The client may want the developer to enter into a non-disclosure agreement. This means that the developer agrees not to discuss any of the work it is undertaking for the company and guarantees confidentiality. The client may also expect the developer to agree to compensate them for any financial loss that occurs if the job is delivered late.

Think about it

Why might a client want a non-disclosure agreement?

Going into production

Having decided on the best idea to take forward, you have to work this idea up into a firm proposal that you will be able to take through the production process to complete the finished product. This will mean working in a very organised way and keeping records of the production stages from the original development files to the final optimised graphics. You will work to specified deadlines which may be set by your client, tutor, or by yourself. These will need to specify what you will produce and when. Milestones should be set not only for the final product but also for key stages during the production.

Building a development portfolio

As you begin to develop your ideas and work through the pre-production stages, start to build a development portfolio of evidence in which you log and record the work undertaken and include supporting information such as developmental images, sketches, thumbnails, ideas sheets, concept drawings and early visual mock-ups.

You will need to show the different software tools and processes you have used. This could be done by taking screenshots at regular stages of your work.

These should be clearly annotated so that they clearly show the progress that you have made and the different processes that you have gone through. If you have difficulty in organising paper-based work you could scan in your drawings and notes and keep your portfolio as a digital blog using sites such as Wordpress or Blogger, but be sure to keep all the paperwork you generate too.

When you are working on projects on a computer, be sure to save your work regularly. When you become involved in a project it can be very easy to forget to do this, but it is worth remembering as it is very frustrating to lose a lot of work if your computer crashes. If you are doing experimental work, save it regularly under different names, for example, version 1, version 2, so that you can easily return to an earlier version if things do not work out.

Creating digital graphics

This section of the chapter is relevant to Unit 19, LO1, LO2 and LO3.

Types of digital graphics

Digital graphics can be found in virtually every example of interactive media. As you develop your interactive media productions, you will need technical knowledge of digital graphics to underpin your practical work. This final section of the chapter therefore concentrates on digital graphics, the theory of how they are created and optimised and their applications in interactive media production.

Activity: Picture perfect

In a group, find and discuss examples from the Internet of as many different types of digital graphics as you can, for example, photographs, graphics, buttons, etc.

Try to find out how each of these graphics might have been produced – what software and input devices (cameras, scanners and so on) might have been used in their creation.

Digital graphics have many uses, including displaying photographs, logos, textures, buttons, animations and so on. There are two main types of digital image that you need to understand. These are bitmap (or raster) images and vector images.

Bitmap or raster images

A bitmap (or raster) image is composed of tiny squares of colour, or pixels. Common bitmap file formats for use in interactive media are jpg, bmp and tiff.

These are the key advantages of bitmap images.

- Bitmap images are good at displaying subtle graduations of colour and are usually used to display photographic images.
- Each pixel can be individually edited so any tiny flaws or blemishes in the image can be edited out.

The key limitations of bitmap images are as follows.

- When you resize a bitmap image to make it larger it can lose quality as the individual pixels will become visible.
- Because the computer has to store information about every pixel, the file size of bitmaps can be quite large.

Here is a bitmap image of some flowers.

This is the same image as the bitmap image – you can see the pixels are visible when the image is increased in size.

The key limitations of vector images are as follows.

- You can only edit individual shapes in a graphics program, not individual pixels.
- Vector images can look 'cartoony' rather than realistic.

Saving files in different file formats use different methods of compressing files to make them as small as possible. Formats like jpg compress the files to small sizes but lose some image quality. These are known as lossy formats. Lossless formats give better image quality but at the expense of larger file sizes.

Some file formats, such as gif, are good at saving vector images with flat areas of colour as small bitmap images for use on the web.

Here is a version of the original photograph, which has been turned into a vector image.

Vector images

Vector images are generated by graphics programs and are made of individual shapes of different colours which are generated by the program using mathematical formulae. Common vector file formats are eps and fla. Some programs will convert vector images to bitmaps for pixel editing when they are imported.

These are the key advantages of vector images.

- Vector images do not lose quality when scaled.
- Images can be very small because a computer saves information about individual shapes or colour areas, not each individual pixel.

When the vector image is increased in size the pixels are not visible but the image can look cartoon-like.

Another example can be seen below with the two cartoon cars which have been increased in size.

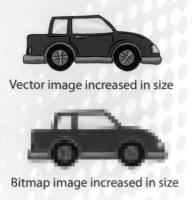

Vector image increased in size

Bitmap image increased in size

Figure 1: When might you use images like this?

Several other factors also affect the quality of your final image on screen. Adjusting these factors to achieve the best image for the intended result, while maintaining a file size small enough for purpose, is known as 'optimising' the images. It would be no use having an image that looked great if it were so large that it took several minutes to appear when viewing it on a web page.

Image resolution

Image resolution refers to how much detail the image holds. This can be measured in dots or pixels per inch (dpi or ppi). As the output of your computer screen is made up of pixels, if the resolution (pixels per inch) of the image is less than that of the screen, the quality of the image will appear reduced. Screen resolutions are generally between 72 and 100 pixels per inch so if you want an image to appear 3 inches (about 7.5 cm) square on screen then it would need to be 300 pixels by 300 pixels.

If the image is to be printed it needs to be of a much higher resolution, for example, 300 pixels per inch, so the same 300 by 300 pixel image could only be printed out at 1 inch square without losing quality.

Bit depth

The bit depth is a measure of how many different colours can be displayed in an image. More available colours results in a more accurate colour representation of the image on screen.

Black and white (monochrome) images can be referred to as 1 bit images.

8 bit images will represent 256 colours or 256 shades of grey. Using 8 bit might be a way to keep the file size down if saving images with limited colour palettes such as vectors.

Most computer monitors today use 24 bit colour, which is capable of displaying over 16.7 million colours and suitable for most applications giving life-like colour representations of photographs and so on.

Colours
RGB format

Screens display colours in an **RGB** format. This stands for red, green, blue, which are the three colours of light which can be combined to make up all the other colours and white.

The images on the next page show how the image of the flowers is composed from three channels of RGB. On the red channel the pink flowers appear very light. This indicates that a lot of red light is visible in these areas. Where all three channels show white areas, red, green and blue light combine to make white. Note that the small yellow leaves are very dark in the blue channel; yellow is formed by combining red and green light, which can also be thought of as subtracting the blue light from white because blue is opposite yellow on the colour wheel.

Key term

RGB – red, green, blue.

Full-colour RGB image.

Blue channel.

Red channel.

Green channel.

HSV and HSL

Colours can also be defined by other methods such as **HSV**, which is a measure of their hue – that is, where the colour lies on the colour wheel (see Figure 2), saturation (a measure of the intensity of the colour; a colour with very little saturation might appear greyscale) and brightness value.

The same image as before is shown on the next page with adjustments made to its **HSL** values.

Key terms

HSV – hue, saturation and value.
HSL – hue, saturation and lightness.

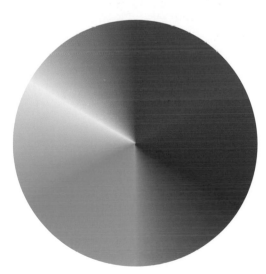

Figure 2: When would you refer to the colour wheel?

Original image.

+75% lightness.

180° change in hue.

Activity: Digital graphics formats

In a group, discuss the following questions.

- What type of digital graphics format would be best suited to represent a photograph?
- What type of digital graphics format would be best suited to represent a logo using two or three solid colours?

−75% saturation.

By the end of your studies you will be expected to have a good understanding of how initial ideas for digital graphics can be taken through from origination to finished product, and you should be familiar with optimising these graphics for a variety of different applications and file formats.

My first role was on the creative team of the multimedia division of a large design agency. It was my job to mock up alternative designs for what a website or multimedia presentation might look like using programmes like Photoshop, as well as traditional marker pen techniques.

After a while I was asked to present the design work in meetings with clients. I was a bit nervous at first, but soon found I had an aptitude for making presentations and progressed to the job of creative account manager. In this role I meet with clients regularly, not only at the final pitches, and I act as the liaison between the client and the creative team. My job now involves less hands-on creative design but I still have to think creatively and translate the needs and requirements of the client to brief the creative team. I also need to liaise with the more technical members of the team such as the programmers and know about what they are capable of, and what might be difficult to achieve – there would be little point in the creative team designing a great looking website if it didn't function in the way the client wanted!

Most of the jobs I work on are websites, but the multimedia division also produces work for interactive DVD presentations and even digital interactive television. The productions I work on might just as easily be for small independent businesses as for branches of large well-known multinational businesses. Often the designs need to take into consideration the client's existing corporate branding or designs created by different divisions, or even different agencies, and used for other media such as print or television commercials.

While my working hours are in theory nine to five, I have to be flexible and I often work outside of these hours, starting early to travel to give presentations, or finishing late to meet with clients in the evenings or to work alongside the design team to put presentations together in time to meet urgent deadlines.

Think about it!

- Think about the last time you gave a presentation to your class. What skills do you think you might need to develop to do a job like Samira's?
- What personal qualities do you think are needed in the role of creative account manager?

Just checking

1. What is copyright and why is it important in the interactive media industry?
2. Which regulatory body is responsible for setting guidelines for web accessibility standards?
3. Identify the two main types of digital graphics.
4. What does HSV stand for?

edexcel

Assignment tips

- Allow some time to ensure that your final portfolio of evidence is well organised and presents your work in the best possible way.

- To achieve a merit or distinction grade, you will need to provide evidence of clear and considered progression from your original ideas and designs through to the completed production work, which will need to be of a good quality and reflect high standards of design and preparation work.

- Explain theory and applications of digital graphics technology with reference to detailed examples to illustrate and explain the points you make. If you hope to achieve the highest grades, it is not enough simply to mention an example. You need to explain the relevance of your examples and use them to support your points and demonstrate that you have carefully researched and understood the issues.

- Keep a thorough log of your practical production work, including any changes you make, and why. The highest grades will be awarded for reflective work showing the ability to make well-judged decisions. You need to explain how you made your decisions, demonstrating that you drew on your excellent understanding of the relevant technical and professional issues to inform your thinking and decision making.

- Remember to include relevant tutor observation records and feedback from your client and target audience with the documentary evidence of your work.

- Use the technical vocabulary of the industry appropriately and confidently in your assignments.

- Make sure any written work is neat, methodical and check carefully for any errors.

Games development

The computer games publishing and development industry can be a very exciting and dynamic place to work. It is an enormous business and is more diverse than might initially be imagined. The computer games industry is one of the fastest-growing forms of media entertainment with annual global sales of approximately £32 billion.

When following this pathway you will experience a wide range of roles in the computer games industry and gain a variety of game industry software skills that will assist you if you choose a career in games. You will also gain basic practical experience in the production and development of computer games, including the application of digital graphics for use in computer games and the communication of your initial ideas through the drawing of concept art.

When following this pathway you may have the opportunity to develop your understanding of why story writing, sound and music are vital areas in game development. Using a range of 2D and 3D software tools the pathway also introduces you to the design and production of game worlds.

This chapter will support your work on two mandatory units for this pathway: Unit 13, Understanding the computer games industry and Unit 20, Computer game platforms and technologies.

These units will help you to develop an appreciation of how the industry operates and why the business of developing computer games ultimately depends on both creativity and finance.

You will also develop an understanding of the capabilities and benefits of the different types of computer game hardware platforms as well as familiarity with specific software technologies and techniques appropriate to each platform.

This chapter is designed to give you an overview of the games development industry and the types of skills you will need for this pathway. You will find details of the learning outcomes and the assessment and grading criteria for the Games development pathway on pages 265–267.

Andrew, Computer Games Art student

I completed a BTEC National Diploma in Games Development and then applied to Teesside University to study a BA in Computer Games Art. I am now in my final year of study and I am constantly developing and learning new skills that will help me secure my dream job in the games industry when I finish my degree this year.

I was able to learn and develop quite a few skills for university while studying for my BTEC National Diploma. The units on 3D environment modelling, animation and game engines gave me a headstart at university because many students had not had the opportunity to study any of these 3D applications. This allowed me to produce better project work and enabled me to develop my skills faster than those who had not used these specialised industry software applications before.

I am currently building a 3D environment model of Dunluce Castle (on the north coast of Northern Ireland) for my final year project. I am modelling the castle as it would have looked when it was lived in during the late 1500s and early 1600s, including some of the buildings that surrounded the castle and the terrain. Staff at Dunluce Castle Visitors Centre are very interested in the project; they would like to have my finished work displayed in the centre.

When I graduate I plan to get a job in the games industry in the UK or Ireland for a few years as a 3D environment artist. However, my dream is to get a job in a games studio in California and once I have established a name for myself, to come back to live in Ireland and work as a freelancer.

Over to you!

- What job would you like to do in the games industry?
- List the skills you might need to do this job.
- What will you need to do to develop these skills to help you do this job?

The computer games industry

This section of the chapter is relevant to Unit 13, LO1, LO2 and LO3.

Set up

Current market trends in games development

Make a list of some games products that members of your class are familiar with.

- Can you categorise these in any way?
- Are there any clear favourites or trends?
- What do people enjoy or not enjoy about the games you have listed?
- Can you agree on the key features of a successful game?

The computer games industry: an overview

All aspiring entrants to the computer games industry need an awareness of the role of each organisation in game publishing. No matter what job you plan to undertake, you will need to learn about organisational behaviour and how to perform in both a corporate environment and in a smaller independent concern.

Production of a new game title starts at the concept development stage where the game ideas are first conceived. The game is then created and produced by a team of skilled people; the size of the team will depend on the type of game being developed.

Development teams used to be mainly independent, but over the years they have increasingly been acquired by publishers and distributors to enable them to develop games in-house. However, the 'small is beautiful' approach often remains the most fruitful way of making good game titles, and creative designers seem to work better and produce better results without interference from a larger corporate structure, so some publishers who have acquired development studios have left the studios largely untouched operationally. This approach has helped large publishers to be more successful and given them the opportunity to produce a large number of titles available on all game platforms.

Publishing houses that have their own internal development studio are known as 'first party' developers. Nintendo has its own internal 'first party' development teams. However, it would be impossible for them to supply enough titles on their own so they contract 'second party' developers to create games for them under Nintendo's label.

Game development studios that are independent or unaffiliated with a particular publisher that create games for a platform are known as 'third party' developers.

Publishing houses

Publishers normally hold the rights for the games delivered to them by the internal or independent developer. The publisher is responsible for marketing the title's launch and its manufacturing process. They will usually be responsible for the title's distribution to the retail stores.

Professional organisations

A number of professional organisations support different aspects of the games industry. Table 1 on the next page lists some of them.

Table 1: Professional organisations for the games industry.

British Academy of Film and Television Arts (BAFTA)	www.bafta.org
Entertainment and Leisure Software Publishers Association (ELSPA)	www.elspa.com
International Game Developers Association (IGDA)	www.igda.org
The Independent Games Developers' Association (TIGA)	www.tiga.org
Mobile Entertainment Forum (MEF)	www.m-e-f.org
Pan European Game Information (PEGI)	www.pegi.info
Women in Games International (WIGI)	www.womeningamesinternational.org

Activity: Organisations

Investigate the roles of the organisations in Table 1 and answer the following questions.

- Where can you find the current official games charts?

- Where can you find news about industry events and new technology?

- Where can you find out about conferences, trade shows and other events for the games industry?

- Where can you find out about anti-piracy law and technologies?

- Which organisations offer student membership or other forms of support and information for students?

- Which organisations offer career development opportunities?

The computer games business

Finance

The successful development of computer games depends ultimately on both creativity and finance, so it is important for you to have some understanding of the financial issues and the current market trends affecting the computer games industry.

Financial planning is important if you need to obtain funding to make your computer game become a reality. It is also required to help secure contracts or partnerships, as you will need to show how good your studio is at money management before backers will invest in the project. Below are three general financial business models.

Equity financing – family and friends might be willing to invest long-term capital in exchange for a percentage ownership and a share of future profits.

Debt financing – the game studio takes out a loan to fund the development of the product. This type of financing will not give the lender ownership control of the studio, but the loan must be repaid with interest. Lending to a game studio is likely to be seen as a high risk by a lender; therefore significant collateral (for example, your house) will help.

Venture capital – funds are raised from investors who expect to get a high return within a short period of time. It is unlikely that new start-up studios will secure funding from this source as those investing will generally focus on more established studios with high potential.

Activity: Financing your studio's next hit game

- Use the Internet to access investment websites to help you research types of financing deals that might be available for game development studios.

- Investigate what type of financing deal might be best suited for a new start-up studio, outlining the reasons for your choice.

- Research the purpose of a business plan and what it may contain.

Keeping in touch with the market trends in gaming

It is important for game developers to be in touch with current market trends, as this knowledge will help to maximise a game's profitability and success. As few as one in ten games is likely to achieve the coveted triple A status, the highest accolade possible for a game.

Massively Multiplayer Online (MMO) games have come to the rescue of developers, with their introduction of a subscription model. Players are given a free-to-play portion of the game, then they must buy a subscription if they want to continue to play. Some developers have also introduced a pay-per-episode model.

Downloadable content is becoming more popular with gamers; developers distribute their full games and subsequent content via the Internet. The availability of fast broadband has helped to popularise this model of distribution.

Games are now also available through online social networks. These micropayment games may be free to play with the revenue being generated from advertising and in-game items. Another method of generating small sums of revenue is to entice players to deepen their gaming experience of the game by buying additional levels, episodes or components.

Activity: Current market trends in games development

Access game industry trade websites or go to the library and find a trade magazine such as *MCV*, *Develop* or *Edge* to research what current trends are emerging.

- Investigate console development and the marketing strategies adopted by the major console manufacturers such as Microsoft, Sony and Nintendo.
- Research the impact market trends have on game developers and publishers.
- Research the industry trends towards the merger and acquisition of development studios by movie studios and game publishers.

PLTS

Undertaking research will help develop your skills as an **independent enquirer**.

The computer games industry and the law

Copyright and piracy

Games technology and software in all formats are protected in law by copyright (see Unit 1). Copyright is an automatic right that protects a piece of written or recorded work from being copied or used by anyone else without the copyright owner's permission. Copyright owners can choose to grant permission or license others to use the work, usually for a fee, while retaining ownership over the rights themselves. Like other forms of intellectual property, copyright can be bought and sold.

As the computer games industry has developed, so too has a parallel illegal industry in the piracy of games software, along with a wide range of counter-measures in the forms of technology security and law enforcement.

One group particularly concerned with such matters is ELSPA's Intellectual Property (IP) Crime Unit, which takes an active role in tackling games piracy. It offers advice to consumers and retailers, hosts a hotline for people to report suspected piracy, and monitors and investigates sales of illegal products on the Internet, at computer fairs, car boot sales and elsewhere. It also works with enforcement agencies such as Trading Standards and HM Revenue & Customs, offering training and helping to investigate suspected offences.

Activity: Piracy issues

Discuss the following with other class members.

- What are the issues surrounding piracy? Is it immoral? Who loses out as a result of piracy?
- How does the IP Crime Unit tackle the issue of games piracy?
- How can you identify counterfeit goods?

Visit the ELSPA website to find out more about the issues surrounding software piracy, and the work of ELSPA's IP Crime Unit.

Classification of games

Unit 1 included a case study of the role of PEGI (Pan European Game Information), which classifies games in terms of age suitability and content descriptors. Look again at that section to remind yourself of PEGI's activities and responsibilities.

Case study: PEGI Online

PEGI Online is an addition to the PEGI system, designed to offer protection against unsuitable online gaming content and to help parents of young people to understand issues of privacy and protection in relation to the online gaming environment.

The PEGI Online Safety Code (POSC) sets out requirements, including a commitment to keep the gaming website free from illegal or offensive content created by users or in the form of unsuitable links, and measures to protect young people and their privacy when they participate in the gameplay.

The PEGI Online logo, displayed on the website, will indicate that the gameplay service provider meets the requirements of the POSC.

You can find out more about the provisions of the Code by visiting www.pegionline.eu

1. What does the display of the PEGI Online logo indicate?

2. What are the key requirements of the POSC?

Working in the games industry

This section of the chapter is relevant to Unit 13, LO1, LO3 and LO5.

Departmental structures and roles

The structure of a development studio or publisher will vary from company to company. The following is a general look at a possible structure of a studio and the jobs presented here are not a comprehensive list. Not every game will require the breadth of skills represented in all the areas in the diagram on the next page.

PLTS

Investigating roles in the industry will help you to become an **independent enquirer**.

Job roles in the games industry

As you can see, the computer games industry offers a wide range of exciting and interesting jobs. As a game tester you may get the opportunity to view a game at each stage of its development, from **first playable** demo to **gold master** (when the game is ready for mass distribution). You may even have some of your gameplay ideas implemented through the suggestions you have made during the testing phase.

Game artists create all the art assets for a game. As a game artist you could create the game world environments that the player will move around in, or

Activity: Roles, responsibilities and working patterns

Research at least one job type from each of the five categories in Figure 1. Find out what roles and responsibilities are involved for each job.

Investigate what is meant by a fixed-term contract.

Research the possible working patterns that you may have to accept.

Key terms

First playable – the first version of a game that is playable; often used to show others outside the studio the game's proof of concept.

Gold master – the term used to indicate that the game is ready for mass distribution by either electronic means or by physical media.

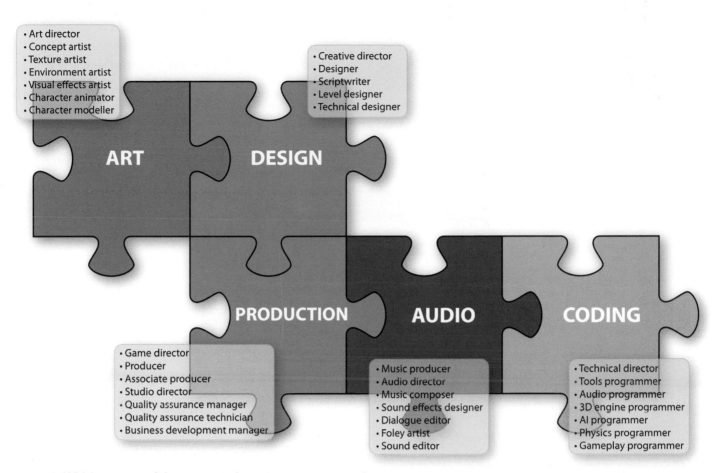

ART
- Art director
- Concept artist
- Texture artist
- Environment artist
- Visual effects artist
- Character animator
- Character modeller

DESIGN
- Creative director
- Designer
- Scriptwriter
- Level designer
- Technical designer

PRODUCTION
- Game director
- Producer
- Associate producer
- Studio director
- Quality assurance manager
- Quality assurance technician
- Business development manager

AUDIO
- Music producer
- Audio director
- Music composer
- Sound effects designer
- Dialogue editor
- Foley artist
- Sound editor

CODING
- Technical director
- Tools programmer
- Audio programmer
- 3D engine programmer
- AI programmer
- Physics programmer
- Gameplay programmer

Figure 1: Which aspects of the games industry interest you most?

the vehicles, pick ups and weapons the player will use during gameplay. You may create the character animations or special animated effects for the game.

The computer games industry also employs people in marketing, finance and legal. These job roles are specifically tailored to meet the industry's requirements, and require both the appropriate business knowledge and a thorough understanding of the games industry context. They can be fascinating areas of the industry to work in.

The development of computer games depends ultimately on both creativity and finance, so it is important to have some understanding of the business models specifically associated with the games industry. You need to gain an appreciation of the costs, turnover and profits available to each company in the development, publishing and distribution of a game.

Understanding the legal constraints, professional considerations and ethical obligations particular to the computer games industry will help you when seeking employment in the industry. Having an appreciation of both personal work contracts and the types of contract

between industry organisations, and the importance of intellectual property rights will be valuable in any possible future career.

It is impossible to go into all these areas in detail in this chapter, but you can access specific information about the industry, including statistics, career options and opportunities through the Sector Skills Council.

Did you know?

Skillset is the Sector Skills Council (SSC) for Creative Media, which comprises television, film, radio, interactive media, animation, computer games, facilities, photo imaging and publishing. Their aim is to support the improvements to the productivity of the media industry and to ensure that it remains globally competitive. Visit their website at www.skillset.org/games

Job roles in the computer game development industry are many and varied, and will be dependent on the size of the organisation. Here we explain what the major disciplines are, and what kinds of job titles they hold.

Game designer – game designers usually determine the overall vision of a computer game and have a large influence on its development, much like film directors have in the production of movies. They influence the direction the game takes, creative or otherwise, from the early concept stage to the game's release date.

The game designer's role is complex, and is more about maintaining, implementing and executing ideas, rather than just coming up with the storyline, some characters and level designs. A designer has to know a lot about the other game development roles within the production team and when to bow to the judgement of others. Since computer game production is a cooperative effort by a group of talented people, it will often result in the designer having to compromise between what they want and what other departments are able to deliver.

Role:	Responsibilities:	Skills:
• collaborate with various departments • determine overall vision of a computer game • maintain, implement, and execute ideas.	• focus on the writing of the game's design document • design levels • work on gameplay • write the game's story and dialogue.	• have a well-rounded education • know about different aspects of game development • ability to manage diverse teams of talented people.

Artist – the vision of the game set out by the designers, art director and producers is visualised and brought to life by the game artists. The concept artist works with the art director to establish the game's style, and 3D modellers realise those concepts. Game artists play a vital role in breathing life into a game.

Many small game studios will require artists who can work in different roles when required. Having a broad knowledge of art is seen as an asset.

Role:	Responsibilities:	Skills:
• work with the art director to establish the game's style • might hold different roles as and when required, e.g. animator, rigger, modeller, texture artist, character artist, environment artist.	• develop concept art • create textures • create or model characters • create game environments.	• familiarity with at least one major 3D software application, such as 3DS Max or Maya • familiarity with 2D graphics tools, such as Photoshop • some understanding of fine arts.

Producer – the producer is the project manager of a video game project. Their role is to manage the development team, to deal with high-level issues, and to oversee the entire development project, although exact responsibilities can vary from studio to studio.

A video game producer can have the following titles: executive producer, producer, assistant producer and associate producer.

Role:	Responsibilities:	Skills:
• organise and facilitate the game's production • act as mediator between departments, studio and the publisher • act as the point of contact for the leads and directors in each department within the studio.	• create and enforce schedules and budgets • assign tasks • make sure deadlines and milestones are kept to schedule • make sure that the team has everything it needs to create the game.	• leadership and communication skills • ability to get along with a wide variety of people • project and game business management skills.

Audio engineer – a game audio engineer (or sound effects designer or audio director) is responsible for creating the sounds and music to match the visuals of a game.

Those involved in game audio may also be the composers, writing and recording original music for the projects they work on.

Role:	Responsibilities:	Skills:
• give the game a distinctive sound and add realism.	• create the sounds and music to match the visuals of a game • record, mix and edit production sound and dialogue.	• familiarity with all the aspects of sound design, from **Foley** (the technique of creating, adding and/or synchronising sound effects with pre-produced animations or full motion video sequences) to production sound mixing and dialogue editing • familiarity with audio recording and editing tools, such as Pro Tools.

Quality assurance technician – a quality assurance technician (or game tester) is considered the last line of defence before a game is released to customers online or in retail stores.

A quality assurance technician role is an entry-level position and is seen as a way of getting into the games development industry. If quality assurance technicians show they have great communication skills and understand how the production process works while developing a computer game they can become leads. From this role, they can sometimes move into associate or assistant producer roles.

Role:	Responsibilities:	Skills:
• help make sure that the quality of a game meets the standards set by the development studio, console manufacturer and the publisher.	• play the game or portions of the game looking for bugs or glitches • record any bugs in a database • take screen shots to help document a bug in detail.	• great communication skills • understanding of the computer game production process.

Key term

Foley – the technique of creating, adding and/or synchronising sound effects with pre-produced animations or full motion video sequences. It was named after Jack Foley, a sound editor at Universal Studios.

Did you know?

A useful way to keep up to date with industry developments and job opportunities is to take out student membership of the International Game Developers Association (IGDA). Visit their website at www.igda.org

The Independent Games Developers' Association (TIGA – www.tiga.org) offers membership for organisations, including colleges. Does your college subscribe?

Marina Howard
Game tester and student

My first experience of testing was when I got the opportunity to test a simple game-based educational product. It really wasn't sophisticated at all, but it had a lot of possible routes through the game, and I had to do all of them, in every possible order. That can be surprisingly difficult, as it goes against your instincts as a player. You usually want to work your way through the best way you can and get it all right.

This particular product was aimed at primary school children and my brief was to imagine a group of them all grabbing for the controls at once, hitting things in any order and basically trying to break it! I had to be really methodical and do everything in all the possible wrong orders as well as in the right order to simulate what could happen in the classroom. The glitches tended to happen when I did things that the game didn't really expect. If you went really wrong in how you're meant to play, you might get stuck or the wrong dialogue box might come up.

I've now also had a short-term summer job as a tester on a commercial game product. Again, it was important to be methodical, and record the glitches in exactly the way the developer wanted the information, in good written English.

I had to be flexible in terms of working shifts, and of course needed to show I'd got a lot of knowledge of console and PC games.

Think about it!

- Which skills will you need to develop to help you apply for a job as a game tester?
- Would developing and testing your own games help to prove to potential employers that you could document and test the functionality and playability of a game?

How much do you know about the job roles that interest you most?

Researching any company to whom you are applying will help you to show your passion and determination to be a part of the computer games industry. Access the Skillset website or go to the library and find a magazine that carries job advertisements for various roles in the computer games industry. *Edge*, *Develop* or *MCV* magazines may be a good place to start. Find a job that appeals to you, and try to find out as much as you can about:

- the company advertising the job
- the kind of work you would be expected to do
- the skills you would need to fulfil the role
- what other job roles exist within the company and how they relate to each other in the production of computer games.

Preparing for a career in the computer games industry

Your portfolio is your personal showcase to present to prospective employers and higher education institutions in support of your planned career moves.

Think about it

- What would be the optimum way to showcase your best work? Have you considered using a wiki or website to demonstrate your skills?
- Explore and become familiar with as many games and formats as you can, and try to learn from what you experience. What do you feel works well, and what does not? Develop your own style and preferences in your own work.
- Build a database of games and technologies that you have found inspiring or useful. Make notes about what you think about them, and use them as a reference resource when working on your own productions.

You need to take your portfolio seriously and prepare it to the highest possible standards, showing the very best you can offer and achieve.

Building up your personal development plan (PDP) is best regarded as an ongoing activity culminating in well-considered action plans and polished portfolios. It is a good idea to identify your career path as early as possible, research the requirements of your preferred role, recognise your skill gaps and develop an action plan to address these.

Activity: Making a start – preparing your PDP

- Research methods of preparing a personal development plan.
- Research the methods and layout of a professional CV, digital portfolio and job application letter. Prepare samples of these that you can develop and customise when job opportunities come up.
- How can you use your PDP to help you identify and achieve your personal goals?
- Continuous professional development is an important aspect of any career. How will you continue to keep yourself up to date?

While your practical portfolio will demonstrate your technical and creative skills, your written applications need to outline your personal skills and explain how they can be used in the industry. It is not enough simply to claim that you fulfil the job specification; you need to demonstrate how you do so with specific examples.

Always remember, when expressing yourself formally in writing, to check your writing carefully for any grammatical, spelling and punctuation errors.

PLTS

Reviewing your learning and achievements and developing a well-presented personal development plan, setting goals with success criteria for your personal career development, inviting feedback on your performance and dealing positively with praise, setbacks and criticism, and evaluating your learning and experience to inform future progress as part of your reflection on your personal development, will help develop your skills as a **reflective learner**.

The technology behind computer games

This section of the chapter is relevant to Unit 20, LO1, LO2 and LO3.

The production process

The game's production usually includes the following stages.

Month 1	Months 2–3	Months 4–5	Months 6–12	Months 13–18	Months 19–21	Month 22	Month 23	Month 24
• Ideas • Design team thinks up new ideas or publisher reviews proposals from developers • Licensing team secures new licences	• Contracts • Developer or publisher decides which ideas to pursue • Publisher legal team enters contract with developer • Publisher decides on best developer for the product • Legal team agrees contract with any licence holders	• Prototype • Developer or design team works on prototypes to verify proof of concept, e.g. technology and game play work as intended • Design document, technical specification and milestone schedule produced	• Games development starts – producer manages the product supported by product manager and designer • Quality assurance (QA) team regularly test product as developed • Game development in accordance with monthly milestones • Producer works closely with the design team or developer throughout development • Feedback from QA is incorporated into the game	• Game development and QA supported by third-party focus testing • PR and marketing team help plan how the game will be marketed • Each milestone is carefully checked against the agreed schedule • Demo produced and PR/marketing commences	• Game development and QA continues • Game is substantially finished and ready to be 'polished' • Demo demonstrated to distributors and retailers	• Approval submission and final testing • Approval by Sony, Microsoft and Nintendo • PR and marketing campaign	• Production and game localisation • Final product manufactured and shipped to retailers	• Game released • Game on sale around the world

Figure 2: Game production stages.

This sets the context for the technologies and processes which are the focus of the specialist mandatory unit for the Games development pathway, Unit 20, Computer game platforms and technologies.

Platforms and technologies

A sound knowledge of present-day game hardware platforms, as well as the latest software technology, is highly desirable when seeking a career in the games industry. You will benefit from having a full understanding of the capabilities and benefits of the different hardware platforms (such as PCs, consoles and mobile devices), as well as familiarity with software technologies and techniques appropriate to each game platform.

To avoid making impossible demands of a game platform, you need to be aware of the function and purpose of each component of the modern interactive game system you are developing games for.

Game systems are dedicated computers, requiring software instructions to organise their processing. Different platforms have particular programming requirements. It is therefore important to examine the features and limitations of the basic software used in typical game platforms.

The games industry is constantly evolving, both creatively and technologically, and it is important that you keep up to date with the latest developments. This means not only studying hardware and software technologies, but also the combination of these components into playable systems for use by single players and interactively among multiple players.

To understand computer game platforms and their associated technologies you will need access to a wide variety of modern game platforms, as well as peripheral devices, both cabled and wireless. You will need access to a wide variety of computer game titles on a range of game platforms. Access to a Local Area Network (**LAN**) and a Wide Area Network (**WAN**) is necessary to enable you to install LAN games and online games. A LAN is a network of computer devices covering a small physical area, such as your home, an office or your classroom. A WAN is a network of computer devices covering a large area – it has to communicate across a large geographical area such as distances in the order of hundreds of kilometres. Access to the Internet is necessary to connect consoles to the World Wide Web. You will require access to computers to be able to install games and drivers for graphics cards, sound cards and game peripheral devices.

Studying the historical developments of game platforms and reflecting on their technological advances is important. This overview of platforms will lead you naturally to deeper study of the enabling technologies, and an appreciation of the operating systems and development software controlling platform actions.

Key terms

LAN – a Local Area Network is a network of computer devices covering a small physical area.

WAN – a Wide Area Network is a network of computer devices covering a large area and has to communicate across a large geographical area.

Activity: Game platforms – a historical timeline

- Investigate the development history of game platforms to help you make a historical timeline of their technical developments.
- Investigate the features and limitations of the various platform types, such as arcade, consoles, PC, mobile and television.

Hardware technologies

Computer game platforms are not all the same. Some are more powerful than others, and the way each game responds and plays will depend on the platform it has been designed for. There are four major platform types used by gamers: arcade machines, consoles, PC and mobile. Digital television is not as popular in North America as it is in the UK, but despite this game publishers have begun to release exclusive variations of the hit titles for digital television to meet the needs of an entirely new type of gamer.

At the heart of every gaming device are four main components: CPU (central processor unit), GPU (graphics processor unit), memory or RAM (random access memory) and an audio processor/sound card.

The table on the next page explains the function of some of the most common hardware components found in the PS3, Xbox 360 and Wii game platforms. It is worth noting that specifications are frequently updated. Have a look at manufacturer's websites for current information.

Table 2: Game hardware components.

Device	Function	Type/Size	Speed
CPU (central processor unit)	This is sometimes referred to as the 'brains' of any electronic device, and is responsible for managing virtually everything that happens in a game, interpreting and executing the commands requested from the computer or game console's hardware and software.	Cell Broadband (PlayStation 3)	3.2Ghz (Gigahertz)
		Xenon (Xbox 360)	3.2Ghz
		Broadway (Wii)	729Mhz (Magahertz)
GPU (graphics processor unit)	This is a dedicated processor used to calculate all the graphics information in a game and display them on the screen.	NVIDIA RSX 'Reality Synthesizer' (PlayStation 3)	550Mhz
		ATI Xenos (Xbox 360)	500Mhz
		ATI Hollywood (Wii)	243Mhz
Memory/RAM (random access memory)	The game on a CD or DVD is streamed into the RAM so that the console can display the graphics. RAM will not hold the game information when the console is not switched on.	256MBs Main XDR DRAM or extreme data rate dynamic RAM (PlayStation 3)	3.2Ghz
		512MBs (Xbox 360)	700MHz
		512MBs Internal flash memory (Wii)	700Mhz

Table 2: *continued*

Device	Function	Type/Size	Speed
HDD (hard disk drive)	A hard disk drive is generally used as a storage device for games and other media such as music, pictures and video files.	2.5" Serial ATA (PlayStation 3)	–
		2.5" Serial ATA (Xbox 360)	–
		None (Wii)	–
APU (Audio processing unit)/ Sound card	Like its graphics counterpart, the GPU, the APU's main function is to help increase overall system performance by offloading complex audio and effects processing from the CPU. Depending on platform capabilities, the APU can output 3D positional sound aspects of a game, DVD or CD in various formats to speakers/earphones.	Dolby 5.1ch, DTS, LPCM (PlayStation 3)	–
		16-bit/5.1 surround sound, 48 KHz sample rate (Xbox 360)	–
		Dolby Prologic II (Wii)	–
Display	A game console display shows the content of the video game on the built-in or external display. The display can be in monochrome or colour and is likely to be liquid crystal display (LCD).	Full High Definition 1920 x 1080p display resolution (PlayStation 3)	–
		Full High Definition 1920 x 1080p display resolution (Xbox 360)	–
		Enhanced Definition 854 x 480p display resolution (Wii)	–

Activity: What's inside the box?

Studying the hardware specifications of at least two hand-held game platforms will help you to have a deeper understanding of their enabling technologies, and an appreciation of the operating systems and development software used to control them.

Investigate the hardware features and limitations of two hand-held platforms, such as the PlayStation Portable and the Nintendo DS.

- What are the advantages and disadvantages of each game's storage medium?
- How might this help with anti-piracy problems?

Software technologies

Game consoles and all other gaming devices require third-party software technologies to make them function, such as operating systems, application software and software tools. Computer games also rely on third-party device driver software tools to enable a game to communicate directly with hardware such as sound and graphics cards. Application programming interfaces (APIs) are also used, and by the aid of software programs the APIs interface between the game and the platform hardware to aid the display of 2D and 3D computer graphics or the production of three-dimensional positional audio as the game is played.

An operating system (OS) acts as an interface between the game platform/hardware and the gamer/user. The OS is responsible for the management and coordination of requests from software applications, hardware devices and actions evoked by the gamer/user.

The most common PC (personal computer) operating systems are Windows, Linux and Mac OS.

Windows

The Windows OS has gone through many iterations. It originated as an add-on to the older Microsoft Disk Operating System known as 'MS-DOS' for the IBM PC. Web and database servers also use the Windows OS, with Windows XP (released in October 2001) currently being the most widely used version of the Microsoft Windows operating systems. Microsoft released a new operating system called Windows Vista in November 2006, which contained a large number of new features. A new visual style called 'Windows Aero' along with a new user interface was introduced with a number of new security features such as 'User Account Control'. In early 2008 the server version was released, 'Windows Server 2008', and in October 2009 Microsoft released Windows 7, a faster and more streamlined OS, together with a Windows Server 2008 R2 server version.

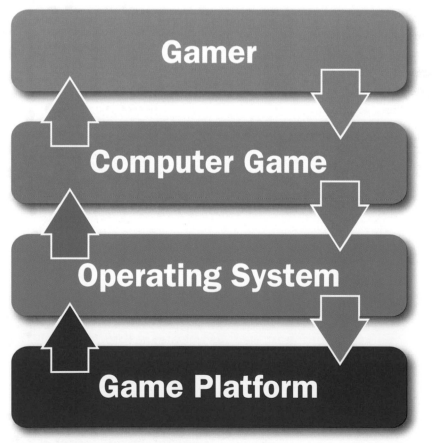

Figure 3: OS coordination of requests.

Linux

Linux OS was created as a hobby by a student at the University of Helsinki in Finland called Linus Torvalds. Linus began his work on Linux in 1991 and released version 1.0 in 1994 under General Public Licence (GNU). The source code was made freely available to everyone. This enabled other companies and individuals to release their own versions of the operating system based on Linux core elements.

Linux is now used as an alternative by some manufacturers and users to proprietary Unix and Microsoft operating systems. A wide range of applications that run on Linux OS has grown over the years, such as OpenOffice and Mozilla web browser. If you are curious to see Linux in operation you can download a live CD version called Knoppix.

Mac OS

Apple Computer Inc, now Apple Inc, manufactured the Macintosh personal computer in January 1984 and shipped it with the Mac OS operating system, known as the 'System Software'. The Mac OS was one of the first operating systems to use an entirely graphical user interface (GUI) as opposed to a text-only interface known as command line interface (CLI). The Macintosh OS is credited with popularising the GUI. Mac OS has also gone through many iterations and currently Mac names its OS X after big cats, for example, Apple calls Mac OS X 10.6 'Snow Leopard'.

Windows CE

Windows CE is an optimised OS for devices that have minimal storage and is capable of working in under a megabyte of memory. Windows CE is no longer targeted solely at hand-held devices. Many other platforms have been based on the CE operating system, such as Windows Mobile designed for use in smartphones and mobile devices.

Symbian OS

Symbian is an open source operating system designed for mobile devices and smartphones, originally developed by Symbian Ltd. It is now owned by Nokia, but it has been set up as an independent non-profit organisation called the Symbian Foundation. The Symbian operating system is now reckoned to be one of the world's most popular mobile OS, accounting for a large proportion of smartphone global sales.

Activity: Operating systems and software development tools

- Find out what application software development tools are used to develop games for three different platforms, such as PC, hand-held and mobile phone.

- Investigate why it is necessary to use device driver software for hardware devices such as a sound card and a graphics card.

- Investigate why an application programming interface (API) is used to display 3D graphics and to implement three-dimensional positional audio.

Configuration

The way a game is intended to be played affects every level of design and planning. There are many possible gameplay configurations, involving different permutations of platforms, console to display, console to console, playing across LANs, WANs, servers, online, peer to peer and so on.

The diagram on the following page illustrates a typical LAN set-up.

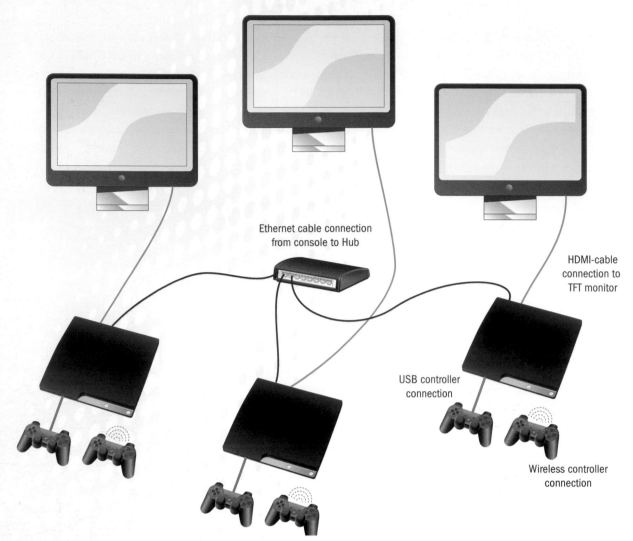

Figure 4: An example of a Playstation 3 Local Area Network.

Activity: Gameplay set-up

What are the limitations of the gameplay set-up in Figure 4?

Sketch a similar diagram for the following configurations:

• console to console (wireless and wired)

• Wide Area Network (for online gameplay).

Prepare a report, log or blog describing how you have physically connected and configured at least two different types of console network.

Jonty Adams
3D digital modeller/animator

I studied IT and interactive media at school, but wasn't sure what to do after that. I was vaguely thinking of going into web design because I wanted to do something creative, not just techie.

By chance, I ended up helping out a couple of friends with a project involving computer animation, and I really enjoyed it. I thought this was something that would really interest me so I found out all I could about digital animation and took the Games pathway for my BTEC. I already knew a bit about 2D animation programs such as Flash but when I started learning about 3D modelling and animation programs such as 3D Max and Maya, I found it really exciting, like another world had opened up.

Getting into the games industry took a lot of effort. I did some work experience at a local company which produced online adver-games. The game they were currently working on was a treasure-hunt type game to advertise a new product. This gave me the motivation to further develop my animation skills in Flash and learn how to make my own Flash games. I got a part-time job as a game tester for one of the larger mobile games companies, by keeping on asking if they'd let me show them the Flash games I had made and tested. I made sure I had lots of notes on how I produced and tested my games. This job was a stepping stone and my way into the games industry. My passion was to be a 3D modeller or animator, I realised to achieve this I needed to have a portfolio of artwork and a showreel of my animations to get into a junior modeller or animator position.

I got my first real job as a general dogsbody where I'd done my work experience. I didn't do much hands-on animation work at first – most of their content was more 2D than 3D anyway – but it was all good experience.

I've found that it's important to build up and hold on to your contacts, as you never know what will lead to the next thing. Through word of mouth I heard about a part-time 3D animation opening at a bigger games company. It felt risky, leaving my regular job for a part-time contract, but in terms of experience and working for a bigger company it seemed the next logical move. Thankfully it worked out well and I've now secured a full-time junior animation role with the same company. And I'm at the point now where I know enough people to hear about other work coming up elsewhere.

Think about it!

- Which aspect of the games industry are you most interested in?
- Do you want to specialise in a particular area, and do you need to build up further skills to be able to do this?

Just checking

1. What is the difference between a development studio and a publisher?
2. What might be a possible departmental structure of a game development studio?
3. What responsibilities is a producer expected to carry out as part of their role?
4. What is the function of an APU?
5. What is a device driver and why is it necessary to use device driver software for hardware devices?
6. What is an operating system and why is it used in a game platform?

edexcel

Assignment tips

- The highest grades are awarded for work that demonstrates a thorough and detailed understanding, using well-chosen examples to clarify your points, and accurate use of the terminology. You need to comment on your examples, showing why they are significant and how they help to support your points.

- Keep a careful log of your work so you can demonstrate how you have followed the production process and explain the decisions you have made. How has your understanding of the theory had an impact on what you have done in practice? Have you got sufficient evidence to demonstrate your thinking and understanding to your assessor?

- When things change, discuss why and how you overcame the problems. The highest grades will be awarded for evidence of reflective work, drawing on your knowledge of theory and professional practice to solve problems and make decisions.

- You will achieve the highest grades if you demonstrate that you can apply your skills competently to a practical task and can show that your work is moving towards the professional quality that would be expected in the industry.

Pathways reference section

This section provides details of the learning outcomes and assessment and grading criteria for the pathways (endorsed routes) featured in this book:

- television and film
- radio
- sound recording
- print-based media
- interactive media
- games development.

In addition to the mandatory units required for your level of the qualification, you will also need to complete units selected from the optional units for each relevant pathway.

Television and film

Learning outcomes

After completing the following two mandatory units in the Television and film pathway you should:

Unit 8, Understanding the television and film industries

1. know about ownership and funding in the television and film industries
2. know about job roles in the television and film industries
3. understand contractual, legal and ethical obligations in the television and film industries
4. understand developing technologies in the television and film industries
5. be able to prepare personal career development material.

Unit 16, Film and video editing techniques

1. understand the development and principles of editing
2. be able to prepare moving image material for editing
3. be able to edit moving image material.

How you will be assessed

The Television and film pathway will be assessed by a number of internal assignments that will be designed to allow you to show your knowledge, skills and understanding of the learning outcomes.

These relate to what you should be able to do after completing the units. Your assessments could be in the form of:

- presentations
- case studies
- productions and showreels
- written assignments.

Remember

Remember that you will need to supply separate evidence for each learning outcome for your assessment.

Assessment and grading criteria

The following tables show you what you must do in order to achieve a **pass**, **merit** or **distinction** grade for Unit 8 and Unit 16 in the Television and film pathway.

Unit 8, Understanding the television and film industries

To achieve a **pass** grade the evidence must show that you are able to:	To achieve a **merit** grade the evidence must show that, in addition to the pass criteria, you are able to:	To achieve a **distinction** grade the evidence must show that, in addition to the pass and merit criteria, you are able to:
P1 describe ownership and funding in the television and film industries with some appropriate use of subject terminology	**M1** explain ownership and funding in the television and film industries with reference to detailed illustrative examples and with generally correct use of subject terminology	**D1** comprehensively explain ownership and funding in the television and film industries with reference to elucidated examples and consistently using subject terminology correctly
P2 describe the characteristics, duties and responsibilities of management, creative and technical job roles in the television and film industries with some appropriate use of subject terminology	**M2** explain the characteristics, duties and responsibilities of management, creative and technical job roles in the television and film industries with reference to detailed illustrative examples and with generally correct use of subject terminology	**D2** comprehensively explain the characteristics, duties and responsibilities of management, creative and technical job roles in the television and film industries showing how they relate to each other, with reference to elucidated examples and consistently using subject terminology correctly
P3 describe contractual, legal and ethical obligations in the television and film industries, with some appropriate use of subject terminology	**M3** explain contractual, legal and ethical obligations in the television and film industries with reference to detailed illustrative examples and with generally correct use of subject terminology	**D3** comprehensively explain contractual, legal and ethical obligations in the television and film industries with reference to elucidated examples and consistently using subject terminology correctly
P4 describe developing technologies in the television and film industries with some appropriate use of subject terminology	**M4** explain developing technologies in the television and film industries with reference to detailed illustrative examples and with generally correct use of subject terminology	**D4** comprehensively explain developing technologies in the television and film industries with elucidated examples and consistently using subject terminology correctly
P5 prepare personal career development material using basic formal language	**M5** prepare carefully produced personal career development material using generally correct formal language	**D5** prepare personal career development material to a quality that reflects near-professional standards consistently using correct formal language

Unit 16, Film and video editing techniques

To achieve a **pass** grade the evidence must show that you are able to:	To achieve a **merit** grade the evidence must show that, in addition to the pass criteria, you are able to:	To achieve a **distinction** grade the evidence must show that, in addition to the pass and merit criteria, you are able to:
P1 describe the development and principles of editing with some appropriate use of subject terminology	**M1** explain the development and principles of editing with reference to detailed illustrative examples and with generally correct use of subject terminology	**D1** critically assess the development and principles of editing with supporting arguments and elucidated examples, and consistently using subject terminology correctly
P2 apply editing preparation techniques with some assistance	**M2** apply editing preparation techniques competently with only occasional assistance	**D2** apply editing preparation techniques to a technical quality that reflects near-professional standards, working independently to professional expectations
P3 apply editing techniques working within appropriate conventions and with some assistance	**M3** apply editing techniques to a good technical standard showing some imagination and with only occasional assistance	**D3** apply editing techniques to a technical quality that reflects near-professional standards, showing creativity and flair and working independently to professional expectations

Radio

Learning outcomes

After completing the following two mandatory units in the Radio pathway you should:

Unit 9, Understanding the radio industry

1. understand organisational structures and ownership in the UK radio industry
2. understand job roles, working practices and employment contracts in the UK radio industry
3. understand the role of the regulatory bodies, legal and ethical issues relevant to the UK radio industry
4. understand developing technologies in the UK radio industry
5. be able to prepare for employment in the UK radio industry.

Unit 17, Audio production processes and techniques

1. understand characteristics of different acoustic environments in relation to recording sound
2. understand conventions in audio production and post-production
3. be able to capture and record sound from different sources
4. be able to mix and edit recorded sound.

How you will be assessed

The units in the Radio pathway will be assessed by a number of internally assessed assignments that will be designed to allow you to show your understanding of the unit outcomes. These relate to what you should be able to do after completing the units. Your assessments could be in the form of:

- radio programmes and radio programme extracts
- recorded interviews
- presentations
- case studies
- practical tasks
- written reports.

Remember

Remember that you will need to supply separate evidence for each learning outcome for your assessment.

Assessment and grading criteria

The following tables show you what you must do in order to achieve a **pass**, **merit** or **distinction** grade for Unit 9 and Unit 17 in the Radio pathway.

Unit 9, Understanding the radio industry

To achieve a **pass** grade the evidence must show that you are able to:	To achieve a **merit** grade the evidence must show that, in addition to the pass criteria, you are able to:	To achieve a **distinction** grade the evidence must show that, in addition to the pass and merit criteria, you are able to:
P1 describe organisational structures and ownership patterns in the UK radio industry, with some appropriate use of subject terminology	**M1** explain organisational structures and ownership patterns in the UK radio industry with reference to detailed illustrative examples and with generally correct use of subject terminology	**D1** comprehensively explain organisational structures and ownership patterns in the UK radio industry with elucidated examples and consistently using subject terminology correctly
P2 describe job roles, working practices and employment contracts in the UK radio industry with some appropriate use of subject terminology	**M2** explain job roles and the effect of employment contracts on working practices in the UK radio industry with reference to detailed illustrative examples and with generally correct use of subject terminology	**D2** comprehensively explain the effect of employment contracts on job roles and working practices in the UK radio industry with elucidated examples and consistently using subject terminology correctly
P3 describe the role of the regulatory bodies, legal and ethical issues relevant to the UK radio industry, with some appropriate use of subject terminology	**M3** explain the role of the regulatory bodies, legal and ethical issues relevant to the UK radio industry with reference to detailed illustrative examples and with generally correct use of subject terminology	**D3** comprehensively explain the role of the regulatory bodies, and legal and ethical issues relevant to the UK radio industry with elucidated examples and consistently using subject terminology correctly
P4 describe developing technologies in the UK radio industry, with some appropriate use of subject terminology	**M4** explain developing technologies relevant to the UK radio industry with reference to detailed illustrative examples and with generally correct use of subject terminology	**D4** comprehensively explain developing technologies relevant to the UK radio industry with elucidated examples and consistently using subject terminology correctly
P5 prepare for employment in an identified role in the UK radio industry using basic formal language	**M5** prepare carefully for employment in an identified role in the UK radio industry using clear and generally correct formal language	**D5** prepare to near-professional standards for employment in an identified role in the UK radio industry using fluent and correct formal language

Unit 17, Audio production processes and techniques

To achieve a **pass** grade the evidence must show that you are able to:	To achieve a **merit** grade the evidence must show that, in addition to the pass criteria, you are able to:	To achieve a **distinction** grade the evidence must show that, in addition to the pass and merit criteria, you are able to:
P1 describe characteristics of different acoustic environments in relation to recording sound with some appropriate use of subject terminology	**M1** explain characteristics of different acoustic environments in relation to recording sound with reference to detailed illustrative examples and with generally correct use of subject terminology	**D1** comprehensively explain characteristics of different acoustic environments in relation to recording sound, with elucidated examples and consistently using subject terminology correctly
P2 describe conventions in audio production and post-production with some appropriate use of subject terminology	**M2** explain conventions in audio production and post-production with reference to detailed illustrative examples and with generally correct use of subject terminology	**D2** comprehensively explain conventions in audio production and post-production with elucidated examples and consistently using subject terminology correctly
P3 produce recorded sound from a variety of sources with some assistance	**M3** produce recorded sound from a variety of sources to a good technical standard with only occasional assistance	**D3** produce recorded sound from a variety of sources to near-professional standards working independently to professional expectations
P4 produce mixed and edited sound tracks working within appropriate conventions and with some assistance	**M4** produce mixed and edited sound tracks to a good technical standard, showing some imagination and with only occasional assistance	**D4** produce mixed and edited sound tracks to near-professional standards, showing creativity and flair and working independently to professional expectations

Sound recording

Learning outcomes

After completing the following two mandatory units in the Sound recording pathway you should:

Unit 10, Understanding the sound recording industry

1. understand organisational structures and ownership in the UK recording industry
2. understand job roles, working practices and employment contracts in the UK recording industry
3. understand legal and ethical issues relevant to the UK recording industry
4. understand developing technologies in the UK recording industry
5. be able to prepare for employment in the UK recording industry.

Unit 17, Audio production processes and techniques

1. understand characteristics of different acoustic environments in relation to recording sound
2. understand conventions in audio production and post-production
3. be able to capture and record sound from different sources
4. be able to mix and edit recorded sound.

How you will be assessed

The units in the Sound pathway will be assessed through a number of internally assessed assignments that are designed to allow you to demonstrate the skills, knowledge and experience you have gained in order to successfully complete the unit outcomes. The grading criteria tell you what you should be able to do after completing the units. Your assessments will relate directly to the media products you must produce, and could be in the form of:

- graphic presentations
- 'real life' recording scenarios
- written assignments
- case studies
- a personal video diary
- IT-based design.

Remember

Remember that you will need to supply separate evidence for each learning outcome for your assessment.

Assessment and grading criteria

The following tables show you what you must do in order to achieve a **pass, merit** or **distinction** grade for Unit 10 and Unit 17 in the Sound recording pathway.

Unit 10, Understanding the sound recording industry

To achieve a **pass** grade the evidence must show that you are able to:	To achieve a **merit** grade the evidence must show that, in addition to the pass criteria, you are able to:	To achieve a **distinction** grade the evidence must show that, in addition to the pass and merit criteria, you are able to:
P1 describe organisational structures and ownership patterns in the UK recording industry with some appropriate use of subject terminology	**M1** explain organisational structures and ownership patterns in the UK recording industry with reference to detailed illustrative examples and with generally correct use of subject terminology	**D1** comprehensively explain organisational structures and ownership patterns in the UK recording industry with elucidated examples and consistently using subject terminology correctly
P2 describe job roles, working practices and employment contracts in the UK recording industry with some appropriate use of subject terminology	**M2** explain job roles and the effect of employment contracts on working practices in the UK recording industry with reference to detailed illustrative examples and with generally correct use of subject terminology	**D2** comprehensively explain the effect of employment contracts on job roles and working practices in the UK recording industry with elucidated examples and consistently using subject terminology correctly
P3 describe legal and ethical issues relevant to the UK recording industry with some appropriate use of subject terminology	**M3** explain legal and ethical issues relevant to the UK recording industry with reference to detailed illustrative examples and with generally correct use of subject terminology	**D3** comprehensively explain legal and ethical issues relevant to the UK recording industry with elucidated examples and consistently using subject terminology correctly
P4 describe developing technologies in the UK recording industry with some appropriate use of subject terminology	**M4** explain developing technologies relevant to the UK recording industry with reference to detailed illustrative examples and with generally correct use of subject terminology	**D4** comprehensively explain developing technologies relevant to the UK recording industry with elucidated examples and consistently using subject terminology correctly
P5 prepare for employment in an identified role in the UK recording industry using basic formal language	**M5** prepare effectively and competently for employment in an identified role in the UK recording industry using clear and generally correct formal language	**D5** prepare to near-professional standards for employment in an identified role in the UK recording industry using fluent and correct formal language

Unit 17, Audio production processes and techniques

To achieve a **pass** grade the evidence must show that you are able to:	To achieve a **merit** grade the evidence must show that, in addition to the pass criteria, you are able to:	To achieve a **distinction** grade the evidence must show that, in addition to the pass and merit criteria, you are able to:
P1 describe characteristics of different acoustic environments in relation to recording sound with some appropriate use of subject terminology	**M1** explain characteristics of different acoustic environments in relation to recording sound with reference to detailed illustrative examples and with generally correct use of subject terminology	**D1** comprehensively explain characteristics of different acoustic environments in relation to recording sound, with elucidated examples and consistently using subject terminology correctly
P2 describe conventions in audio production and post-production with some appropriate use of subject terminology	**M2** explain conventions in audio production and post-production with reference to detailed illustrative examples and with generally correct use of subject terminology	**D2** comprehensively explain conventions in audio production and post-production with elucidated examples and consistently using subject terminology correctly
P3 produce recorded sound from a variety of sources with some assistance	**M3** produce recorded sound from a variety of sources to a good technical standard with only occasional assistance	**D3** produce recorded sound from a variety of sources to near-professional standards working independently to professional expectations
P4 produce mixed and edited sound tracks working within appropriate conventions and with some assistance	**M4** produce mixed and edited sound tracks to a good technical standard, showing some imagination and with only occasional assistance	**D4** produce mixed and edited sound tracks to near-professional standards, showing creativity and flair and working independently to professional expectations

Print-based media

Learning outcomes

After completing the following two mandatory units in the Print-based media pathway you should:

Unit 11, Understanding the print-based media industries

1. understand organisational structures and job roles within the print-based media industries
2. understand working practices and employment contracts commonly used in the print-based media industries
3. understand financial issues and market trends affecting the print-based media industries
4. understand legal, ethical and professional obligations in the print-based media industries
5. be able to prepare personal career development material.

Unit 18, Producing print-based media

1. understand print-based media production techniques and technology
2. be able to develop ideas and originate designs for print-based media products
3. be able to produce print-based media products
4. be able to reflect upon own print-based media production work.

How you will be assessed

The units in the Print-based media pathway will be assessed by a number of internal assignments that will be designed to allow you to show your understanding of the unit outcomes. These relate to what you should be able to do after completing the units. Your assessments could be in the form of:

- presentations
- case studies
- practical tasks
- written assignments.

Remember

Remember that you will need to supply separate evidence for each learning outcome for your assessment.

Assessment and grading criteria

The following tables show you what you must do in order to achieve a **pass**, **merit** or **distinction** grade for Unit 11 and Unit 18 in the Print-based media pathway.

Unit 11, Understanding the print-based media industries		
To achieve a pass grade the evidence must show that you are able to:	**To achieve a merit grade the evidence must show that, in addition to the pass criteria, you are able to:**	**To achieve a distinction grade the evidence must show that, in addition to the pass and merit criteria, you are able to:**
P1 describe organisational structures and job roles in the print-based media industries with some appropriate use of subject terminology	**M1** explain organisational structures and job roles in the print-based media industries with reference to detailed illustrative examples and with generally correct use of subject terminology	**D1** comprehensively explain organisational structures and job roles in the print-based media industries with elucidated examples and consistently using subject terminology correctly
P2 describe working practices and employment contracts in the print-based media industries with some appropriate use of subject terminology	**M2** explain working practices and employment contracts in the print-based media industries with reference to detailed illustrative examples and with generally correct use of subject terminology	**D2** comprehensively explain working practices and employment contracts in the print-based media industries with elucidated examples and consistently using subject terminology correctly
P3 describe financial issues and current market trends in the print-based media industries with some appropriate use of subject terminology	**M3** explain financial issues and current market trends in the print-based media industries with reference to detailed illustrative examples and with generally correct use of subject terminology	**D3** comprehensively explain financial issues and current market trends in the print-based media industries with elucidated examples and consistently using subject terminology correctly
P4 describe legal, ethical and professional obligations of those working in the print-based media industries with some appropriate use of subject terminology	**M4** explain legal, ethical and professional obligations of those working in the print-based media industries with reference to detailed illustrative examples and with generally correct use of subject terminology	**D4** comprehensively explain legal, ethical and professional obligations of those working in the print-based media industries with elucidated examples and consistently using subject terminology correctly
P5 prepare personal career development material using basic formal language	**M5** prepare carefully produced personal career development material using generally correct basic formal language	**D5** prepare personal career development material to a quality that reflects near-professional standards using correct formal language

Unit 18, Producing print-based media

To achieve a **pass** grade the evidence must show that you are able to:	To achieve a **merit** grade the evidence must show that, in addition to the pass criteria, you are able to:	To achieve a **distinction** grade the evidence must show that, in addition to the pass and merit criteria, you are able to:
P1 describe different forms of print-based media production techniques and technology with some appropriate use of subject terminology	**M1** explain different forms of print-based media production techniques and technology with reference to detailed illustrative examples and with generally correct use of subject terminology	**D1** comprehensively explain different forms of print-based media production techniques and technology with elucidated examples and consistently using subject terminology correctly
P2 produce ideas and originate designs for print-based media products working within appropriate conventions and with some assistance	**M2** produce ideas and originate effective designs for print-based media products to a good technical standard, showing some imagination and with only occasional assistance	**D2** produce ideas and originate designs for print-based media products to a technical quality that reflects near-professional standards, showing creativity and flair and working independently to professional expectations
P3 produce print-based media products using appropriate technology and processes, working within appropriate conventions and with some assistance	**M3** produce print-based media products to a good technical standard, showing some imagination and with only occasional assistance	**D3** produce print-based media products to a technical quality that reflects near-professional standards, showing creativity and flair and working independently to professional expectations
P4 comment on own print-based media production work with some appropriate use of subject terminology	**M4** explain own print-based media production work with reference to detailed illustrative examples and generally correct use of subject terminology	**D4** critically evaluate own print-based media production work in the context of professional practice, with elucidated examples and consistently using subject terminology correctly

Interactive media

Learning outcomes

After completing the following two mandatory units in the Interactive media pathway you should:

Unit 12, Understanding the interactive media industry

1. understand the organisational structures and job roles in the interactive media industry
2. understand current market trends within the interactive media industry
3. understand contractual, regulatory and ethical obligations in the interactive media industry
4. know about employment opportunities in the interactive media industry
5. be able to prepare personal career development material.

Unit 19, Digital graphics for interactive media

1. understand theory and applications of digital graphics technology
2. be able to generate ideas for digital graphics for an interactive media product
3. be able to create digital graphics for an interactive media product following industry practice.

How you will be assessed

The units in the Interactive media pathway will be assessed by a number of internal assignments that will be designed to allow you to show your understanding of the unit outcomes. These relate to what you should be able to do after completing the unit. Your assessments could be in the form of:

- presentations
- case studies
- practical tasks
- written assignments
- interactive media products
- digital images.

Remember

Remember that you will need to supply separate evidence for each learning outcome for your assessment.

Assessment and grading criteria

The following tables show you what you must do in order to achieve a **pass**, **merit** or **distinction** grade for Unit 12 and Unit 19 in the Interactive media pathway.

Unit 12, Understanding the interactive media industry		
To achieve a **pass** grade the evidence must show that you are able to:	To achieve a **merit** grade the evidence must show that, in addition to the pass criteria, you are able to:	To achieve a **distinction** grade the evidence must show that, in addition to the pass and merit criteria, you are able to:
P1 describe organisational structures and job roles in the interactive media industry with some appropriate use of subject terminology	**M1** explain organisational structures and job roles in the interactive media industry with reference to detailed illustrative examples and with generally correct use of subject terminology	**D1** comprehensively explain organisational structures and job roles in the interactive media industry with reference to elucidated examples and consistently using subject terminology correctly
P2 describe current market trends in the interactive media industry with some appropriate use of subject terminology	**M2** explain current market trends in the interactive media industry with reference to detailed illustrative examples and with generally correct use of subject terminology	**D2** comprehensively explain current market trends in the interactive media industry with reference to elucidated examples and consistently using subject terminology correctly
P3 describe contractual, regulatory and ethical obligations in the interactive media industry with some appropriate use of subject terminology	**M3** explain contractual, regulatory and ethical obligations in the interactive media industry with reference to detailed illustrative examples and with generally correct use of subject terminology	**D3** comprehensively explain contractual, regulatory and ethical obligations in the interactive media industry with reference to elucidated examples and consistently using subject terminology correctly
P4 describe employment opportunities in the interactive media industry with some appropriate use of subject terminology	**M4** explain employment opportunities in the interactive media industry with reference to detailed illustrative examples and with generally correct use of subject terminology	**D4** comprehensively explain employment opportunities in the interactive media industry with supporting justification and elucidated examples and consistently using subject terminology correctly
P5 prepare personal career development material using basic formal language	**M5** prepare carefully produced personal career development material using generally correct formal language	**D5** prepare personal career development material to a quality that reflects near-professional standards consistently using correct formal language

Unit 19, Digital graphics for interactive media

To achieve a **pass** grade the evidence must show that you are able to:	To achieve a **merit** grade the evidence must show that, in addition to the pass criteria, you are able to:	To achieve a **distinction** grade the evidence must show that, in addition to the pass and merit criteria, you are able to:
P1 describe theory and applications of digital graphics technology with some appropriate use of subject terminology	**M1** explain theory and applications of digital graphics technology with reference to detailed illustrative examples and with generally correct use of subject terminology	**D1** comprehensively explain theory and applications of digital graphics technology with elucidated examples and consistently using subject terminology correctly
P2 generate outline ideas for digital graphics for an interactive media product working within appropriate conventions and with some assistance	**M2** generate detailed ideas for digital graphics for an interactive media product with some imagination and with only occasional assistance	**D2** generate thoroughly thought-through ideas for digital graphics for an interactive media product with creativity and flair, working independently to professional expectations
P3 create digital graphics for an interactive media product following industry practice, working within appropriate conventions and with some assistance	**M3** create digital graphics for an interactive media product to a good technical standard, following industry practice, showing some imagination and with only occasional assistance	**D3** create digital graphics for an interactive media product to a technical quality that reflects near-professional standards following industry practice, showing creativity and flair, working independently to professional expectations

Games development

Learning outcomes

After completing the following two mandatory units in the Games development pathway you should:

Unit 13, Understanding the computer games industry

1. understand organisational structures and job roles within the games industry
2. understand financial issues and current market trends affecting the games industry
3. understand contractual, legal and ethical obligations in the games industry
4. be able to use project management techniques commonly used in the games industry
5. be able to prepare personal career development material.

Unit 20, Computer game platforms and technologies

1. understand game platform types
2. understand hardware technologies for game platforms
3. understand software technologies for game platforms
4. be able to connect and configure platforms and devices to enable gameplay.

How you will be assessed

The units in the Games development pathway will be assessed through a number of internally assessed assignments that are designed to allow you to demonstrate the skills, knowledge and experience you have gained in order to successfully complete the unit outcomes.

Reports and presentations might be suitable assessment vehicles, though more innovative approaches might also be chosen – for example, to provide content for a website explaining the structures, issues, trends and obligations of the computer games industry with a section on the legal and contractual issues to recruits entering the games industry.

Logs recording application of project management techniques to a project of around 20 hours' work is a suitable assessment vehicle for this learning outcome. The project can be attached, of course, to another unit.

Remember

Remember that you will need to supply separate evidence for each learning outcome for your assessment.

Assessment and grading criteria

The following tables show you what you must do in order to achieve a **pass**, **merit** or **distinction** grade for Unit 13 and Unit 20 in the Games development pathway.

Unit 13, Understanding the computer games industry

To achieve a **pass** grade the evidence must show that you are able to:	To achieve a **merit** grade the evidence must show that, in addition to the pass criteria, you are able to:	To achieve a **distinction** grade the evidence must show that, in addition to the pass and merit criteria, you are able to:
P1 describe organisational structures and job roles in the games industry, with some appropriate use of subject terminology	**M1** explain organisational structures and job roles in the games industry with reference to detailed illustrative examples and generally appropriate use of subject terminology	**D1** comprehensively explain organisational structures and job roles in the games industry with reference to elucidated examples and consistently using subject terminology correctly
P2 describe current market trends and financial issues in the games industry with some appropriate use of subject terminology	**M2** explain current market trends and financial issues in the games industry with reference to detailed illustrative examples and generally correct use of subject terminology	**D2** comprehensively explain current market trends and financial issues in the games industry with reference to elucidated examples and consistently using subject terminology correctly
P3 describe contractual, legal and ethical obligations in the games industry with some appropriate use of subject terminology	**M3** explain contractual, legal and ethical obligations in the games industry with reference to detailed illustrative examples and generally correct use of subject terminology	**D3** comprehensively explain contractual, legal and ethical obligations in the games industry with reference to elucidated examples and consistently using subject terminology correctly
P4 apply project management techniques to direct a project with some assistance	**M4** apply project management techniques to direct a project competently, and with only occasional assistance	**D4** apply project management techniques to direct a project to a quality that reflects near-professional standards, working independently to professional expectations
P5 prepare personal career development material using basic formal language	**M5** prepare carefully produced personal career development material using generally correct formal language	**D5** prepare personal career development material to a quality that reflects near-professional standards consistently using correct formal language

Unit 20, Computer game platforms and technologies

To achieve a **pass** grade the evidence must show that you are able to:	To achieve a **merit** grade the evidence must show that, in addition to the pass criteria, you are able to:	To achieve a **distinction** grade the evidence must show that, in addition to the pass and merit criteria, you are able to:
P1 describe game platform types with some appropriate use of subject terminology	**M1** explain game platform types with reference to detailed illustrative examples and with generally correct use of subject terminology	**D1** comprehensively explain game platform types with elucidated examples and consistently using subject terminology correctly
P2 describe hardware technologies for game platforms with some appropriate use of subject terminology	**M2** explain hardware technologies for game platforms with reference to detailed illustrative examples and with generally correct use of subject terminology	**D2** comprehensively explain hardware technologies for game platforms with elucidated examples and consistently using subject terminology correctly
P3 describe software technologies for game platforms with some appropriate use of subject terminology	**M3** explain software technologies for game platforms with reference to detailed illustrative examples and with generally correct use of subject terminology	**D3** comprehensively explain software technologies for game platforms with elucidated examples and consistently using subject terminology correctly
P4 apply techniques to connect and configure platforms and devices with some assistance	**M4** apply techniques to connect and configure platforms and devices competently with only occasional assistance	**D4** apply techniques to connect and configure platforms and devices to a technical quality that reflects near-professional standards, working independently to professional expectations

Glossary

Acoustics – the study of sound and the way it behaves in different environments.

Active consumers – the audience is able to read and interpret media texts for themselves.

AM – Amplitude Modulation: one of the ways in which radio waves are propagated.

Audience research – the collection and analysis of information about the target audience for a particular media product or sector of the media industry.

Blog (or weblog) – an online software package that allows the user to record text, graphics and images via the Internet.

Budget – what your production is going to cost.

Call sheet – details the specific plan and resources needed for a single day of production.

Closed questions – limiting in terms of the potential answers that can be given.

Compression – a means of reducing file size to accommodate more material.

Constraints – the limits put on your production.

Contingency – the back-up plan or reserve pot of money.

Continuity – ensuring that sequences in individual programmes and programmes in a schedule are broadcast in sequence and with no noticeable interruption.

Copyright – an automatic right that protects a piece of written or recorded work from being copied or used by anyone else without the copyright owner's permission.

Curriculum vitae (CV) – a summary of your education and qualifications, any paid or voluntary work experience, and the names and contact details of referees.

DAB – Digital Audio Broadcasting.

Demographics – a way of describing a group of people according to factors such as age, gender, ethnicity, occupation, social class and sexual orientation.

Demo material – a sample of work to demonstrate your practical skills, whether as a presenter, a technician, a journalist or writer, or in some other role.

Digital processes – widely used within the commercial printing industry; include photocopying and the use of desktop publishing (DTP) software.

Distribution – distribution companies own the rights to a film and publicise it; they also make and deliver the prints or files for projection in each cinema.

DRM – Digital Radio Mondiale.

Dry sound – capturing audio with no acoustic environment properties at all; often referred to as a skill in recording, editing and mixing 'dead' sound.

Ethical – ensuring that you are working within the accepted social 'norms' and that rules and values are upheld.

Exhibition – the business of showing films to audiences; what cinemas and cinema chains do.

First playable – the first version of a game that is playable; often used to show others outside the studio the game's proof of concept.

FM – Frequency Modulation: one of the ways in which radio waves are propagated.

Focus group – a group of people drawn from the target audience who are invited to assess proposed products.

Foley – the technique of creating, adding and/or synchronising sound effects with pre-produced animations or full motion video sequences. It was named after Jack Foley, a sound editor at Universal Studios.

Genre – literally means a 'kind', 'sort' or 'type'.

Geodemographics – a way of describing a group of people based on where they live, sometimes organised according to postcode.

Gold master – the term used to indicate that the game is ready for mass distribution by either electronic means or by physical media.

Hand-operated processes – usually used today for producing pieces of art and design rather than for commercial media production; include etching and screen printing.

HSL – hue, saturation and lightness.

HSV – hue, saturation and value.

LAN – a Local Area Network is a network of computer devices covering a small physical area.

Linear – files that can only be accessed from the beginning of the file.

Market research – the collection and analysis of information about the market within which a particular product will compete with other products for an audience and for revenue.

Mechanical processes – involve the use of some form of machinery and include offset-litho and gravure.

Minutes – notes that record what has been discussed and agreed at a meeting, usually in a succinct or bullet-pointed format.

Mise-en-scène – the literal translation from French is 'putting on stage'; it means creating a setting for a scene in a production on stage or screen.

Non-linear – files that may be accessed at any point on the time line.

Open questions – allow the person answering to give their own views and opinions on the subject.

Parody/spoof – a send-up that pokes fun at a genre.

Passive consumers – the audience accept what the text contains.

Pastiche – a copy of a genre.

Pitch – a verbal presentation that allows for the expansion of the key points of a proposal.

Post-press or **print finishing** – the processes that take place on the printed material before a product can be distributed.

Pre-press – the generic term for all the work needed to get a product ready for print.

Press – the term for the actual printing process.

Primary research – original research to obtain new information using techniques like interviews, questionnaires and focus groups.

Production – where films are developed and made.

Production diary – a way of recording all the activities undertaken on a day-to-day basis.

Production documentation – all production paperwork from pre-production to post-production.

Production research – the collection and analysis of information for the content and production of a media product.

Production schedule – a planning document that brings together all of the information needed for a particular production. It gives an overview of the whole production.

Proposal – a document that sells an idea for a media product to a client.

Psychographics – a way of describing a group of people based on their attitudes, opinions and lifestyle.

Qualitative research – research based on opinions, attitudes and preferences rather than hard facts and figures.

Quantitative research – research based on measurable facts and information that can be counted, producing numerical and statistical data.

Recce – a planned and structured visit to a potential production location during pre-production to ascertain its suitability for use.

Reverberation – characteristic of sound in a reflective environment.

RGB – red, green, blue.

Risk assessment – the identification of potential risks to staff, the public and equipment in a production.

Secondary research – research using existing information that has already been gathered by other people or organisations.

Statutory – having the force of law.

Surround sound – the effect of creating sound around the listener by the use of multiple speakers.

Talent – the professional people who feature in a production such as actors, presenters, dancers and voice-over artists.

Target audience – the people you want to consume your product.

Treatment – the initial outline of a moving image production.

USP – unique selling point. Often used in advertising, it relates to the originality of your idea or concept that will make it different to anything else already on the market.

WAN – a Wide Area Network is a network of computer devices covering a large area and has to communicate across a large geographical area.

Wet sound – capturing audio with elements of the acoustic environment present.

Index